What Leaders in Family Law Have to Say About
The Co-Parents' Handbook

"*The Co-Parents' Handbook* contains the most powerful and important advice for any parent going through a divorce. If you are considering or starting down the divorce path, whether you are male or female, straight or gay, whether you have younger or older children, then this book is for you. It provides a roadmap to healing and carefully crafted directions about how you can protect your children throughout. It will teach you step-by-step how to dismantle your spousal relationship and build a co-parenting relationship. It is rare that we find a user's manual for major life transitions, but Bonnell and Little have created a master accomplishment in this easy-to-digest handbook with concrete examples that all readers can begin using the same day they pick up the book. It includes a healthy dose of hope and love at its core, making sure the reader understands that Bonnell and Little are with them throughout this transformation from spouse to co-parent.

I assist clients with some of the most difficult divorce cases. While I will counsel them through the legal portions of their divorce, I firmly believe that the best possible outcomes require the skills set forth in *The Co-Parents' Handbook*; I will wholeheartedly recommend it to each of my clients in lieu of any other book on these subjects. The skills it teaches will not only benefit their families from an emotional standpoint, but also helps to substantially improve a client's ability to prepare themselves for the legal system by following some of the sage and concrete advice provided."

—Justin M. Sedell, Principal Attorney at Lasher Holzapfel Sperry & Ebberson, PLLC in Seattle, Washington; Adjunct Professor at Seattle University School of Law and University of Washington School of Law

"Karen Bonnell, with the assistance of Kristin Little, has done a phenomenal job in *The Co-Parents' Handbook*. It speaks to all parents facing the transition to co-parenting: those doing this difficult task well, those who are struggling, and all those in between. The book addresses complex issues in a straightforward, easy-to-understand language. Karen and Kris tackle high-conflict emotion while assisting with the practical guidelines. They provide a compass, navigation skills, and everyday here's how tools to meet the day-to-day challenges of two-home family life. They address real family life challenges including new romantic partnerships without casting blame. They provide clear examples from a variety of families navigating this new and challenging territory—learning to do what's best for kids and creating a better future for all. I will buy this book in bulk!"

—Nancy Cameron, Q.C., Attorney; Mediator; Author; Founders Member of Collaborative Divorce Association of Vancouver, BC, Canada; Past President, International Academy of Collaborative Professionals

"Until now, parents did not receive an owner's manual for how to raise kids after divorce. *The Co-Parents' Handbook* is that owner's manual—a clear and practical guide on how to create and maintain a successful co-parenting relationship. It is filled with wisdom about how to make the most of post-divorce co-parenting, and covers both the common questions—such as how to tell the kids about the divorce and how to sensibly introduce new romantic partners—to the equally important questions that are less commonly asked—such as how to make residential schedules really work and how to effectively stay on track as co-parents after divorce. If you want your children to thrive after your divorce, you owe it to yourself to read this book."

—J. Mark Weiss, JD, Attorney; Mediator; Collaborative Law Trainer; Former Chair, Washington State Bar Association Family Law Section; Fellow and former President of Washington chapter, American Academy of Matrimonial Lawyers

THE
Co-Parents'
Handbook

Raising Well-Adjusted, Resilient, and Resourceful Kids in a Two-Home Family from Little Ones to Young Adults

Karen Bonnell, ARNP, MS, Co-Parenting Coach

with Kristin Little, MS, MA, LMHC, Child Specialist

Cover and Interior Design: Kathryn Campbell

*The Co-Parents' Handbook: Raising Well-Adjusted, Resilient, and Resourceful
Children in a Two-Home Family from Little Ones to Young Adults*

"The Seven C's of Resilience" is used with permission of the American Academy
of Pediatrics, Building Resilience in Children and Teens: Giving Kids Roots and
Wings, 2nd Edition, Copyright © 2010 American Academy of Pediatrics.

ISBN-10:1495345866
ISBN-13: 978-1495345869
LCCN: 2014905100

Printed in the United States of America by CreateSpace
Published in the United States of America by
CMC Publishers, Bellevue, Washington
www.thecoparentshandbook.com
www.coachmediateconsult.com

DEDICATION

We dedicate this book to our children—

Karen's

Ali: for your amazing strength to stand your ground, and for teaching me about the invincible mother-daughter bond

Ben: for your call to justice, your strength to walk along a change-filled path, and your courage to face life even when it is nothing that you expected

Kristin's

Sebastian: for teaching me that life is bigger than I am, and showing me that it's more fun than I ever imagined

—and to your children.

The
Co-Parents'
Handbook

**Raising Well-Adjusted, Resilient, and
Resourceful Kids in a Two-Home Family
from Little Ones to Young Adults**

CONTENTS

WHY THIS BOOK?

The question for the child is not "Do I want to be good?"
but "Whom do I want to be like?"

—Bruno Bettelheim, internationally renowned child psychologist

I'VE NEVER MET a parent who didn't want what was best for his/her children. As a professional working every day with parents and co-parents, and a parent who navigated a difficult divorce, I've experienced first- and second-hand a body of knowledge, skills, protocols, and practices worth sharing.

I've dedicated my work to digging deep and learning everything I could about adults in the transition from parent to co-parent: figuring out what works and what doesn't, and finding ways to help them heal. This book contains the teaching stories and principles shared everyday with parents going through some of the scariest, most uncertain, and change-filled transitions of their lives.

Kristin Little draws on her own experience with divorce and co-parenting as she listens daily to children tell their stories of changing families. As a child specialist, Kris has the vital role of helping children understand their experience of change, normalizing some of their concerns about divorce, and bringing information to parents about their children's needs, feelings, and adjustment.

About four years ago, I watched the magic happen when Kris first brought the "voice of the child" into the room—helping parents understand better what their children were thinking, feeling, hoping for, and hurting from. Our teamwork began. Kris has woven the voices of the children throughout these pages, helping us all to remember where our focus belongs: on the kids. *The Co-Parents' Handbook* shows how co-parents can turn a very difficult transition into something that strengthens kids and expands their sense of family.

We remind parents every day that, for a child, the freedom to love and be in relationship with each of his/her parents is unquestionably enriching when a parent is capable of caring for that child. "Whom do I want to be like?" *My parents! Whether in two homes or one, my parents are the two most important people in my world.* We're here to support you to be those co-parents—working together, knowing how, and succeeding.

—Karen Bonnell, ARNP, MS
May 2014

A NOTE ABOUT FAMILIES

There is no such thing as a "broken family." Family is family,
and is not determined by marriage certificates, divorce papers,
and adoption documents. Families are made in the heart.

—C. Joybell C., author of *The Sun is Snowing*

WHILE WE ARE writing to a broad audience here, we are always mindful about you and your unique circumstances. Please know that we invite you to exchange words and translate to what best represents your experience. We may rely on the word "married" when "coupled" or "partnered" might better describe your particular experience. We combined "divorced" and "separated" into "divorced/separated" to include parents who never chose (or may be prohibited from having) legal marriage. We generally refer to "spouse," but recognize that "intimate partner" or "my kiddo's Mom/Dad" or some other descriptor may more comfortably reflect your situation.

We work with LGBTQ couples, heterosexual couples, and parents who never had a committed partnership. We have stay-at-home dads as well as stay-at-home moms and surrogate moms. Some of our families have "steps" and "halfs," adopted and foster children, multi-generations, and four-leggeds as well as two-leggeds that count in the family profile.

Our goal is to support family—not *define* family—and to assist loving, caring parents like you to go forward with confidence and optimism. We aim to help you do what's best for kids when forming a two-home family. We offer useful suggestions that are applicable whatever your situation and family constellation might be.

Your family circumstances may result in questions and concerns not found here. We support you in reaching out to a co-parent coach, child specialist, legal counsel, and/or mental health professional to get support and guidance. Any steps you take to constructively reduce conflict, solve problems collaboratively, and look to a positive future *are best for both children and adults*—best for family.

Note: We have illustrated many situations and feelings throughout the book with examples from parents and children we have worked with, in order to give concrete, real-world evidence. However, all names and defining characteristics have been changed in order to safe-guard privacy and confidentiality. We are grateful for their example.

INTRODUCTION

YOU'RE SEPARATING AND/OR getting divorced. Your whole life is about change. You're thinking ahead. What will my life look like with my children moving back and forth between two homes? What do I need to think about, consider, prepare for? How do others do this? What are the pitfalls? I just want some way to get perspective and balance. Or....

You've finished shooting the rapids—you're officially divorced/separated. You have boxes packed or unpacked; you have documents that describe your financial launch pad and a parenting plan to guide life with your children. You have a heart that is still mending whether from heartbreak or release from a marriage/relationship that ended, broke, didn't work. You're beginning a new life, with new rules, a new sense of home. You're forging a new co-parenting relationship with an old spouse/partner, armed with your commitment to do whatever is in the kids' best interest.

"What exactly does that mean?" you ask. How on earth do I navigate all the feelings, the inconvenience, uncertainty, awkwardness? How do I put my best foot forward after months of struggling to drag one foot behind the other? I knew what it meant to be a good parent when we all lived together, but how do I use those skills as a co-parent now that everything's different? This book helps answer your most pressing questions, gives you a roadmap and provides tools for co-parenting post-divorce/separation.

WE WILL SHOW YOU WAYS TO:

- Successfully work through difficult feelings while forming your "business of co-parenting relationship"

- Build a mutually respectful co-parenting relationship

- Keep your children front and center while protecting them from adult conflict and concerns

- Understand your children's needs as they navigate the loss and change of divorce

- Help your children build resilience and competence in the face of family change

- Implement strategies and protocols for day-to-day living in a two-home family that work

Whatever the circumstances behind your new life as a co-parent, this book provides ideas, guidelines, and information to help you navigate the transition from one home to two for your children. Divorce may be the most common path, but certainly not the *only* path to a two-home family. There are parents who've had a child and have never lived together, parents who once lived together and now don't, etc. You're reading this book because you want to learn how to help your children grow up strong and resilient with roots in two homes—co-parenting even as life moves forward and relationships change. For your children, you two will always be their parents—part of their sense of family. We help answer questions about how to provide a safe, secure two-home family-life.

At the core, this book is about your children. The heart of the matter is helping children maintain or reclaim their carefree childhood in the wake of divorce/ separation.

> When it comes to a child's sense of family, what divorce breaks apart, solid co-parenting rebuilds.

In order to co-parent, you'll need to know how to take care of yourself, your emotions, and have the tools to build and maintain a respectful, cooperative co-parenting relationship.

As new parents, we all joked about our amazing bundle arriving without an operating manual. So we read parenting books and magazines; we did our best; we made loving mistakes, our kids grew. We sometimes learned the hard way: through experience. Co-parenting after divorce/separation throws another level of complexity into the already challenging job of raising kids. A whole set of new skills are needed under the best of circumstances. More often than not, we need serious guidance to successfully navigate awkward situations fraught with emotional landmines. We wrote this book because both of us understand how difficult, complicated, and uncertain the process of co-parenting can be. We also know about emotional landmines and how easy it is to make not-so-loving mistakes in the aftermath of a difficult divorce/separation.

What might have been loving mistakes in the past, after divorce/separation often take on the emotional tenor of our "unloving feelings" toward our children's other parent. We call those not-so-loving mistakes. This guidebook helps prevent not-so-loving mistakes and recognizes that although every parent wants to do what's best for their kids, they often have no idea what to do or how to accomplish it. With clear protocols, helpful tools, and a little support, parents can avoid the pain borne of not knowing how to do better, and move right into providing a healthy, supportive, loving foundation for their kids through skillful co-parenting.

Our goal is to help parents develop confidence in their ability to create a positive, resilient family even with the challenges of living across two-homes and in the aftermath of a broken adult/spousal relationship. As a co-parent coach and child specialist, we help parents build new foundations—as independent adults finding new footing, as co-parents, and as transformed families. We watch how children reflect confidence in their parents' ability to establish a secure and loving sense of home and family through their day-to-day activities/relationships, and we listen for the freedom to *just-be-kids-growing-up* in how they speak about their family. We see more than our fair share of parental conflict, and children's tears and anger as they struggle to make sense of loss and change. However, we also see parents' unfolding courage, amazing growth as people and parents, and their love and commitment reflected in their kids' stories. This was captured beautifully by a six-year-old girl when she responded to the query if both her parents had attended her recent ballet recital:

· · · · · · · ·

Turning hand on hip, looking as if an adult should
understand something so very simple and true, she declared,
"Weeelll, of course! We are still family, you know."

· · · · · · · ·

This is our hope for your children: that they will experience confidence in your ability to sustain their sense of family even in the face of change, and that you will find the guidelines and tools that support YOU as you grow stronger and become a skillful co-parent. This book offers practical, hands-on ideas for creating your own sense of a two-home family. Some may work and some may not; you are the expert on your homelife. Our hope is that you focus on what can help—that you find power and hope in the possibilities suggested, even if more time is needed before you and your co-parent are ready to give them a try. We hope to guide you in discovering skills that build a positive, resilient, and hopeful view of the future for yourself and your transformed family.

[7]

Your "brain trust" through your separation/divorce process and beyond will likely include an attorney. Choose wisely. Hire someone who will represent your interests in preserving your child(ren's) childhood. An attorney who believes in family and preserving the co-parenting relationship as much as possible. Consider learning more about Collaborative Divorce and collaboratively trained attorneys to find out if that option meets your needs and situation. Talk with mediators and divorce coaches who will help guide you. Divorce can be safe and civil—and we hope for you to have that experience. (For more, see the Appendix *Choosing a Family Law Attorney.*)

Let's get started.

THE POWER OF STORY

People are as healthy and confident as the stories they tell themselves…
Without stories we would go mad.
Life would lose its moorings or orientation….
Stories can conquer fear, you know.
They can make the heart larger.

—Ben Okri, Nigerian poet and novelist

THINK FOR A moment about the story of your own family, your own beginning, that brought you to where you are now. There may be themes of love or strife, lessons about commitment and hard work, emphases on people's weaknesses and strengths. The stories that carry these memories and beliefs help shape how you see yourself, your place in this world, and your understanding of human nature.

Our history gives us not only meaning about the past, but also context for how we see the present *and* our future. We create understanding and meaning by weaving together our experience with the words and actions of those closest to us, the ones who have traveled life's path with us—*our family*—however "family" is defined.

Divorce/separation may not be a foundation for happy stories, but emerging from divorce/separation holds the potential for shaping the way children see and learn to navigate crisis and change. They provide a child's window into parents' capacity to navigate transition, struggle with emotion, accept loss, and grow through change. They catalog their own experiences of rebounding from a family crisis they have no control over, restabilizing their own lives, and growing in the face of uncertainty. The task is not easy, but rich with opportunity.

Take a moment and ponder how these children have started their "family life story" about divorce/ separation:

Mattie, age 10: *"I don't know really what happened. One night Dad was here and the next morning he was gone. When I went downstairs for breakfast, Mom was in the living room, crying. I didn't want to ask her what happened. I didn't like to see her like that; it made me scared. I still don't know what happened because Mom and Dad don't talk about it, so I don't ask. I see Dad now, but he lives in a different house. The house I live in with my Mom feels sad now."*

Carrie, age 15: *"Mom and dad got a divorce a year ago. It was hard, but they sat with us and told my brother and me that they tried, but they couldn't get along living in the same house. I was sad and really scared, but they told us they would always love us, that we would still see them. They said they would share taking care of us just like always. I don't like it still; it's hard living in two different places, but I really think it's better—they don't fight like before. They might actually like each other better. We even have fun like a family, like on my birthday. Sometimes I feel different from my friends, but it's really not that bad. I love my parents and they love me. We're still mostly a family, it just works a little different now."*

* * * * * * * *

These stories illustrate the power that parents have in creating their children's understanding of what is changing in their family and what remains the same—what they can count on and how being able to talk about their experience and ask questions helps them piece together an upset present and ultimately build a secure and loving future.

For many parents the biggest question is "how can I guide my kids when I don't know myself what is happening?" While this is a very honest question, think about how you might react if you are lost in the woods on a hike with your children. Would you panic and begin expounding on the danger of bears, tragic stories of people lost for weeks starving in the wilderness? Of course not. You would most likely take a reassuring tone, find your strength and focus on the positive: you have plenty of snacks and water, people know you went out hiking in this area, and although it may be a while, you will be found. And in time, you will all be home safe and sound. You would act as a guide and source of confidence/comfort. You would keep your head about you and make sound decisions; you would listen to concerns, answer questions if you could, and reassure when you had no answers. You would not dwell on blame, but focus on solving the problems ahead and instill faith and confidence.

This approach we call "the loving guide" and while nothing fancy, it is a significant task to find your own confidence, a strong voice and sure footing on a journey that is scary and confusing for you.

In doing so you can help create a family life story for your children, which may include struggle but also includes hope and strength. Your children will experience sadness and fear—can they look to you as a source of help and comfort? Not in every moment because there are *no perfect parents*, but in the overall arc of family recovery, can they see you developing skills, growing, being there for them, and emerging from one of life's difficult changes?

Our deepest hope is that this book helps you find the skills and guidance that contribute to your own ability to create a healthy family life story. A story of personal resilience and family resilience for your children. The practices and protocols are here as a compass—pointing you in the direction of constructive co-parenting, leading you forward out of those moments when you feel lost in the woods—emerging into two-home family life safe and sound.

Chapter 1

The Journey from
Spouses to Co-Parents

DURING AND AFTER divorce/separation, adults often struggle with feelings—feelings that disrupt, confuse, frustrate—and often interfere with co-parenting effectively. We hope to provide guidance on how to manage feelings and shorten the duration of upset to help you recover your "self" and develop as a strong co-parent. Part of what makes this transition so hard is that although spouses divorce/separate, parents don't. Parents emerge from divorce/separation in a new relationship, which we call "co-parents"...and your new job is the business of co-parenting with your former spouse.

What Keeps Us Connected?

The opposite of love is indifference—not hate. Hate is the *other side* of the "love coin" and can be an equally strong energetic connection of the heart to someone who has hurt us, betrayed us, wronged us. Hate and conflict grow out of frustrated love or a fight against the grief over losing something or someone truly important. These losses can include life-long dreams about how life would unfold, our sense of family, financial security, lifestyle, identity, relationships with children/extended family/community, etc.

By acknowledging how hateful feelings and conflict actually connect and involve us with another person, we open the door for more constructive responses—responses that will allow for disengagement, release, and freedom of choice. We come to realize that as much as we protest and claim we want little to do with this other person, we simultaneously engage with them at every turn. Recognizing this pattern, pausing, pulling away from the impulse to engage/strike back (*no matter how RIGHT you may be!*), provides the platform for steps and strategies that promote healthier, more constructive interaction—and a new business-of-co-parenting relationship. This can happen, believe it or not, even as we grieve losses and come to grips with a new reality.

> Managing our very human emotions allows
> us to more fully engage opportunity and
> innovation over limitation and negativity.

Divorce/separation is a crisis—a crisis of change: change in family, identity, roles, security and dreams for the future. However, even during this crisis, we are called to make important decisions. How we make decisions can be influenced significantly by the way we think and feel.

- Like any crisis, divorce/separation unleashes potential for opportunity and innovation. With loss and change come opportunities for rebuilding, strengthening, renewal and re-creation.

- Divorce/separation may also set into motion a lifetime of limitation and negativity—with a danger of trapping ourselves in bitterness, resentment, angry and rigid thoughts—thoughts that prevent us from growing and finding joy on the other side.

- We choose which way we go—consciously or unconsciously. And guess what?

- Your children are going through a crisis as well. They will need your help learning to manage their emotions and by leading the way you can model for your children not only how to grieve but also how to find possibility in the face of change.

The more equipped you are to work with and understand your own emotional experience, the more capable you'll be at working with and helping your children understand theirs. Humans create meaning together—it's *in relationship* that context and meaning emerge. Your children will look to you as parents to make meaning out of what is happening in their family and glean cues to what will happen in the future. Just as if you were on an airplane flight experiencing turbulence, you might look to the flight attendants to see if there was reason to be worried or reassured. You read facial expressions, listen for their words of direction and watch their actions as the plane navigates the bumpy air. Similarly, your children look to the two of you.

That doesn't mean that you deny or fail to acknowledge there is something sad or difficult facing your family—children don't want to be alone in their sadness or difficulty with the separation/divorce. But realize that *to feel safe,* your children also need to witness confidence, hope and resiliency. Sound like a big job? It is, but you can get there by taking some basic steps to reduce the interactions that trigger big emotions, separate partner-level thoughts and emotions from parenting children, and learn to care and support yourself from the inside out.

Key to Managing Your Emotions: "Un-Coupling"

You "coupled." Divorce/separation requires that you "un-couple." Before we go any further with jumping into emotions, let's get clear about the complexity and levels of "uncoupling." That way, you'll know what skills you'll need, ideas to help ground you, strategies for self-soothing along the path. You were married, committed, involved day-to-day, and wrapped together in dreams of the future. You slept next to each other, your breathing found a rhythm together, your biology intertwined. This may have extended across many months or many years. The journey from coupled to uncoupled includes some or all of the following:

- If you were legally married—legal uncoupling, or "divorce completion"
- If you were religiously/spiritually married—religious/spiritual uncoupling with or without actual ceremony
- Emotional connection—emotional uncoupling which often occurs over time through "letting go"
- Physical/physiologic connection—physical/physiologic responses to uncoupling which often requires physical separation and time to heal and settle your heart/nervous system
- Other possible connections: owning a business together—restructuring the business, extended family/community involvement—negotiating participation in shared groups and shared relationships, etc., resulting in unique and potentially complicating circumstances to resolve.

Untangling your adult/spousal relationship has many dimensions with the potential for far-reaching impact. And because you have children, you're called to do this "uncoupling" *while* building a "co-parenting relationship." This can present difficult challenges.

You're called to break the spouse/intimate-partner bonds—the practices and patterns of "coupling." You'll need to re-configure many of the ways you've related to one-another—the shortcuts in decision-making developed out of efficiency, the re-cycling conflicts, the familiarity, pet-names and "we-ness." We hope to support you in abandoning *the old* and rewriting your co-parenting process for *the new*. No small task, and often accompanied by a great deal of wrestle, loss, anger, grief and sadness.

"Uncoupling" takes time and you and your co-parent may be on a different time-line. For the spouse who chooses to leave, he/she may have been "leaving" the marriage mentally, emotionally, physically for two to five years before requesting a divorce/separation. This is disconcerting to understand; startling to realize. Consequently, the "leaver" is often in a very different emotional state than the person who is "left." This discrepancy can be a huge source of pain—especially if the "leaver" moves forward and into a new relationship while the other parent is attempting to find his/her bearings.

Sensitivity to the emotional process of your co-parent in the early stages can go a long way in establishing a strong, positive co-parenting relationship for the long term. Recognizing the value of "uncoupling" and working together to "uncouple" benefits *everyone*—including your children. While the "leaver" often experiences relief and readiness to *move on*, the spouse who feels "left" and the children are generally much further behind in adjustment to the divorce/separation-related changes. When the "leaver" moves forward too quickly for the other's emotional adjustment, particularly with respect to a new relationship, the former spouse and children often feel "invisible" or abandoned—and that what they had relied on as "family" *yesterday* has been *deleted* today. This dynamic can create enormous pain for those who feel left behind. Your co-parent is likely to feel on his/her own to do all the uncoupling alone, picking up the pieces of what often feels like a shattered family… which is actually a family in *divorce/separation transition*.

> "Un-coupling" skillfully while parenting provides continuity in family life for kids. Unskillfully, it exposes conflict.

You're called to do this "un-coupling" while simultaneously interacting with your former spouse about and for the children. Done skillfully, you both provide an integrated sense of family for the kids, or done unskillfully, exaggerates the rift in the family. If we're successful, you'll learn to tease apart your feelings about this person as a former-spouse, from feelings about this person as the kids' other parent. By separating your feelings for your former-spouse from your feelings about him/her as a parent, you have a much greater chance of maintaining an integrated sense of family for your kids.

Key to Un-Coupling: Separating "Spouse Mind" from "Parent Mind"

Imagine that your mind works like a radio. You can tune into different thought-stations that elicit certain moods, inspirations, or experiences. Imagine that you have a thought-station where you rethink, review, and remember all the things about your former spouse that are disappointing and hurtful. This station may be filled with lots of difficult emotion, may remind you of where you are in your divorce adjustment and grief process, and may take you away from focusing on your child. We might identify this station with getting lost in "spouse mind" thoughts. Now, imagine you have a thought-station where you notice the anticipation and excitement your child feels when he/she does something fun or learns something new with his/her other parent. On this station you hear reminders of how important both parents are to a child; you hear helpful tips on how to support your child's other parent to be the best parent he/she can be; you follow important guidance on how to be a constructive co-parent—this is when you know you are tuning into "parent mind." Learning the difference between these two thought stations allows you to begin to choose— to exert control over difficult thoughts and feelings that disrupt your parenting and delay your divorce/separation adjustment. You can learn to intentionally change the station and develop thought patterns that support your co-parenting relationship and children's future.

Next, we invite you to notice which of your thoughts about your co-parent have to do with your former spouse ("spouse mind") and which are about your children's other parent ("parent mind"). For example, "He/she's the best advocate for Frannie; I'm so thankful he/she shows up at doctor appointments." *Parent mind.* Versus: "I can never count on him/her—after the deception, the things he/she's said to me..." *Spouse mind.* Sometimes *spouse* and *parent mind* seem to blend together, "I would never want my children to be a person who acts the way he/she has acted toward me or with other adults." Whoa. Which is it?

If we look at our thoughts through our children's eyes, we find important guidance about what's "former spouse-related" thinking, and what's "parent" thinking. Children don't know (or actually care) about our adult relationship behavior or issues. They care about whether they'll be loved, cared for, and remain connected to both parents free of distress, guilt or conflict. When you express thoughts that intentionally or unintentionally have the consequence of disrupting your children's sense of safety, love and caring with their other parent, or involves them in adult-related issues—you're likely in *spouse mind.*

Now, notice the kinds of feelings that follow upset "spouse mind" thoughts— not so comfortable, hard on your heart, hard on nervous system, and hard on your *co-parent* relationship. It's perfectly fine for you to know your values and to have a critical eye on what you believe to be 'right' and 'wrong' in adult relationships. However, that's not what your children need to see in their relationship with their mom/dad, nor what they need to hear from you about their other parent. Your efforts to reduce turmoil, settle the conflict, separate adult matters from children's experience/relationships directly focus on *what's best for kids.*

Even if you're right about some aspect of what your former spouse is or isn't doing, negative thoughts, harsh judgments, and conflicting feelings don't help kids. In their own time, children will come to their own understanding and conclusions about relationships, family, and imperfect parents. You can teach values without damaging your children's relationship with their other parent. Children at a certain point in their development need to begin to see their parents in a more realistic light—the good and the not-so-good. It's an important tool for them to pick and choose what kinds of traits or behaviors that they wish to use to create their own unique sense of self. Our children are not only born of their biology, but also learn from our personal strengths, weaknesses, triumphs, and failures.

Nurture a positive "parent mind" and learn to limit the negative "spouse mind" to diminish painful and uncomfortable feelings. Acknowledge the difference between thoughts and feelings that come from "spouse mind" versus "parent mind." Notice how they either build positive, even hopeful thoughts and feelings, or negative, sometimes catastrophic thoughts with related feelings. Regardless of your emotional turmoil over the divorce/separation, your children need another parent who loves them, cares for them, feeds, nurtures, disciplines, teaches, and responds to them. They benefit from two parents who already function as great parents or parents that can rise to the occasion, share information, develop skills and learn from one another. Hopefully you'll acknowledge those strengths or appreciate your co-parent's attempts, support his/her learning/success. And from parent mind, share in your children's joy!

* * * * * * * *

Tim was so excited to see his Dad—and the smiles they shared with each other were amazing.

Mom is good at many things; she sure created an awesome costume—Jill looked beautiful and proud.

* * * * * * * *

Parents sometimes equate positive "parent mind" with accepting a former partner's choices, behaviors, or decisions. To be positive toward him/her in any way is to let him/her off the hook, to excuse him/her, to just roll over as if what happened doesn't matter. Positive "parent mind" is something you build for your child. If your former partner benefits in some way, it doesn't matter. This is something you do for your kiddos and for your own future. Your anger and judgement won't change your former partner—there's no amount of punishing thoughts that will change the outcome. Making the journey through loss, hurt and pain in order to co-parent with your former partner for your children's sake is the goal.

But what if I can't manage my emotions gracefully or can't hold on to a "parent mind" right now? Or worse, I simply can't bear the sight of him/her? It may take time, it may take some creative thinking to find ways to find more peace within yourself and between you and your co-parent. You may need to limit your interactions with him/her and take care of yourself first. There's no shame in not being able to do this gracefully—be honest with yourself, know your limits, acknowledge what you need, and continue to move forward. Keep reading. We have some ideas to help.

Key to Healing: Avoid or Manage Triggers, Rage, and Meltdowns

• • • • • • • •

"I'm so angry about what he's/she's done to us, I can hardly stand to see his/her name come up in my inbox or hear his/her voice on the phone. My heart races, I get short of breath, I think terrible things to call him/her. Transitions are nearly impossible as I can't stand to look at them— they're all smiles while I'm left like roadkill on the side of their life choices. After I drop the kids off, I have no idea what to do with myself."

• • • • • • • •

Does any of this sound familiar? Co-parenting with someone who still provokes or triggers strong emotion can be challenging, and also *re-wounding*. Employing constructive strategies to protect your healing heart, soothe your raging thoughts, and relax your exhausted body (*who's sleeping?*) will help you weather these early weeks and months of adjusting post-divorce/separation with increasing resilience and self-care.

Protect your healing heart. Limit your contact with your former spouse in ways that allow for supportive co-parenting without unnecessary contact. Communicate what's going on with the children, be respectfully cordial and business-like and resist the urge to engage about other tangential subjects. This may mean backing off on emails to once or twice a week with simple updates on how the children did during their residential time. Perhaps you want a separate "co-parenting" email address so your daily email is not affected by incoming mail from your former spouse. Recognize and honor your need for some "separation" to heal before progressing forward into a "friendly" co-parenting relationship. With time, it's very likely that you'll achieve a cordial, easier relationship with your kids other parent. Forced friendliness too soon results in prolonged healing and in scar tissue from repeated emotional fall-aparts.

Soothe your unsettled emotions. Oh dear, we are creatures of habit! When that hamster gets going on the hamster-wheel-in-our-brains, thoughts go a-spinning. One thought can lead to a cascade of memories that pile on a heaping bunch of hurt, anger, upset and unproductive, emotionally draining, not-particularly help-ful reminders that you're *divorced/separated*. For example, use distraction: watch a good, funny movie; turn on your favorite upbeat music; go for a walk, lift weights, do some work, call a friend and talk about *something else!* There's a time and a place to process your feelings, and a trusted friend, counselor or post-divorce/separation support group can be a lifeline. Quieting the hamster, soothing your emotions, is an important job, done gently, with understanding, support, and a healthy dose of distraction is often needed.

Pacing and restless energy are part of the grief reaction. If you find you can't sit still, pacing around the island in the kitchen, or wandering through the mall aim-lessly, understand that this is part of your grief reaction. Some experts see this as searching behavior—searching for what's been lost. Within reason, no harm is done by allowing yourself to walk and reduce the anxious energy. Return to the list above for other options for self-care and healthy distraction.

Go on an "anti-rage" campaign and commit yourself to disrupt, interrupt, and change your thinking as often as you can when the raging thoughts come roaring in. You are the architect of your future; let that include a meditation to breathe in *peace* and breathe out *calm*. Even if that's only a moment here and moment there, over time and with practice, those moments will link together and you'll find yourself on the other side of this crisis, feeling better.

Relax your exhausted body. Sleep is important—our bodies actually regener-ate in our sleep, and that includes our "emotional bodies." The longer disruptive sleep goes on (weeks into months), the more prolonged our recovery. Get help sooner than later. Read up on healthy sleep habits (http://healthysleep.med.har-vard.edu/need-sleep) and include the suggested steps as you can.

- Shutdown technology an hour before bed. As distracting and enticing as Facebook may be, it's very likely to be an "energy gain" rather than helpful preparation for sleep. Similarly, save your exercise for during the day or early in the evening. Read uplifting and inspirational messages before bed. Gentle background music can help soothe 'the hamster' and distract your mind as you fall asleep. Remember to "let the meat hang on the bones" in the moments that you're laying awake—practice relaxation, allow your body to feel fully supported by the mattress, let go of as much tension as possible while waiting for sleep to return.

- Your healthcare provider is an excellent person to connect with if your sleep remains disrupted and you realize you're "running on adrenaline," running short on patience, running scared of an uncertain future. It's likely that for a brief period of time, you'll benefit from something (like counseling or medication or meditation) that can in a healthy, non-addictive way, help you break the sleep disruption and return to renewing sleep. With adequate rest you're more likely to have the resilience to parent lovingly, and plan for a positive future. (On that note, this is a particularly important time to avoid alcohol, which often makes matters *worse*.)

- Focus on FUNCTIONING, not perfection. Learn to ask for help. Maybe you are one of those people who up until now prided themselves on exceeding expectations and giving help instead of receiving. Learn to readjust your expectations, accept accomplishing only what is of utmost importance, and accept less than perfection for a time. Give yourself space *to feel* and become aware when you have reached your limit. For a while, your *max point* or your *limit* may be significantly less than you ever imagined—and this is completely understandable. Give yourself permission to take a break, find time for yourself or lean on your friends, family and other supports.

We hear from children how they feel the brokenness: hurt, anger, distress. You can't be someone you're not, and creating more discomfort by "acting as if" is *not* good for kids. Kids see right through us!

* * * * * * * *

Milly, age 9: *"I don't like it that I have to get out of the car all by myself when I go to Mom's but Dad says he doesn't want to see her."*

Daddy might respond this way: *"I know this is really hard for you to run up to the front porch by yourself—I'm gonna sit right here and blow kisses at your back. And pretty soon, Daddy will feel better enough and we'll both walk up to the porch. Have fun with Mommy!"*

* * * * * * * *

Reassure children that you will take care of your feelings and their feelings, that you will be OK with a little more time. Let them know clearly that you're there to parent, support and love them through this difficult time no matter what—and things will get better.

Grief isn't a Straight Path: Anger, Tears, and Acceptance

We can't tell you there's a "right way" or a "wrong way" to grieve and adjust to divorce/separation, but we can tell you it's a process that involves layers of emotion. We can also tell you, that by understanding what you're going through, by digging down deep to find your grit in the face of adversity, by moving toward self-care and acceptance, you can shorten the length of time and impact of the distress for you and your children. Let's take a look at what might be involved in grieving.

Shock and disbelief: For some, the first wave of emotion can actually be "an absence of emotion." This is the period of time when you "don't miss a beat" and carry on with daily life and simply *add in* the details of divorce/separation or divorce/separation adjustment. You may wonder to yourself, *why is this so hard for other people?*

Cooperation or bargaining? Then we sometimes see a period of "congeniality" and a "cooperative spirit" surrounding the divorce/separation. When this is born of a genuine, mutual agreement regarding the ending of the relationship, and a true desire to make things as amicable as possible, then the two adults and their children are extremely lucky. But all too often, this "honeymoon" period is a desperate, hopeful time of bargaining in a sincere attempt to *reverse the outcome*—a plea to the spouse who is leaving to change his/her mind, to "wake-up," to come back home, and resume again as a couple.

Anger and rage, common in divorce/separation, can continue well into post-divorce/separation adjustment. So much change, so much loss, and often a feeling of helplessness to stop what's out of your control. It's a very normal reaction to struggle and fight against these unwelcome truths. Along with anger—and often underneath anger—we find sadness and grief.

Sadness may feel slower and deeper than anger and it has an energy all its own. Unlike the energizing emotion of anger, which comes with an adrenaline rush, sadness lays heavy on our hearts, drains energy out through our toes and color out of the day, and replaces our normal sense of self with feelings of vulnerability, loneliness, and loss. Then there are the tears, difficulty concentrating, anxiety about the future, and sleeping more than normal, which makes day-to-day activities increasingly difficult to accomplish. You may feel like a shell of a person, going through the motions.

Remember that grief is a journey that doesn't last forever, and you don't have to travel alone. Divorce/separation can be like traversing a glacier of emotion. It's easier to bring along necessary support (trusted friend, counselor, post-divorce/separation support group) and allow ample time to work through emotion. Most consider the first two years post-divorce/separation the most significant in adjusting and the first five years part of the adjustment territory. We caution you about lingering too long in a crevasse of anger, fear, or sadness. You can ask for help and lean on others when you find yourself stuck, recycling the past, resentful, rigid, bitter, blaming, or if you become unyielding to a new, more hopeful path.

At the end of the journey awaits acceptance. We discussed above the layers of emotions that you may wander through and visit again from time to time during your grief process. We can remind you that what awaits on the other side of all these difficult emotions is the view of your future through the lens of *acceptance*, which is well worth the arduous journey. There is no straight path or "right path," but we hope for you to reach, in time, that new place of acceptance. And acceptance may even include forgiveness.

Forgiveness: Is it Worth it? Is it Possible?

Apology can be an important part of acceptance and may or may not lead to forgiveness. Having talked to hundreds of divorcing/separating couples, we're often asked about the need for *apology* and the role of *forgiveness*. At the end of the day, divorce/separation is the result of our inability to love each other in the way that we needed to be loved, whether it was humanly possible to provide enough love, whether it was from a place of not knowing how to do any better, and whether it's true for one person or both.

Most of the issues surrounding divorce/separation are about love falling short, through our actions, our words, our connection, communication, or our inability to meet our commitments. You may feel blameless or filled with guilt. Either way, there's probably an apology due. *"I'm sorry I was unable to love you in a way that met your needs, to take care of you in the way that you expected, and to be the person you wanted me to be."* There may be other very specific things to be sorry for as well, and in an ideal, thoughtful, empathetic world, those apologies are delivered.

Acknowledgement and apology are salve for the emotional wounds of rejection, failure, and loss. When we can come to a place of acknowledging each other for not only our negative contributions to ending/losing our marriage, but also the ways the other person enriched our lives, contributed to family life, or *tried* in whatever ways he/she may have tried, we move a step closer to acceptance and a more balanced perspective on life. It's very rare that someone is all good or all bad. When we can recognize our shortfalls and apologize for the ways we wish we had been able to do better, we set the stage for taking down the walls of hurt and anger, blame and enmity.

Can I forgive and/or do I need forgiveness? Whether we get the apology we think we deserve—and give the apology our former partner deserves—we're left with the question of forgiveness: "Can I/will I forgive him/her for leaving?" or "Can I/will I forgive myself for actions I'm less than proud of?"

> Forgiveness does not mean agreement. It does not say that you felt another made the right choices or behaved in an acceptable way. What it means is acceptance of the other person and/or yourself as **less than perfect**.

Forgiveness is possible when we are able of take the energy of "looking back" and wishing the past could be different and turn it to "looking forward" and creating a meaningful future. In making that shift forward, we often find that we've unearthed valuable learning—we've mined the gold from the coal—cherished wisdom, deepened compassion, strengthened sense of self … there are many possibilities. That said, most parents who have walked through the fire of divorce/separation, need many months—if not *many years*—to unwind the complicated emotions, and sort out the divorce/separation experience for *the learning*. Be gentle with yourself.

As stormy seas subside, keep your eyes and heart on the lighthouse of raising competent, happy, secure, loving children, and you will find your way to increased stability, growing acceptance, and perhaps, in time, even forgiveness. Ultimately, you choose when and if forgiveness feels like the next natural step on the journey.

Highlights in Review

- You author your family life story and design your future.

- Your confidence and resilience will inform your children's family life story.

- Remember that although spouses divorce/separate, parents don't divorce or emotionally separate from their children.

- Understand your emotions—that will help you to move forward.

- Work diligently toward "un-coupling."

- Tease apart "spouse mind" from "parent mind" to reduce negativity and set the stage for positive co-parenting.

- Manage triggers and rage so your body, mind and spirit can recover.

- Develop an understanding of where you are in the grief process; consider where your co-parent might be, and how grief is impacting your children (More on children and grief in Chapter 2).

- Ask yourself if there are elements of forgiveness that support your divorce/separation adjustment and healing.

- Step into your role as "co-parent" and embrace your job, *the business of co-parenting;* work with your former-spouse in the best interest of your kids.

What you can't do today, you will find your way into over the weeks, months and years ahead. And for the little ones at whatever age, your efforts and accomplishments will mean a great deal. Children understand broken things—and they understand when things don't work right. Our job is to talk and walk through the brokenness to a *new wholeness* with them as family life changes and re-stabilizes. Let them know that you're working toward feeling better, doing better, and learning new things, too.

Chapter 2

The Journey for Kids through Divorce/Separation

THERE'S NO SUCH thing as a perfect family, a perfect childhood, or a perfect residential schedule. Our job, as co-parents, is to take an imperfect situation and smooth out the rough edges as best we can.

> Growth and development are the underlying rhythms of life that we all experience even in the midst and aftermath of divorce/separation.

Parents often wonder if children adjust more easily to divorce/separation at certain ages or stages of development than at others. The answer is that children adjust differently to divorce/separation and have different concerns based on their age and developmental needs. Change reminds us that life continues, and although it can be a struggle to envision meeting their needs during divorce/separation and helping them adjust to a two-home family, it can be done. What helps parents support their children is reliable information about needs and concerns at different stages of development. Your child is definitely one in a million, but some general landmarks can give you a place to begin asking and answering important questions.

Child Development and Adjusting to Divorce/Separation

The differences in how children react to divorce/separation are due in part to their capacity for cognitive and moral understanding, their developmental stage, and the makeup of their social lives. The other factor is the uniqueness of each child, their temperament and personality. For each stage there are vulnerabilities and opportunities.

- Infants' first and most important need is attachment to their caregivers. They can be well cared for in a two-home family if Mom and Dad can stay focused on the needs of the infant for bonding, stability, and an ongoing atmosphere of gentleness and love with each parent.

- Toddlers are working on their own well-managed separation from and regular return to parents as part of strengthening their individual selves. Co-parents who understand the toddlers needs for regular contact and predictable rhythms continue to support healthy growth and development.

- Preschoolers worry about losing parents, with accompanying sadness and fear.

- School-age children bring their own concerns for justice/fairness/rules and grief over losing family stability.

- Pre-teens are torn between lunging forward into adolescence and falling back into childhood behaviors under the stress of change.

- Early teens often feel betrayed by divorcing parents as they ride the roller coaster of their own unfolding puberty.

- Older teens look for the loopholes in their co-parents' relationship, and may be vulnerable to falling through the cracks as parents imagine that they're more independent and mature than they actually are.

- College students may take the news of divorce/separation very hard. They are likely to experience family changes as if their launch pad is disintegrating after take-off, just when they are trying to find their own footing in young adulthood.

- Adult children interestingly often respond with the harshest judgment to the news that their parents are divorcing. Adult children may question their family's history, wondering "if it was so bad why did it last so long?" They struggle to begin their new relationships and regret that just when they long to reunite as adults, their parents' secure and uncomplicated support is now vastly more complicated.

Just as we consider developmental needs of children in a one-home family, we're called to consider the developmental needs of children as they negotiate change in their family and expansion into two homes. What kids need most at any age along with concern about their well-being, their developmental needs, appropriate structure, responsibilities and discipline, support for/involvement in their play, school activities, and peer relationships, is *love*.

What Your Child Needs Most (At Any Age)

From a child's perspective, what they need most is quite simple: To love openly and feel loved by both parents. Love is best demonstrated through actions as well as words—it means time with, involvement in, and traveling through experiences with your child. This is important for your child with each parent.

Kids benefit from kid-level explanations for the changes they face, so they can understand and have reassurance about the future. That said, from a grown-up perspective, meeting these needs is often quite complicated. How do we explain the end of our marriage in a way that they can understand, that does not undermine their love or respect for either parent, or leave them questioning whether they are the cause?

Working through your own feelings and giving children confidence that adults come together to work through family change can be immensely reassuring. One mom we worked with was vehemently opposed to divorcing—making it almost impossible for her to imagine telling her children she had anything to do with the decision to divorce/separate. As trusted guides, we could validate her concerns, her values, her deeply held beliefs. We recognized and honored how important the "truth" was to her. And in time, she was willing to see that these *adult, emotionally mature concepts* had little to do with the work of being parents and emotionally supporting the kids. Ultimately she was ready to meet with her children's father, so that they could talk together with their children about the divorce/separation.

Explaining Divorce/Separation in Kid Language

＊＊＊＊＊＊＊＊

"Dad and I are getting a divorce, which means we won't be married anymore. I'm sad, but we both can't be happy living together in one house. Sweetheart, this is an adult problem, not a kid problem—I don't want you to worry that you have caused this or you should try to fix it. I'm so sorry this has to happen. Just know that even though we won't be married anymore and living in the same house, both Dad and I will have a place where you will live with us—you'll have a home with Mom and a home with Dad. And we'll work together to make sure you feel loved and cared for by both of us."

"Honey, Mom's right, and I'm sorry about having to make these changes. But, we can tell you that you're still going to go to your school, you're still going to get to see your friends, and you're still going to have one of us there for you to read bedtime stories and help with homework—sometimes it will be Mom and sometimes it will be me."

＊＊＊＊＊＊＊＊

Your children are forming their "family life story"—they've listened to what you've told them, they've overheard conversations, they've felt the changes/tensions/concerns, and they've hoped for the best. It's never too late to go back and help them understand a more positive, constructive message about divorce/separation. Perhaps you didn't know what to tell them before, and now, you'd like a do-over. Examine in your heart what you want your children to hold on to for their family life story, and share with them your hopes and dreams about what they will experience, learn, and grow through as you all adjust to divorce/separation.

KEY CONCEPTS—
When Parents Talk to Kids about Divorce/Separation

- This is a grown-up issue that has to do with two adult partners—and as co-parents, you will work together to make this change.

- Kids and parents don't divorce/separate; kids don't cause divorce/separation.

- Regardless of how we might feel as adults, children don't benefit from blaming one parent for the divorce/separation—judging a parent as bad, irresponsible, or breaking the family is harmful.

- Children benefit from reassurance about the integrity of their family in two homes.

- Children feel supported knowing that you'll be going through this with them with love and support.

- Reassuring children that they will emerge from this change with both of you is central to their security.

Over time, the basic concepts may need to be repeated as variations on these themes emerge in the first year. As children adjust and grieve, they may go through periods of confusion, protest, or express deep hope or wishfulness that everyone could live together again, just like it used to be. Helping them to understand their feelings, while providing gentle reminders that this is an adult decision, the decision has been made, and "We will work together to take good care of you" paves the way for acceptance of a new future.

Sometimes you'll have to fake it until you make it—as long as you're not causing distress. This includes digging deep to find balance, soothe anger, and quell fears. You may need to step back to give the other parent space—or perhaps, be the parent who steps forward to do what needs to be done, whether or not your efforts are acknowledged or the effort required feels "fair." This is all part of doing what's in the kids' best interest.

Consider what children want most. Every child's needs are unique, but what children commonly need (and have often expressed to us), is to be able to:

- Love, enjoy and learn with both their parents.They don't want to feel like they will hurt one by loving the other or having to make things "equal," keeping secrets or editing what they say.

- Have parents that listen to their feelings and comfort them, not the other way around.

- Know their parents can take care of themselves, that they won't fall apart in anger or sadness or have to struggle to afford the basics.

- Continue to support them in their lives, their social activities, their school, their sports and activities and not have to do chores or make decisions that are beyond their skills, capabilities, or age.

- Count on their parents to take care of kid-related details without dropping the ball or arguing. It's hard on kids to be the one telling each parent important "parent" information because their parents won't talk.

- Spend their special times (like birthdays) with both parents when possible. Kids want parents to "really get along, not just pretend, because I can tell." So, if you're going to try and do this together, do it well.

How can we know this? Kids tell us in their own words.

* * * * * * * * * * *

"I don't like to talk about Mom because it makes Dad sad."

"It's hard now, I have to ask Dad and ask Mom because they won't talk."

"I'm scared that the divorce is going to mess up my life and everything I've planned for."

"I worry that Mom won't be okay, so I don't tell her I'm sad."

* * * * * * * * * * *

Those are just a few of the poignant messages children share when asked about their feelings and worries in the midst of divorce/separation. As hard as it is to hear, parents need this information so that they can take simple, loving and direct steps to reassure and guide their children to talk openly. You'll take care of your feelings;

they don't have to worry that you're upset. Help them trust that they can love their other parent freely and openly. Remember as you reassure your children that home is where the heart is, and it's also where the heart feels safe to love you both.

Helping Children Work Through Emotions

Everyone's grieving and the expression of grief may take different forms and emerge at different times. Grief is a process, and comes and goes in and out of awareness. Your completely content seven-year-old can suddenly become sullen playing with Legos. Unbeknownst to you, she just had a memory of when she and Mommy built a Lego castle together—and sadness comes to visit. Your teens were having a great time at Thanksgiving dinner, and as you put dishes in the dishwasher, you find one of them silently crying into a pillow on the couch...he/she's missing Dad. Your four-year-old sits down to breakfast and complains that she never wanted THAT breakfast, she hates you, and kicks her brother—a big mad just rose up over *too much* change, over *difference*, over *all her feelings* in general.

Children need help naming their feelings. As parents, we may have a sensitive spot when it comes to our kiddo's upset—guilt that we've caused this, we're to blame—or, it's the *other parent's fault*, stirring up anger we're already struggling to subdue. Hopefully, we can manage our own feelings so that we can make time and space for our children's feelings. *Listen, listen, listen*...then let them know you understand their feelings/concerns.

· · · · · · · ·

Matt, age 13: *(lying on his bed playing X-Box and making no attempt to get things ready for Mom's pick-up, which is now 15 minutes away.)*

Dad: *"You've had it with packing and unpacking. You hate going to the apartment. It all feels so strange. I get it, Matt. We're all still adjusting— and it IS strange that Mom isn't living here anymore. You know, over time, packing will get faster and easier—and being at the apartment will feel more familiar and more settled for you and Mom. I know this is no 'walk in the park.' How can I help? Let's pull your things together, TOGETHER."*

· · · · · · · ·

* * * * * * * *

Brandie, age 5: *"I hate you, I hate you, I hate you—you should have NEVER gotten this stupid divorce."*

Mom: *"You're so mad at me—and you don't know what to do with all those mad feelings. And you wish Daddy was here and you wish none of this had happened: no new bedroom, no new house, no new ANYTHING. You want things to feel better—and I do, too. We're going to figure this out, Brandie...one step at a time. Would you like to call Daddy? Would that help? Or we could just curl up on the couch together and snuggle—maybe that would help."*

* * * * * * * *

Children respond positively to knowing that what they're going through is shared, understandable, normal, and not something they need to hide, be ashamed of, run from, be punished for, or something that *disappoints us*. As parents, we didn't come to the decision to divorce/separate easily; regardless of how it looks from the outside, no one's having a walk in the park; everyone is adjusting, learning a new way of life, and grieving. Here are tips on of how to lovingly guide your children emotionally.

- Listen—set aside what you're doing to be present and undistracted
- Name the upset—help children develop emotional intelligence/understand their feelings
- Acknowledge how hard certain kinds of change can be
- Help him/her find an example of a challenge that ended with achievement, strength, or personal accomplishment
- Reassure that things will get better, get easier, get more *normal* again soon
- And remind him/her that *we're all in this together.*

Children, like adults, experience grief and sadness—only kid-style. However supportive you might be, doing ALL the right things, children will experience some level of difficulty adjusting. Children experience strong emotions in divorce/separation. However, children generally lack experience and skill in expressing and coping with *big* feelings. Parents should be sensitive and responsive to children's emotions while addressing negative behavior with consistent, appropriate discipline. Although difficult for children and parents, the following reactions can be considered normal for kids.

- Irritability: Younger and older children may have difficulty adjusting to change and may show resistance by fussiness, changes in sleeping or eating patterns, mood swings, being argumentative or defiant.

- Anger: Children may show anger and resentment with one or both parents for disrupting their sense of normalcy. They may express anger overtly with angry outbursts, arguing or challenging parent's efforts to maintain established or new rules and routines.

- Anxiety: Children may have increased fears or nightmares or anxiety regarding changes in their lives and daily routines. Children may be "clingy" or resist separation from one or both parents, ask repeated questions about schedules or express worry about schedule changes. Children may also experience physical complaints such as headaches or stomach aches.

- Sadness: Children may express sadness directly by crying or making statements that express feelings of helplessness. Older children who have learned to cover less socially accepted feelings might express sadness as anger, irritability or withdrawal.

(If you worry that your children are emotionally struggling, please consult with his/her healthcare provider or a mental health provider. For more on Signs of Kids' Distress, see the Appendix.)

Children benefit from understanding your emotional responses on "kid terms" and in "kid-size" doses. You are one of your children's most valuable and beloved teachers about so many aspects of life. This includes how to face adversity, change, disappointment, and emerge healthy, happy and whole. The journey through adjustment and grief takes time. It may include some difficult moments, days, weeks, months, even years. Here are some guidelines for what's best for kids regarding adult emotions.

- Children know you are hurting. How you manage your hurt in their presence can help them to have confidence in your ability to be okay, and most importantly, have confidence in your ability to take care of them in spite of all the challenges.

- Showing honest, appropriate emotion coupled with reassurance is helpful to kids. Witnessing your emotions, the full range of happy to sad, in appropriate intensity and duration, helps guide children through their own grief process. Pairing those expressions with reassurance that you will be okay (and they will too) gives children the message that these feelings are normal and won't last forever. Moving quickly from your own feelings to focus on their emotions or questions gives children confidence that you can put aside your own grief to take care of them.

"Yes I'm crying, I'm going to miss this house and all the good times, but I'll be okay, and I know we will have special times in our new home. Do you feel sad about moving, too?"

- Managing your emotion even in unexpected moments impacts your child's sense of freedom to be her/himself and enjoy important relationships. We hold the lead on establishing emotional safety. Our children will often look first to us to see if we can handle big challenges and they will likely protect us if they feel we cannot. Managing our emotions can free them from the responsibility of protecting us emotionally and allow them to enjoy the other people and events in their lives without hesitation or concern.

Rochelle, age 13, *expressed a lot of worry about the awkwardness of her father dating a friend's mother in their small community. She recounted seeing her friend with her mom by chance at the library: "I waved to Jenny without thinking, and felt really bad. I looked back at Mom, and she saw what happened; she told me 'It's okay, you can say hi to Jenny, I am okay, don't worry about me, I'm fine' and she gave me a little push and even gave a small wave to Jenny's mom. It turned out so much better than I expected."*

Justin, age 10: *"I kinda forgot and told my Dad about going to see Grandma with Mom. I felt bad that he doesn't get to see Grandma anymore and I thought he would be sad, but he said he loved Grandma and was really happy I got to see her. I guess it's okay to talk about the good stuff."*

Healthy divorce/separation provides opportunities for building important strengths. Children can learn from adversity. Sad feelings are not permanent. Children who walk the path from family brokenness to wholeness with their changing family develop confidence in themselves and in their family to handle challenges and stress. They learn flexibility and resilience—and expand their concepts of love, family and commitment. How we describe the changes in the family structure and inspire hope of a future where the transformed family nurtures and supports... yes, *differently... but still in the context of family*, can offer children strength.

Jesse, age 16: *"I don't like having to go between mom and dad's house, but it's not as bad as I thought and they both seem happier—they get along better. I'm kinda proud of them."*

Lizzie, age 22: *"Something I want to tell you—I don't think I understood this when I was a teenager and you and Dad got divorced. But, now, looking back, I know that what you guys did was truly courageous—everything you went through—it took a lot of strength. I learned a lot from you."*

· · · · · · · · ·

Answering Kids' Difficult Questions

"Can you and daddy get married again?"

"I'm sorry, sweetheart, but no, Daddy and I aren't going to get married again. It's hard for all of us to get used to, but it will get easier with time and working together. Just remember, we are still your family, even though we've changed to a two-home family."

"Why can't I stay with you all the time?"

"Oh, Buddy, I love being with you, too. So does Mommy. It's hard to say goodbye but I know that when you're not with me you are being loved and having fun with Mommy. I'm happy that you have both of us that love you so much. I'll see you really soon, and we'll have a great time on Thursday."

"Do you and Mommy still love each other?"

"Mommy and I LOVE being your parents. We're the luckiest mommy and daddy in the world. We don't love each other like married people do, but I love that she's your mom. We both love you and always will."

"Whose decision was it to get a divorce/separation?"
(older child/teen)

"Honey, that's a big question. Remember we told you that we both worked hard to be married but couldn't because we disagreed about too many things and argued too much? Just like you, we both feel sad sometimes that it couldn't work, but we don't think of it as one person's decision."

"Did Dad/Mom have an affair?"

"Asking about *an affair* sounds like you're looking for a 'reason' why Mom and I decided to get divorced or if one of us is to blame. It's okay to ask, but it's really an adult-type question, not really a kid-type question. Just know that being married is a partnership and we both tried really hard and we didn't succeed—no need to blame anyone."

(If however the child is inadvertently exposed to information about an affair it may be good to address it more directly and give just enough information to help the child make sense of what he/she already knows.)

"I know that you know that Mom fell in love with Jesse. Mom and I weren't in love the way a husband and wife need to be. That's why we decided to divorce. I know it's hard; there are a lot of changes. Let us handle the adult stuff and you enjoy being a kid."

• • • • • • • •

Children in divorce/separation often have questions; they can come at the least expected moment. For parents adjusting to the challenges of single parenting, such questions can strike at the heart of emotional vulnerabilities and trigger uncertainties: *What's going on with the other parent? Am I doing something wrong? Are my kids OK if they're asking these things?* Kid questions, if responded to thoughtfully, provide valuable opportunities to help children adjust to *real changes* while instilling confidence in both parents' continued commitment to listen, guide, and give comfort.

How does any parent handle the difficult emotions that come up with these sorts of questions? With a lot of deep breaths and practice. We're not going to suggest there's anything easy about separating adult issues from kid questions, but we do know with thought, practice, and clarity that children don't belong *in the middle* of adult relationship issues, you'll find yourself much more successful than you ever imagined.

Expecting these kinds of questions can help you feel confident and prepared. Children often ask questions when and with whom they *feel safe*. Consider it as a sign of strength for your relationship. Children may be seeking information, deeper understanding, or simply reassurance—try to discern which it might be.

- Younger children often ask questions about their daily lives—changes or concerns that are causing anxiety. Provide simple, brief responses that reassure and clarify.

- Older children may ask direct questions about their parents' relationships.

They are often seeking reassurance for themselves—reassurance that they can continue being children, and reassurance that they don't have to take care of parents or take sides.

- Older children may also ask questions about a parent's relationship in order to form their own concepts and expectations of their future romantic relationships—they have more general questions about love and family.

- Because children don't have the emotional maturity to understand adult relationships, be thoughtful that your answers are age-appropriate. Teens may ask very direct questions, seeming to be ready for *the truth*, and you may find it wise to say, "That's something time and experience can teach you. For now, your dad and I…." (providing a simple, respectful answer.)

When questions arise:

1. **Center:** Take a deep breath and calm yourself before responding.

2. **Listen:** For younger children get on their eye level and pay full attention. For older children, give signals that you are listening but know that a little activity may make them more comfortable. You be the judge. Ask open-ended, neutral questions to get a fuller understanding of their feelings before offering a response.

* * * * * * * *

"You sound worried/sad/mad. Is that right or is it something else?"
"That's an important question. Tell me more."

* * * * * * * *

3. **Understand:** Ask yourself what they are really expressing/wanting/needing. Are they primarily expressing emotion? Do they need comfort/reassurance? Are they asking for basic information that they have a need to know? Are they asking information to gain a deeper understanding? Sometimes children repeat the same question because they're wondering if things will change again. They're just testing *(still the same today?)*.

4. **Respond with care and follow with comfort:** If the message is an emotional bid for comfort/reassurance, answer the question with a brief, direct response:

* * * * * * * *

"No we will not leave you. Either Daddy or I will take care of you even if we live in different houses."

* * * * * * * *

If they are asking for information that clarifies uncertainty or corrects a misunderstanding, give an honest, simple, and neutral (not blaming either parent) answer:

✳ ✳ ✳ ✳ ✳ ✳ ✳ ✳

"No, Mom and I are not going to get married again: I know that's
what you want. I'm sorry, Mom and I have made this decision."

✳ ✳ ✳ ✳ ✳ ✳ ✳ ✳

If they are seeking a deeper understanding, first clarify your understanding of their deeper question and give honest, brief, and neutral information:

✳ ✳ ✳ ✳ ✳ ✳ ✳ ✳

"I think you're asking if you were made from love—you were.
Even if Dad and I care for each other differently now than
we did then—our love for you will never change."

✳ ✳ ✳ ✳ ✳ ✳ ✳ ✳

If your answer to their question is possibly harmful or "adult business," reassure them that *it's okay to ask,* but that their job is to be a kid—not be involved in adult issues:

✳ ✳ ✳ ✳ ✳ ✳ ✳ ✳

"It sounds as if you are asking if anyone is to blame. I know
you want to understand, but marriage and divorce/separation
is adult stuff. We're all going to be okay. Know that we love
you; you don't need to worry or take care of either of us."

✳ ✳ ✳ ✳ ✳ ✳ ✳ ✳

If the question is "adult business" (for example, an affair) asked by an older teen/young adult, they may be wondering about their own future. Clarify first and then provide an answer that instills hope and possibility:

✳ ✳ ✳ ✳ ✳ ✳ ✳ ✳

"I wonder if you are really asking if because we got a divorce/
separation that you question if love lasts. Many times it does.
Every relationship is different and you will get the chance to
make your own choices about love and who you marry."

✳ ✳ ✳ ✳ ✳ ✳ ✳ ✳

Children's ability to navigate the shifts of daily life and make sense out of the bigger questions are essential parts of healing in divorce/separation. With each question, children begin to build a framework of understanding. They learn what *changes* with divorce/separation and what *remains the same*. They develop a more flexible, durable, concept of family and love. Children's questions can be hard, but listening and responding with care and gentle guidance surrounds a child with love and reassurance in times they need it most.

Parents' Feelings: Pacing the Process

For the parent who made the decision to leave the marriage. As we wrote about in Chapter 1, you may have done much of your grieving before you left the marriage. You may have moved on emotionally—and you may actually be happier today than you've been for years. Please, please, please keep in mind that your children are *not* in that space yet—and your co-parent is probably *not there, either.* Your children need you to straddle a gulf between where you are in your new life and where they are in accepting a life that's ended. They need you to dig down deep and reach across that chasm—letting them know that they are not left behind, unimportant, or required to make adjustments that they're simply not capable of making without more time and support. The hike proceeds at the speed of the slowest hiker, *unless we risk someone getting injured.* For children, being pushed well beyond their emotional capacity often results in deep (often invisible) emotional wounds.

If you're the parent who is attempting to make sense out of the divorce/separation, the devastation, and/or any number of reactions to the unexpected and unwanted, you're likely to be parenting with a bellyful of emotion most of the time—whether tears, anger, fear, anxiety or sheer exhaustion. You know you're preoccupied and at times overwhelmed. In our previous chapter, we focused on managing triggers and emotions. For now, know that with time things will get better. For now, get support (whether from a counselor, trusted friend, or through a post-divorce/separation support group) and be gentle with yourself and your children; allow the passage of time and acceptance to bring healing to your heart.

Co-Parenting Goals

Co-parents often disagree about the ending of their relationship, and they may disagree about protocols, but they rarely disagree about wanting what's best for their kids. We like to capitalize on this one nearly guaranteed truth. It's the place where parents will meet and agree. In our discussions with co-parents, we ask them to establish goals together for the post-divorce/separation joint venture of raising their children.

Here are some examples:

- We want our kids to feel loved, listened to, guided, and supported in their various interests, activities, and academic pursuits.

- We want our children to always know that our homes are safe harbors for them emotionally when their lives are stressful, peer pressure feels overwhelming, or their own expectations of themselves get the better of them.

- We want our kids to "be kids." We want them to know that we'll take good care of them and not the other way around. Especially *emotionally*, we want to be sure they know we're *here for them.*

- We want our kids to have access to education and educational/enrichment opportunities, when affordable, and provide a reasonable amount of money to make that happen if we can.

- We want to raise strong, clear thinking, capable, responsible kids who know they make a difference in the world and believe in themselves.

- We value our caring, emotionally healthy, and connected sense of extended family and want the kids to maintain their relationships with family on both sides.

- We believe that a child's strength and positive sense of self is directly related to an engaged and active relationship with each of us—we want to do everything we can to maintain positive relationships for the children—and support their relationship with the other parent.

There are dozens of different goals parents have written and set in front of themselves as "lighthouses" to guide their behavior and decision making. The key is that they've taken the time to think about the platform they stand on together for *however many years* until the children are adults—and *beyond.* What you set into motion today begins to support your children for the rest of your family life. There will be high school graduations, job accomplishments, engagement announcements, births, and deaths. *What platform do you want in place to best support your children through these very real, significant life-cycle events?* You're beginning to build that platform *right now.* Your goals are the planks.

Your Co-Parenting Goals

Take a moment and write your Co-Parenting Goals. Ask yourself, *"what do I need to do to help ensure these goals are met for our children?"* Jot notes underneath your goal to remind you of *your* contribution to success.

_____

_____

_____

_____

_____

_____

_____

_____

_____

Perhaps your co-parent would be interested in writing his/hers as well. If possible, share them with each other. You could compile your list and staple it to your parenting plan when you want to remember: *this is what's* really *important to us as co-parents!* This is not an invitation to "compete with one another," but rather to join together in the *best interests of your kids.*

Highlights in Review

- Children take cues from their parents on the safety, security, and acceptability of changes in their lives—we want to instill confidence and reassurance even when life is hard.

- Children build their "family life story" along with parents—we want to provide positive interpretations and messages of resilience; *help them make lemonade out of lemons.*

- Individual growth and development informs how children respond to divorce/separation.

- Ideally, growth and development continues unfolding, providing parents normal developmental challenges that have nothing to do with divorce/separation.

- Children benefit from holding many of their routines, familiar locations, and routine daily practices in place as they adjust to change. Structure, love, age-appropriate responsibility, and discipline should continue to be cornerstones of healthy parenting.

- Children want to love and be loved by both of their parents freely, without guilt or shame.

- Children grieve in their own "kid" ways—learning their emotional language is helpful in supporting them through family changes.

- Kids ask questions as a way of making sense of their world. They may need repeated reassurance about basic changes until trust rebuilds and stability takes hold.

- When kids struggle in prolonged or distressing ways, parents should talk with the child's health care provider or seek the help of a mental health professional.

- Taking the time to write your co-parenting goals keeps your most preciously held values front-and-center, even when life is tumultuous and stressful.

With shared goals in mind (or individual goals if your co-parent isn't ready to participate), you'll move ahead to some of the practical aspects of settling into a two-home family.

Chapter 3

Settling into a Two-Home Family

IN THIS CHAPTER, we step away from a focus on emotional adjustment to literal steps in setting up your two-home family. You are both 100 per cent parents on duty per your parenting plan agreements. We'll provide guidelines on how to manage your residential schedule in ways that reduce conflict, provide stability, and help kids adjust. We'll show you how to use role definition, predictability, and boundaries to facilitate kid-centered transitions and create secure home bases for your children. We'll provide "Rules for the Road" to deal with many of the common concerns that arise for parents living in separate homes. And lastly, we'll touch on how to integrate other people and pets into a two-home family.

New Routines Take Time

Divorce/separation changes the most basic routines and connections in family life. Everyone's daily schedules change, relationships may feel strained, and children and parents alike may fear a loss of daily connection and relationship with one another. Even among siblings, children may have different views and concerns about the changes, which can further a sense of isolation for a child: *no one understands me*. Unfortunately, your kids need more emotional support and time with you when you have less energy and attention to give. It's a collision of needs, reality, stress, and adjustment.

Yet you have enormous power to help your children cope with change and grieve their loss in healthy ways, even as you adjust and care for yourself. Over time, you and your co-parent will be guiding your children to a new sense of routine and "normal" in their two-home family. The small things matter: the words you say, your body language, your calming gestures throughout the day. It can also be big things such as working to manage your emotions, freeing them from conflict or modeling healthy coping strategies for handling stress, strong feelings, and difficult changes. When you emerge into a two-home family, you need time to establish new patterns. Children, in particular, need time to trust that their new sense of home and relationship with each parent is stable and secure.

Building a Secure Home Base in a Two-Home Family

Ritual, routine, and predictability help build a new normal. When my daughter was a toddler, her dad would carry her downstairs to bed in the evening, and they had a nightly ritual: my daughter would say about being put to bed, "And Blankie, too?" and he would answer, "'Of course!' said the horse." These simple routines allow children to build trust and mastery over an ever-changing self and world. So, consider how you can retain these comforting routines as you settle into a two-home family and, over time, create new ones together that become part of the fabric of your new sense of home.

How much time does it take to stabilize after divorce/separation? It depends; it really varies from family to family. Most experts would suggest about a year, maybe two.

What Does it Depend On?

For parents, we know that emotional adjustment is often the primary focus. Maintaining physical health (eating well, sleeping enough) is basic to a secure future. A sense of confidence in or mastery over an adequately secure financial present and future goes a long way to stabilizing homes and creating security post-divorce/separation. And dramatic shifts in day-to-day life post-divorce/separation will increase adjustment time. For example, is the once stay-at-home-parent now returning to school or workforce full-time resulting in daycare or dramatic schedule changes? Is a new partner being integrated into one parent's life simultaneously?

For kids, along with things like a) age, b) temperament, and c) other concurrent loss, change, or stress the child may be experiencing, factors include:

- Level of conflict (if any) in each home and between households/between co-parents—the longer open conflict persists, the longer it will take to build stability.

- Change in familiarity—did they move? Is there a new adult, additional children that are part of the family now?

- Sense of control—does each child have an age-appropriate amount of input about simple things like choosing bedding, or deciding what photos he/she can have by the bed, where the toys will be stored or homework done?

- Relationship with each parent—are both parents still physically and emotionally available to be concerned about the child and his/her feelings? Can they emotionally support the child?

Looking at the whole picture of your child's adjustment supports his/her development. Children may appear to be adjusting better in one home over the other, or with one parent over the other. When both parents commit to a healthily adjusted child not only in his/her house, at school, with peers, in extra-curriculars, but also in the other parent's household, they fully support their child. Keep in mind, that children go through rough times with one parent and then the other depending on age, gender, issue, etc., as part of normal growth and development—and in divorce/separation we simply need to scaffold and support those rough patches across two homes.

The parent who remains in the family home is faced with assisting his/herself and the children in dealing with "what is not there anymore"—the absence of the familiar *whole family*, a loss of the way things were. Although this can be easier than starting over, staying in the family home is not without challenges. The sadness and loss may be more disguised but not less important. Having simple, occasional check-ins with the kids on how they are feeling opens the door for sharing feelings and acknowledging the loss and change.

For the parent who moves out, his/her first new living situation is often less-than-ideal, temporary, or makeshift in some way—and is often followed by a second transition later, when finances are more stable. This can be challenging in the first six to 12 months when trying to establish routines with your children and a sense of home. For the kids, everything from their favorite toys to their special pillow becomes a focus of their 'OK-ness' and comfort, especially when someone may be sleeping on the couch at Aunt Anne's, where a parent is staying, or the breakfast room table seconds as a fort where sleeping bags get tucked for adventurous overnights in a parent's first living space.

The more we can honor a reasonable amount of recreating the familiar in the face of building a new future, the better. Patience, understanding, involving the children (age appropriately) in establishing their new digs can bring some enthusiasm and freshness to an otherwise uncertain situation. Reassuring the children that you feel the newness, too, that creating memories and a sense of home takes time, that you're aware that it's a big change. Appreciating their efforts at adjusting and accepting the changes can go a long way.

When both parents move into new living situations, the children are simultaneously saying goodbye to their family home while creating a new sense of home with each parent. Our hope is that both parents consider the comfort and well-being of their children in each home when planning to launch their two-home family.

Until both parents settle into permanent housing, and while co-owning the family home during your separation/divorce process, respect the boundaries of the parent who remains living in the home. Sometimes the parent who is living outside the family home feels entitled to enter the home at will: "I pay the mortgage; this is still my home." This is a very tough time; you co-own the home, but it's now occupied by your soon-to-be ex partner. Respecting his/her boundaries, just as you would a renter, with due notice and receiving permission to enter, are essential guidelines for civility.

Two 100% Parents

There is no way to get divorced/separated without changing the fabric of your family. We remind parents that it is rare that children arrive in this world without some tearing apart as well—it's one of the realities of how humans experience profound life-change. Painful as it can be, we recover, we heal; we grow and thrive. Even in divorce/separation, with separating homes, being separated from your children on some sort of residential schedule, your goal is to remain two 100% parents.

Early in the co-parenting, during residential schedule days, parents often struggle with missing their kids and feeling like they do not have enough time with them. You go from daily contact to something less than that as the other parent takes over duty. There can be an impulse to compete for time, to count hours, to become overly concerned with an extra-overnight here, or a Saturday lunch visit there. Competing and counting hours is not the answer. Grieving the loss and change is part of the answer. And building a workable residential schedule for the future is part of the answer.

Although difficult to believe, once healthy recovery happens, both parents and kids recalibrate to the new schedule, the new normal, and a new sense of expectations. There are many things that help with this resetting of expectations and finding a different, even comfortable, rhythm of family life:

- You are a 100% parent—whether you are on duty or not, you are always your child's parent. All the other loving adults that may enter your child's life will never substitute for you. We have watched this for years: the fear and concern about losing connection with a child, missing an important moment, or the other parent getting something special that you want a piece of. Unless you simply do not show up, your child(ren) will always have a special place in their hearts and lives for you. You will share amazing special moments, and yes, the other parent will, too. And, that's OK. So start by reassuring yourself: there's enough time, enough contact, enough wonderful experiences, and enough love to hold you and your children in a strong, bonded, and enduring place.

- Practice generosity. Look for opportunities to include the other parent in your child's life when appropriate. Keep in mind that this is for your kiddo as much as it is for the other parent. Go back to the good-old-fashioned golden rule: treat the other co-parent the way you hope to be treated.

One family demonstrated this spirit of family togetherness by the residential parent planning the birthday and "inviting" the other parent and his/her partner and even former in-laws to the celebration. Their child experienced his birthday with all the important people in his life showing their ability to work together and focus on the joy of the occasion. When this is possible, it's a great example of open-heartedness in meeting a child's needs.

- Create realistic rituals with your children when they are with the other parent. Be sensitive about randomly intruding on your co-parent's and children's residential time; consider how often you call, the impact, the value; consider the other parent's schedule. For older children, an occasional text message may be a good way to be in touch without involving yourself in the other household. Perhaps it works best to let the kids contact you, trusting that they will do so when it's comfortable for them. Remember that calling or connecting is not a measure of how much they care for you. Your ability to trust them to find their way of calling/connecting with you is often a measure of how much you care for them. With younger children, co-parents often work out ways to Facetime, Skype, or similar, which allows little ones a chance to connect with Mommy/Daddy in a way that supports their development. With our itty-bitty ones, parents should find ways of creating visits in the other parent's home, maintaining breast feeding, etc. Keep your eye on the mark: determine what meets each child's developmental needs and what works best for the kids—which, as they get older, can include settling in with their other parent without worrying about connecting with you.

A Clear Residential Schedule

A residential schedule is designed ideally by both parents (or with both parent's input) and takes into consideration the children's developmental stage, special needs (if any), and designates enough time with each parent for an engaged and positive relationship. You may work with a co-parenting coach or your legal team to determine your children's residential schedule. This is an important task that serves co-parents well when done properly. Your residential schedule should be clearly written, understandable by both parents, be specific in terms of transition times, and address special events, holidays, school breaks, and vacation time. The residential schedule is one portion of the larger parenting plan that describes your co-parenting agreements and responsibilities.

The residential schedule defines parental responsibility for the care and feeding of your children. The residential parent is "on duty" while the non-residential parent is "off duty." A residential parent has day-to-day decision making for and with his/her children when the kids are scheduled to be with that parent in his/her home. Even in co-parenting agreements where parents have 'joint decision-making,' typically that does not cross into day-to-day structure and function of an individual parent's life with his/her children. This division of parenting responsibility is an important boundary to know, honor, and respect.

> Weilyn's mom called on Thursday to ask if Anisha could spend the night on Saturday. Grace wanted to say, "Sure!" but knew that Anisha would be with her father on the weekend. So instead, she offered Weilyn the phone number to contact Anisha's dad regarding the invitation on his residential time.

Co-parents, not kids, are in charge of the residential schedule. This comes up often: Do children get to decide where they live when they're 13? If you're asking us, the answer is unequivocally "NO." Children need the safety to pushback, argue with, resist, and protest during certain developmental stages. Healthy co-parents recognize that these temporary, often difficult periods require skillful parenting in a one-home family—even more so in a two-home family. When a parent involves a child in adult-level issues/concerns or sides with a child against the other co-parent, he/she is pulling the child up into the parental subsystem of the family—in other words, *out of his/her childhood* and into adult business that may eventually compromise the child's normal, healthy growth and development.

> Co-parents who work together and reassure children that parents are in charge of the residential schedule ensure that children have the freedom to move through their positive as well as difficult developmental stages safely and securely until they're ready to leave home after high school graduation.

This is not to say that parents can't agree on a child living with one or the other parent during particular points in the child's growing-up years for good reasons. The key here is: *both parents come to agreement* to what's *in the child's best interest* for the short- and long-term residential schedule. The child is not *used* to further one parent's needs or agenda over the other, or meet a parent's emotional needs at the cost of the child's own childhood, or threaten the child's relationship with his/her other parent.

• • • • • • • •

Will, age 14: *"I hate you. You're the worst mother—you're just a basket case! You better give me back my XBOX. I can't believe you. You're so full of *&%@; I'm living with Dad and you can't stop me. He never does crap like this!"*

Mom: *"You'll get your XBOX back when those missing assignments are completed and turned in. I get that you're really mad right now—and I can deal with that. Your Dad and I have already talked. And he completely agrees: assignments need to get done. This week. You're welcome to call Dad."*

Will (3 hours later): *"They're done. Here. Look. Both of them. Happy now? ….Mom, can you take me and Josh to the community center?"*

• • • • • • • •

Mom (to Dad): *"Sam, Kelsey got the lead in the school musical. She's so excited, but she's also really worried about how she's going to manage the play practices, her three AP classes, and work on the school newspaper schlepping back and forth between our houses. Has she mentioned anything to you? I'm wondering how you'd feel about just letting her stay here with me for the next two months until the performances end to provide some relief in her schedule."* (Mom lives closer to school than Dad.)

Dad (to Mom): *"Hmmm, she hasn't mentioned it to me yet, but I can imagine that might be hard for her to bring it up for fear of hurting my feelings. She's hardly ever home—it's kind of crazy, isn't it? I'm really happy for her and I know she's doing such a great job. OK, let's offer that to her and see what she says. What I'd like to suggest is that she and I make weekly dinner plans and I'll take her to a late breakfast on Sundays if that would work for you—just so she and I stay in touch over the next two months."*

Mom (to Dad): *"That would be great. Sundays are fine. OK with you if I tell her we've talked?"*

Dad (to Mom): *"No—let me tell her, OK? I'll see her tonight at home."*

Dad (to Kelsey): *"Hey Sweetie, Mom and I talked and we're wondering if it would help you if you stayed at her house for the next two months during play rehearsals—you know, until the performances are over and not switch back and forth. We want to do whatever will help you feel like you can focus and be* *less stressed. I'm thinking we could plan dinners during the week when it can work and definitely a late breakfast every Sunday. What do you think?"*

Kelsey (to Dad): *"OMG, that would be so helpful, Daddy! Are you sure? Thank you so much!"*

* * * * * * * *

> The residential schedule provides the backbone and rhythm for your children's daily lives.

This is not to say that it's rigid and unyielding; rather, that the clarity and specificity serve important purposes. A good residential schedule provides predictability and security—ensuring connection with parents on a regular and reliable basis for kids—as well as diminishes negotiation, change and conflict for parents as they settle into new routines, stabilize households, and find their footing in new lives with the kids.

The residential schedule may change over the course of child-rearing depending on the ages of your children, their developmental needs, and your relationship with your co-parent. Whether changed over time, or not, children learn to relax into the clarity of a residential schedule, knowing where they belong when, with whom, and how to resolve questions about meeting needs for time and attention. Effectively implemented, young adult and adult children often continue to borrow from the residential schedule rhythms as they plan holidays home from college and into *their* future family life leaving them free from fear of disappointing someone they love very much.

* * * * * * * *

Brad, age 21: *"Hey, Mom, is Thanksgiving this year with you or Dad?"*

Mom: *"It's a 'Dad year'—enjoy!! Will you bring the pecan pie again?"*

* * * * * * * *

Co-parents may feel completely comfortable with children moving back and forth at will through the gate in the back-yard that separates their two-homes. The key is that co-parents together feel comfortable, secondly, that children are safe and supervised, and thirdly, that children are thriving. Whenever these three criteria are met, you and your co-parent have a winning combination!

Guidelines for Managing
Your Residential Schedule

Stability First / Flexibility Second

Slowing down all the change during the first six months to a year, settling into a pattern that's predictable, allowing your children a feeling of mastery over their whereabouts in their two-home family has great value. Do what you can at the front end to balance parental needs, unanticipated schedule changes, and children's predictability needs. Err on the side of holding to the schedule when possible.

Trading Time / Covering Time

Parents also work together to manage changes in residential schedules through trading time and covering time. "Trading time" refers to exchanging residential time for like residential time. This means: weekend time for weekend time, and weekday/evening/night time for weekday/evening/night time. It's not hours for hours, but rather similar *quality* of time. Evenings during the school week have a different quality from weekend day times. Trades are negotiated, keeping in mind that these are requests and not mandatory. You'll work out how you do trades together. Similarly, "covering time" refers to offering your co-parent the opportunity to be with the children in lieu of babysitters without any request to trade. (If you find you and your co-parent regularly trading or covering time in an ongoing way, you may want to consult with your legal team about potential impact on your parenting plan or renegotiate your residential schedule.)

"But I Have to Work"

Your co-parent is not "on call" for you, or your back-up unless expressly agreed upon. Be respectful of each other's time. Making and keeping commitments regarding schedule and time is important for your co-parenting relationship—vital if you or your co-parent need to show up to work on time or other important commitments—and for your kids sense of security. Being "on duty" per your residential schedule is all part of the formal business contract that you two designed to ensure the well-being of your children. In a one-house family, parents often back each other up, rely on each other, maybe even take each other for granted. Those days are gone: report on time and be prepared for your job: taking care of the kids!

Right of First Refusal

This is a term found in some Parenting Plans that refers to a requirement that the residential parent must offer residential time to the other parent before contracting for childcare with a babysitter or any third party. Sometimes there's a specific amount of time that triggers the right of first refusal, for example, "over four hours" or "overnights." If this is part of your parenting plan agreements, as with any contractual arrangement, keep your agreements with integrity. If you're wondering if this *should* be a part of your parenting plan agreements, we would offer this consideration: when you're getting along with your co-parent, you will generally want him/her to care for the kids whenever reasonable (exception: when Grandma wants a special chance to have Junior with her). When you're in conflict and not getting along with your co-parent, the right of first refusal often results in fighting— or another tension filled transition for your children. Please seriously consider the short and long-term implications of tying yourselves together and limiting your choices through a provision like right of first refusal.

"Mom, Can MacKenzie Babysit Us?"

Children who move back and forth between parents on a regular basis can benefit from the fun and familiarity of a babysitter without facing another transition. We encourage co-parents to recognize the value of good judgment and allowing each other some privacy. Rather than counting hours you could be with your children when they are left with a babysitter during your co-parent's residential time, relax and trust that the use of competent babysitters can enhance your children's sense of home and normalcy. Allowing grandparents the chance to provide childcare in a parent's absence creates the opportunity for a secure sense of extended family—and sometimes the kids will go to a friend's for a sleepover when Mom or Dad has plans. When co-parents can trust and create space for all of these typical ways of caring for children in daily life, rather than the non-residential parent insisting he/she should be offered time with the children, *kids and parents benefit.*

"Dad, Can We just Stop at Mom's and Pick Up...."

Establishing boundaries and teaching good guest protocols are part of raising children in a two-home family. Parents often ask if children should have keys to both parent's homes and whether children should be encouraged to 'just drop by' the off-duty parent's home. We take a practical approach to this complicated question. Yes, we want children to experience that both homes are *theirs.* However, if children learn right from the beginning that stopping by can happen only after:

1) Calling/texting first and,

2) Getting permission from the off-duty parent.

...then you're never faced with kids dropping by at inconvenient or potentially adult-only times. That can include being awakened from a dead sleep, or your child being experienced as an *intruder!* Just because you're a parent, when you're *off-duty*, it's OK to have boundaries, control over who comes and goes from your home, and privacy. Talk with your co-parent; together you'll establish what's appropriate for each of your homes and individual comfort zones.

Child-Centered Transitions

> Transitions represent a changing of the guard, a letting go of one parent's hand while reaching to take the other parent's hand.

How you and your co-parent manage transitions punctuates your kiddo's lives. Are they filled with question marks (uncertainty?), exclamation points (anger/hostility/conflict!), empty space (where they make the transition alone), or a bridge where the movement from one home or parent to the other is smooth, integrated, and without concern? Parents are in charge of this experience; we sustain the calm, even steps through transition.

- Ensure respectful (on the part of the adults) transitions.

- Some parents utilize "natural" transition spots that don't require contact with each other, such as school/activity pick-up/drop-off. This way, the children experience letting go of one parent into a familiar environment like school or daycare, and meeting the other parent at the other end of their day. For parents who are having difficulty seeing each, this is a useful way to minimize upset until more healing occurs and contact is less painful.

- Others meet in a neutral location for a quick transfer and hand-off of children's belonging. For the parent who prefers that their co-parent not come to his/her home, this works well. Examples include grocery store parking lot, park, neighborhood coffee shop, or similar neutral, familiar place. When children are having particular difficulties leaving the "family home" to be with their other parent, this transition plan often assists the children with letting go of home first and parent second.

- Similarly, when children are having difficulty leaving home in either direction, having the current residential parent help children pack up, get into his/her car and drive to the receiving parent's home can ease the sense of disruption, of being taken away by the receiving parent.

- For some particularly difficult or conflictual co-parenting relationships, parents employ a third party to assist with transitions. One parent drops off to a third party and the other picks up from the third party. Given a choice between allowing someone to assist your children through the transition or having your children experience arguments or violent emotions between parents—the former is definitely preferable until both parents are capable of a more calm, respectful, neutral transition.

- Do what works—respectfully and as calmly as possible.

- Transitions can be a time of cordiality and brief sharing. A quick positive story, a brief reminder to the kiddo to tell Dad about the spelling test (*that you aced!*), or positive wishes for a good weekend and fun with Grandma is appropriate. Lingering, long conversations, multiple hugs beyond typical, or any negative exchanges, are confusing and not helpful to kids. If you have a difficult report from school to share, WAIT. Email or call later.

- Sometimes children want one parent to enter the other parent's home to see something important during a transition. Be a respectful guest. Always get prior permission from your co-parent. Asking in front of your child is a set-up and not nearly as respectful as encouraging your child to wait with reassurance that you'll "talk with Mom/Dad about this first," before making plans to enter your co-parent's home.

RESISTING TRANSITIONS

If a child resists the transition from one parent to another, parents should work together to reassure him/her and/or address legitimate issues, rather than allow the child to refuse to spend time with that parent. Encourage your children to enjoy times in both homes. Children will have complaints—they may from time to time test your conviction that having a strong, engaged relationship with their other parent is important. A child may be having a struggle with his/her other parent and hopes that you'll take sides, solve his/her problems, and/or provide an escape hatch from taking responsibility for his/her behavior. A young child may simply be expressing the pain of separating—today from you, tomorrow from his/her other parent.

Discern the nature of the complaint and seriousness of his/her reluctance. Helping children develop self-advocacy skills, supporting them in approaching another adult (even their other parent) to solve problems, stepping in to advocate for them are familiar skills. You've faced similar concerns when your child comes home from school with complaints about a teacher. Your first inclination is not to agree that he/she doesn't have to return to school! There are many steps that begin with discerning the seriousness of the problem and developing a plan for conflict resolution. (See Chapter 4: Communication Protocols that Work.)

Refusing time or rejecting a relationship with a parent is too heavy a burden for a child to carry. Parents need to maintain responsibility for big decisions, and only if there are clear, serious safety issues should a parent step in and do whatever is necessary to protect the child through restricting time or supporting a child in refusing time. Even then, the goal is to eliminate the risk, solve the problems, and resolve the conflict to facilitate a child's unrestricted relationship—love, caring, and the opportunity to work out issues—with both parents. (See also the Appendix "What if You need a Parenting Plan Modification—Advice from an Attorney".)

KEYS TO SUCCESSFUL TRANSITIONS

Help children succeed at managing the challenges of their two-home family. Children's capacity for tracking belongings, organizing time, and maintaining focus can be more challenged in a two-home family at the outset. Help your children by building strategies and processes for navigating across two homes. Create age-appropriate routines and rules that make their job easier:

- Allow children to take important belongings between homes. This works best if both parents acknowledge the need for things to get returned and redistributed as needed. It's fine to request that the toys at Mommy's new apartment stay at Mommy's, while allowing older, familiar toys to travel back and forth.

- The right gear makes all the difference in the world. Packing Junior's life into a backpack may not feel big enough, and a suitcase may feel too traveling salesman-like. Try a nice square plastic tote with clip on lid. It holds everything from library books to X-box games, extra tennis shoes and swimming trunks, plus Madeline can decorate hers with pens that draw on plastic, stickers, and a checklist slipped into a clear plastic sleeve taped securely to the inside lid for guidance when packing. Transitioned items may require coordination with your co-parent if kid transfers are happening at school or after-school care. Parents may drop off the tote or extra items at the other parent's home at a designated time arranged in advance.

- Stuff gets forgotten! Particularly in this first year, accept that there will be a few extra trips between households to regather something important that was left behind. No need to blame either your child or the other parent, just focus on doing better next time. Rome wasn't built in a day. Children in two-home families tend to build superior organization and self-management skills over time.

- Create workable routines and practices for packing and preparing for their transition. Just as you and your child developed a bedtime routine when she was three, and a "clean-up-your-room, make-your-bed" routine by the time he was seven, you and your child will develop routines for packing and preparing for transitions. Similar to the child who resisted getting ready for bed, your child may want to resist preparing for his/her transition. It's not easy; convenient; or *his/her choice.* Be patient, persistent, and practical. Time will help turn a potentially bumpy time into a no-brainer.

- Help children manage their daily life activities such as homework between two homes with coordinated co-parenting protocols (See Chapter 4: Communication Protocols that Work).

- If possible, parents should try to find some basic areas of agreement regarding discipline and daily routine that help children feel some continuity between homes. Some good examples: morning and bedtime routines, homework practices, meal times (within reason), and similar bedtimes.

Good Co-Parenting Hygiene: Rules for the Co-Parenting Road

CO-PARENTING BASICS

A co-parenting relationship, like any relationship, takes work and takes effort to build familiarity, trust, and goodwill. You aren't starting from a clean slate. There's a lot of history, some of it positive, some of it not so good. Hold onto what worked and let go of what didn't. You have an opportunity to build a better co-parenting relationship if you don't allow the frustrations of the past to inform the present.

Primary parents are often surprised by the changes in parenting interest and energy by a parent who was previously focused on work or personal interests, when parenting was a side gig. We see this all the time. This stepping-up, stepping in, and wanting a recognized co-parenting role is often felt to be disruptive, threatening, a day late and a dollar short ("Where were you when I needed your help? golfing!" "You've never been to a parent-teacher conference, *ever!*"). History aside, the newly interested and sometimes not-so-prepared co-parent is stepping up to directly meet your kids' needs. No better time than the present to help him/her successfully engage as the children's other parent. He/She may not know *how*, but he/she can *learn.* From your "spouse mind," you may want to push back and not allow the other parent to suddenly come to the parenting party; from "parent mind," you recognize how much your children will benefit from a strong, positive, nurturing relationship with *each of you*, allowing you to relax and help your co-parent succeed. Skill-building takes time, so you may need patience and perseverance through this stage of co-parenting development.

When sharing information with your co-parent be constructive not instructive. A father will never be a "stay-at-home-Mom" nor vice-versa. Parents, whether two moms, two dads, or a mom and a dad, will each be unique, bringing strengths and weaknesses to parenting. Parents often divide duties in a one-house family that can result in one parent having more of certain kinds of information about children than the other. Getting helpful information "downloaded" and shared between co-parents helps kids feel like their lives are more similar than different as they move from home to home. Have a conversation about what kind of information would be helpful to share and when. Would your co-parent like you to put information in an email or talk with him/her? Help each other prepare to be good parents—keeping in mind that co-parenting is a relationship between equals regardless of history or current skill-set.

> Addie, a typical four-year-old eater, had stumped Mommy on lunch packing. After the second day of Addie's full lunch box returning home untouched, Meg, her mom, decided she needed some information. She asked her ex, Hugh, "What do you put in Addie's lunch? She seems to love them!" Hugh kindly offered to email her a list of Addie's favorite lunch foods. Meg was so relieved, and Addie got the nourishment she needed.

Building a functional co-parenting relationship takes time; treating your former romantic partner in a business-like manner can feel awkward. Starting with a renewed perspective gives you the chance to create something constructive and sustainable—and most importantly, something that works in the here-and-now and for the future in the best interest of your kids.

Keep adult emotions separate from kids' emotions. Adults and children have a very different experience of divorce/separation. You've divorced/separated from your former spouse; kids aren't divorcing ANYONE. Your kiddos shouldn't carry the flag for your hurt, angry, betrayed feelings. You don't want to embroil them in a loyalty battle—it's a *lose-lose* for children. Most importantly, allow them to love their other parent openly and without reservation. Allow them to do the same with all the loving people in their lives—*even new partners*. Allowing children to maintain a full range of loving connections, and protecting their precious childhood from our adult issues demonstrates enormous respect and caring for them, and helps them stay healthy emotionally.

- Strive to model cordial, respectful communication about the other parent, both verbally and nonverbally.

- Speak positively about the other parent's traits, skills, or interests to your child. Remember, for the first years of your child's life he/she heard others make admiring comments like, *"That's JUST LIKE your Dad...You smile JUST LIKE your Mom!"* Our children want to *be like us* in important ways, and we want them to continue to be proud of both of us as they grow up to become who they are.

- Give your children direct messages about enjoying a great relationship with the other parent; repeat it often.

- Help your children with preparing for the other parent's birthday, Mother's/Father's Day, and other special holidays.

- Facilitate the kids maintaining healthy relationships with family members on both sides of the family.

- Accept your children's relationship with your ex's new partner (when that time comes), despite your own feelings.

- Reassure children in words and actions that you are okay when they are not with you. Children don't need to worry about their other parent being lonely, or sad, or in some way "not OK" by being alone.

* * * * * * * *

Abigaile, age 4: *"Mommy, do you miss me when I'm at Daddy's?"*

Mommy: *"Of course, Pumpkin; but I'm so glad that you're having 'Daddy time' that I'm happy in my heart even when you're at Daddy's."*

Abigaile: *"Well, Daddy's sad all the time when I'm not there...he misses me."*

Mommy: *"Oh Pumpkin, Daddy does miss you, but you can be sure that Daddy will take care of Daddy's big-man feelings; he knows how to do that. You don't have anything to worry about."*

* * * * * * * *

Encourage children to enjoy their residential time in each home and share experiences. Children in a two-home family may feel disconnected and anxious. They can have difficulty understanding the "rules" of family relationships. Children benefit when we actively encourage them to fully engage and enjoy each parent during their residential time. We want kids to feel comfortable sharing information about their life/experiences with either parent. The more freely they can discuss activities and relationships across both homes, the more relaxed they can be that their life is whole, OK, and that there's nothing they should hide, be ashamed of, or fear causes pain *for you* or other grown-ups.

- Show pleasure when children share their positive stories about time with the other parent.

- Maintain healthy skepticism when they share negative stories about their time with the other parent. Children are famous for speaking to the choir. If they suspect that you enjoy hearing that Mom's "bad," they'll bring you stories of just how "bad" she is, however exaggerated, inflated, or completely inaccurate the stories actually are. If you have a genuine concern, handle it respectfully with the other parent off-line from a place of curiosity (more on this in Chapter 4: Communication Protocols that Work).

- Children live in a "secret-free zone" with parents. We teach them from an early age to talk with us, to tell us what's most important to them, to share their biggest worries, and to own their scariest mistakes—knowing that *nothing will be made worse by talking with us about it.* Divorce/separation changes none of these cornerstone teachings. Please do not ask your children to keep secrets from their other parent.

- Reassure your children in words and actions that *they are safe, loved, and well cared for when with the other parent* even if that care is different than what you provide.

Help children feel connected with both parents, regardless of schedule. Regular and consistent schedules help children and parents function well and feel connected. However, there will be times when keeping to the schedule means children miss out on special events with the other parent. From a child's perspective, schedules are their time for being loved and cared for by each parent, not a parent's right to his/her time with the children. *Children are not possessions.* Ideally you and your co-parent share the following values:

- Both parents are free to attend children's public events (athletic games, school events, etc.) even though they occur during one parent's residential time (see Chapter 8: The Kids' World Outside of Home—Co-Parenting in Public Spaces).

- Each parent encourages children's interaction with their other parent when they attend special events.

- Within reason, parents strive to be flexible when needed for children to participate in special events with the other parent or parent's extended family, or avoid long stretches without seeing the other parent, when possible.

- Children need to have reasonable phone access to either parent when desired.

- Encourage your children to keep photos or mementos of their other parent in their room or by their bed; maintain scrapbooks with family photos. *The household has changed, but their family history wasn't deleted.*

SOVEREIGN TIME: INDEPENDENT PARENTING

Respect each other's parenting time. Each parent is responsible for caring for children during his/her residential time. It interferes with effective co-parenting when one parent makes plans for the kids during the other's residential time, makes rules for or discipline to be carried out during the co-parent's residential time, or attempts to change the co-parent's residential schedule without agreement. Nine times out of ten, the other parent will push back, disappointment/conflict will ensue, and both co-parents will backslide into greater distrust and conflict. Kids lose another step toward stability and calm in their two-home life.

- Safeguard your co-parenting relationship by 1) checking first, 2) discussing as needed, 3) confirming agreement, or respecting the lack of agreement. You and your co-parent each have the right to say "no" and have the other accept your boundary gracefully.

- Plan activities for your residential time only and respect the other parent's freedom to plan activities on his/her time. If activity schedules cut across both residential times, both parents agree *first* before involving children in discussions or enrollment (see Chapter 4: Communication Protocols that Work) .

- Be mindful that this is a business relationship of equals. Neither of you are in control of nor should you negatively impact the other's scheduled time with the kids—this *includes* when you're both with your children in public spaces (see Chapter 8: The Kids' World Outside of Home—Co-Parenting in Public Spaces).

Respect each other's independence in parenting. In divorce/separation both parents find their way into independent households, with rules, practices, and protocols independently deemed appropriate for each parent's home. Children need love, discipline, connection, and structure for meeting the demands of daily life in each home. Parents don't need to be in agreement on every aspect of the children's daily lives as long as children are thriving, progressing through their developmental stages, and are safe and secure in each home.

- Both parents share in the work and play of caring for their children. No Disneyland parenting; no more "wait til your Dad/Mom gets home." You may need to stretch and carry more "Mom energy" when the kids are away from Mom's house, or "Dad energy" when away from Dad's. That's what is *best for the kids*. In practical terms, you may find that you have to be more nurturing, a little bit softer, more conscientious about safety; or, you may have to channel your inner-boss with more ease, or push yourself to be more adventurous— accepting your child's occasional bumps and bruises that come from testing appropriate physical limits.

- Both parents create a positive plan for discipline and routines in each home— don't rely on the other parent for discipline issues in your home.

- Both parents take individual responsibility for obtaining information from academic, recreational and social resources. You both want to be on all the emails from the "Little Bears Basketball" league, both know the password to your child's academic website where teachers post grades and assignments, and both begin to develop a call list of your children's friends' parents to arrange play-dates and respond to birthday invitations during your residential time.

- Support your children's peer relationships by maintaining contact and engagement, if possible and reasonable, across both parent's residential time.

- Respect differences in parenting style or practices. You can discuss concerns, but remember: *it's a discussion*. If you two cannot agree, and it is not a safety concern, it may be best to accept the difference. A simple difference in parenting style will have less impact on your child than on-going conflict between the two of you. Choose your battles wisely. (Safety concerns may need intervention, and we encourage you to consult your child's healthcare provider, your attorney, or the authorities depending on the level of concern.)

Co-parents often provide different levels of attention to nutrition, TV or screen time, tidiness, and bedtime routines. As a mom told me recently,"he may be the mac-and-cheese Dad; I just want him to be the best mac-and-cheese Dad to our daughter he can be." That's acceptance.

FACILITATING ONE-ON-ONE TIME WITH A PARENT

Helping each other have precious one-on-one time with each of your children can be an important gift to both parents and kids after divorce/separation. The residential schedule sets into motion a series of back to back single-parenting stretches for kids. Gone are the days when Dad was available to hang with for one thing; Mom was around doing something else; a child could run out on an errand with a parent by him/herself leaving siblings behind. Figuring out how to have parent-child time that *celebrates* that one-on-one relationship with each of your children can be a challenge, but with creativity and strong co-parenting, it can happen with occasional ease and much pleasure.

CO-PARENTS WITH PARTNERS

Parents should remain the parenting leaders even with new partners. Introducing new partners is a big transition for *everyone*. This can be a time of heightened anxiety, concerns about "what's going to happen next," who's in charge, and how will this *impact ME?* The children and your co-parent will likely need reassurance that all will not be *changed* regarding the hard-earned or budding family stability. The new partner/adult in the children's lives has his/her own anxieties and uncertainties. There may be other children to consider as well. To the extent that it's possible, hold your co-parenting relationship in a primary position with regard to your children. As enticing as it may be to switch co-parenting loyalty to your new partner or try to create a happy threesome (your new partner, your co-parent and yourself), that may result in enormous disruption without respectful planning and sensitivity to timing. (See Chapter 9: New Adults in Your Children's Lives.)

- If possible, inform the other parent of your intention to introduce a new partner. Dating information may be hard to hear as an ex-partner, but is useful to know as a parent who provides children positive emotional support and reassurance that everything's OK when they return from residential time with their other parent.

- Parents remain the leaders on behalf of their children and make the important kid-related decisions, even if new partners become part of the family. Until there's adequate time to assess how the adults will work together, new relationships are built, and new agreements are forged from a place of respect, trust and goodwill, the co-parenting agreements in place between the two of you remain the cornerstones for your children's sense of security and family life.

- Parents should help their new partners become familiar with the co-parenting arrangements and agreements, and support him/her in finding a role in the family that respects his/her place in the household as well as existing family relationships across the two-home family.

What About Grandparents: Helping Extended Family Join the Team

Divorce/separation requires everyone to adjust—including grandparents, extended family, and our closest friends. Some of your extended family may need guidance for adjusting to the new norm of "collaborating" and "cooperating" over behaviors of exclusion and open expressions of unresolved anger typical of divorce/separation in the past.

- Share information with your closest allies and your children's extended family group about your hopes for respect and calm, your needs for support, and their role. Let them know how they can rally and be part of a constructive post-divorce/separation team.

- You may find yourself having to manage conversations within earshot of your children. In spite of loved ones intention to support you by expressing anger/disappointment and their own feelings of betrayal, they may be inadvertently complicating feelings for your kids. Help others recognize that bad-mouthing, taking sides, or criticizing your former spouse is hard on children who love their other parent, someone who is very special to them.

- Let each parent be the natural gateway to their extended family. Until and unless otherwise expressly agreed upon, allow the bloodlines to provide useful, respectful boundaries whenever there's a question of whether you should or your spouse should contact his/her family members.

- Lead by example, and hopefully grandparents and significant family members and friends will follow the same guidelines of respect and cordiality you value when interacting with the children and your former spouse at family or public events.

What about Miss Kitty and Fido?

There are many ways to deal with a family pet(s) in a two-home family. Because there are both practical and emotional considerations, please be sure that your children are involved (in age-appropriate ways) with your decisions about family pets. Some families have the beloved pet follow the residential schedule. For other families, that's not possible nor would the pet thrive under those conditions. Sometimes with all the other changes, what's best for the family pet is to be re-homed where the pet can have his/her needs best met for socializing, exercise, etc. The sensitivity and skill used to handle a family pet telegraphs a lot to your children about your understanding of how change impacts each and every member of the family.

Highlights in Review

- Adjustment takes time. Familiar routines and predictability help build a "new normal."

- Many elements impact a child's adjustment. Conflict and stress will consistently prolong settling into a two-home family.

- Your parenting plan residential schedule provides a backbone to your children's daily rhythm.

- Parents are in charge of the residential schedule.

- Supporting each other to be the best co-parents you each can be is what's *best for kids*.

- Transitions are important for kids. They hope parents are able to stay calm and make the transition as smooth as possible for them.

- Healthy boundaries between homes and respect for each other's parenting style is critical for a constructive co-parenting relationship.

- Co-parents remain the central figure in kids' lives as decision makers; new partners may enhance and expand the circle of nurturing, but most co-parents do best when their primary roles with their children are respected and upheld.

Chapter 4

Communication Protocols that Work

Technically, co-parenting exists with any parenting arrangement, regardless of its formal designation. In whatever way each parent is involved in raising the child, the parents co-parent. Most effective co-parenting arrangements contain the following characteristic dynamics between the parents: cooperation, communication, compromise, and consistency. These dynamics often grow over time and typically take a period of years to evolve effectively.

—Michael Scott, Mediator/Marriage and Family Therapist

Taking the High Road

All healthy communication originates from and is guided by respect and civility. We're going to write that again: *All healthy communication originates from and is guided by respect and civility.* Wow, SO MUCH EASIER SAID THAN DONE. We know it; you know it. That is the most important lighthouse in each and every communication with your former spouse—your children's *other parent.* Let's get clear about what we mean by respect and civility in both written and verbal communication:

- *In your kids' best interest:* remember, you're writing/speaking to your children's other parent, not your ex-partner.

- Pleasant tone (*you'd use that very same tone to your BOSS*).

- Appropriate word choice (this is not the time for four-letters or other expletives).

- Judiciously use ALL CAPS for highlighting and ease of reading—not for *shouting* at the reader.

- Be brief, informative, well-organized.

- Use the subject line of an email effectively.

- Be thoughtful about how many communications you send; repetitive texts or emails are intrusive and ineffective.

- Respond in a timely manner to *appropriate* communications received, even if all you say is, "Got it. Will get back to you tomorrow" or whenever is appropriate and possible.

- Ignore unproductive emails, texts, or voice messages. Think of any response to negative/unproductive communication as kindling on a fire you're hoping will die-out. *Don't feed the fire.*

When angry or triggered, go quiet. Your least productive interactions will occur when you're angry or triggered, so, to the extent that you can, excuse yourself, take a break and step away from interactions when you are in those states of mind. Go for a run, sit in meditation, take a nap, do some work, watch a funny movie. Re-engage and/or respond when your perspective is unclouded by difficult emotions and when productive problem-solving can resume. If you and your co-parent are in an entrenched cycle of high-conflict conversations, consider using a family specialist to facilitate communication while you both build skills and learn to soothe emotions. After a few problems tackled successfully, you'll have more confidence to fly solo.

Protect your children from witnessing/overhearing/participating in unhealthy/protracted adult conflict. Arguments scare kids. Conflict undermines their sense that parents can take care of them; often causes kids to feel they need to take care of parents by taking sides, solving problems or caretaking emotionally rather than expressing and managing their *kid-level feelings*.

- Keep parent conversations respectful and calm when kids are present.

- Allow children to enjoy their special events by being respectful and cordial to the other parent.

Get comfortable waiting and editing your email before sending—allow enough time to pass to ensure a neutral tone. Find a way to save messages to your Draft folder and re-read emails to check that they meet the above criteria. *Breathe* before responding to a text message. This is a skill! Practice makes better, not perfect. When the wheels fall off the bus, regroup. That may mean soothing your own feelings, clarifying information or intent, or even apologizing for your misstep. Over time, communication will smooth out and difficult interactions will turn around more quickly.

Even when only one person can maintain civility, the path to respect and co-operation is shorter and less arduous. Whether your co-parent shares these values, ideas, protocols or not, we encourage you to strive to bring your *best self* to your communications.

> We understand as well as anyone the impulse to fight fire with fire, just know we're in it with you to **stop, resist the fight, breathe,** and **practice civility.**

The power of "No, thank you" Whether communicating verbally or in writing, practice the art of *confident clarity*. When you say, "no, thank you" or "no, that doesn't work for me," stop before you find yourself justifying or defending your position. There are times when a gentle explanation, or a bit more information provides a useful context for your answer, but learning to be comfortable with a simple, polite "no, I'm sorry, that doesn't work for me" is constructively powerful. Similarly, receive a polite "no" from your co-parent without pushing for more or assuming the worst.

The value of "Yes, of course" And, "Yes, of course, I'd be glad to" generates good-will. A simple act of generosity can turn a difficult situation into a reminder that you're actually *on the same team* when it comes to your kids! Practice generosity.

Individual styles and technology preferences will drive how co-parents accomplish effective communication. We're writing from the 'Silicon Valley of the North' where the newer the gadget, the more immediate and expedient, the better. However, remember you and your co-parent are working on uncoupling, creating more spacious, healthy boundaries between you while building an effective co-parenting relationship. Notice how modes (phone, text, email, etc.) and styles (spontaneous/planned, brief/detailed, etc.) themselves affect your communications. Take care to use and develop those communication practices that support your ultimate goals as follows:

- Healthy boundaries—*respect privacy; unobtrusive*
- Effective—*desired outcome*
- Agreed upon—*works for both of you*
- Respectful—*slow down, consider, manage emotions*
- Sustainable—*works over time*

Communication Protocols

Co-parents work well together when they have protocols for both routine and non-routine communication, a way to document/track agreements about parenting responsibilities, and the skill to communicate important information in a clear, concise, business-like manner. We hope to offer guidance and suggestions on these necessary communication components to make co-parenting smoother and easier as you care for your children.

Face-to-Face/Skype Co-Parent Business Meetings

The "Tri-Annual Co-Parenting Business Meeting" serves many needs for planning, decision-making, and designating tasks. Effective co-parenting requires coordination and planning. Attempting to manage the myriad details, decisions, and schedule exceptions through daily (even weekly) contact often results in many more communications than feels comfortable along with difficulty keeping all the messages straight! The Tri-Annual Business Meeting was designed to increase effective planning and decrease the back-and-forth through email/text that often results in miscommunication and conflict. Parents may need to meet *face-to-face* more often than three times a year, but we recommend that co-parents develop a rhythm of meeting predictability in August, January, and March (adjustable). The meetings have specific agendas (a full template is provided in the Appendix).

- August: Plan the school year from September through early January. This includes discussion regarding holidays, days off from school, academic requirements, fall and early winter extracurricular activities, health care appointments, and any other specific residential, kid, or parent considerations occurring in the fourth-month arc.

- January: Similarly, sit down together to plan the second semester of school. This agenda includes mid-winter and spring break plans, holidays, days off from school, school events, health care appointments, kid, or parent considerations occurring in the second semester through end of school.

- March: This is your summer planning meeting. Co-parents can determine the best time for this meeting according to scheduling needs; some co-parents may prefer earlier, others later. You'll plan vacations, summer events, camps and day-care considerations to the extent that you can. This also gives co-parents a chance to check in on academic performance and the spring activity/sport/extracurricular planning.

Co-Parenting Business Meetings are just that: well-planned, complete with agenda, timelines, problem-solving and cooperative attitudes. They are generally held at a coffee shop or similar neutral environment. Rotating responsibility for meeting planning (one parent in odd years, the other in even for example), helps keep both engaged and positively participative. Share tasks—if one parent planned the meeting and drafted an agenda, the other parent could take notes and prepare for distribution. Review minutes, make corrections and confirm in a timely manner. Keep your notes to refer to for shared decisions, designation of tasks and timelines established. Refer back to your notes to help with keeping agreements made and following up on commitments. You and your co-parent may expand this model to better fit the unique features of your lifestyle, rhythms, and children's needs. We encourage you to experiment and discover what works best for you.

Transition Updates

Children also benefit when you communicate/coordinate with your co-parent on the day-to-day through transition updates. Typically accomplished through email (or voicemail), the parent going off duty provides information to the parent coming on duty, covering topics such as:

- health changes (physical and emotional)
- appointments needed or scheduled
- school/day-care issues/information
- significant family events affecting children
- changes or concerns regarding peer relationships
- changes in activities of daily living (ADL's: sleep patterns, eating etc.)
- anything additional that is relevant for smooth, integrated transitioning for the parent coming on duty to care for the children

If there's nothing in particular to report, simply send an email: "Smooth few days; nothing in particular to report—all good." To aid your co-parent in identifying this information easily, consider a subject line such as: "Transition Update." Let's look at an example from Kathy to Patty:

Subject Line: Sunday 9/8 Transition Report

Hey, Patty,

Health: I gave Chelsea Tylenol every 4 hours or so this weekend after having her braces adjusted on Friday. Last dose was at 9 this morning. She seems over it and doing fine now.

Appts: I scheduled her next ortho appt on my time—no worries—in two weeks (Friday 9/19 at 7:30 AM); you're welcome to join us if you'd like.

School: Max has school pictures on Tuesday—just a reminder—the flyer is in his backpack; he'll need a separate check from you. I ordered the "B" grouping; my check's in the envelope—so I'm covered.

ADLs: Both kids seem to be doing OK with getting up earlier with alarms. Hard to let go of summer sleep-ins.

Lastly, Chelsea came home from hanging with Mikaela, and they've both decided to become vegans—good luck with that!

I'll see the kids Wed after school. Thanks.

Kathy

In some families, the transition update may need to be expanded. For example, children with learning differences may need more focus on transitioning homework from household to household. Similarly, a child with a medical condition requires co-parents to communicate effectively on the parameters of health maintenance/medication management needed. Once you begin to implement the "general template" for transition updates, you will become skillful at tailoring transition reports to successfully meet the needs of your family.

Transition Updates—Homework

Supporting children's academic success across households works best with routines, supportive communication, and accurate information. Although each parent has the responsibility for and right to create their household rules and schedules, homework is one area where similar routines across households can be very helpful. The development of self-discipline and independence in homework management starts with patterns and practices that support success. These include: predictability/habit (how, when and where), age-appropriate parental guidance/monitoring along with adequate parental support, interest and feedback. We encourage each parent to participate in parent night, curriculum night, meet-the-teacher opportunities, parent-teacher conferences (even if you schedule separately with the teacher) and to access academic information such as online sources that verify assignments and progress.

If both parents have a daily routine, understand mechanisms for tracking homework (many schools implement a daily planner as well as website information for homework tracking), and are engaged in their children's school life, communication between co-parents regarding homework is typically easy and limited. Once a good foundation is set, both parents develop competence as "homework monitors" with a shared understanding of what their child needs to succeed. Communication is usually a courtesy heads-up regarding important tasks or events, coordinating work on a larger project, and/or addressing behavioral issues that affect homework.

Subject: Schoolwork

Hi Frank,

FYI—Amy has the big math test on Friday and will need her calculator. I've been working with her to be sure she returns it to her backpack after completing her homework, but she's still struggling with leaving it on her desk (which results in a desperate phone call before third period). If you can follow through with building the habit as well, that would be a great help.

Sarah continues to try the "I finished all my homework at school" with me. I remind her of our expectation that she read for an hour if she has no assignments, but she's pushing—and funny enough, she generally comes up with some unfinished spelling assignment or similar. We're not out of the woods yet with this one.

Thanks.

Peg

Requesting Changes to the Residential Schedule

By developing a clear, easy way to request changes to the schedule, parents can plan more efficiently and support each other in the vicissitudes of family life. Place schedule requests in separate emails to assist your co-parent with efficient responses. Consider a subject line that's simple and clear: "Schedule Change Request for Saturday 10/6." In the body of the email be clear about whether you're requesting a "trade" or asking for "coverage." You determine how much disclosure you offer behind your request (none is required or needed)—some parents find it easier to make requests for work-related obligations over personal commitments. Keep in mind that a schedule request is a *request*. Your co-parent is free to answer "sure; happy to do that" or "no, that doesn't work for me" or offer an *alternative* without justification or explanation. Make an effort to respond promptly to schedule change requests. Here's an example:

Subject: Schedule Change Request - Weekend Feb 2 - 4

Matt,

I will be out of town on Feb 2 - 4 and it's my regularly scheduled weekend. Would it work for you to swap either the w/e before or the w/e after? I would drop the kids at school Friday morning and would ask you to go on duty at 9AM that day. Since they would normally transition back to you at 7 PM on Sunday, I assume they'll just stay with you on Sunday. Please let me know. I appreciate your consideration.

Brenda

Subject: RE: Schedule Change Request - Weekend Feb 2 - 4

Hey, Brenda,

I'm happy to help that w/e, but I don't want to trade either of those other w/e's. I've already made plans. Please let me know if you'd like me to have the kids from the 2nd - 4th and we can trade a weekend in March.

Matt

Subject: RE: Schedule Change Request - Weekend Feb 2 - 4

Matt,

Perfect. That works fine. Thank you. I'd love to have the kids the w/e of 3/9. Let me know. I've changed the residential calendar for Feb 2 - 4.

Brenda

Matt and Brenda did an excellent job of the following:

- Being clear and concise—Matt knew exactly what Brenda was requesting

- Using a cordial, easy, factual style

- Showing respect—no pressure, a simple request

- Practicing generosity—Matt looks for an alternate solution that worked for him that he hopes works for Brenda to give her back a w/e in the future

- Expressing appreciation

Triggering unproductive communication can be remarkably easy if difficult emotions override the issue to be resolved. Let's look at another example of Mom requesting some additional time with their children—this email reflects difficult emotions and unresolved hurt.

Subject: The Kids

Sam,

As you may have heard my graduation is next Saturday. This is a really important day for me and I want the boys there to celebrate. The boys tell me you have been working most weekends and they've been with babysitters. Obviously coming with me would be more beneficial for them. I hope you can be reasonable and not make this any more difficult than it needs to be.

Kristi

Let's examine the problems with this email:

- Kristi makes assumptions about Sam's time with the children and his knowledge of her personal life.

- Kristi doesn't make a clear and respectful request that would include details of exactly what she's asking for—rather she attempts to "push" Sam into agreeing to something without details of times, dates, and transitions.

- Kristi adds additional information about Sam's work schedule and use of babysitters, which comes across as provocative/critical. If Sam's work schedule is an actual concern, Kristi could discuss with Sam directly in a separate conversation.

- She uses a disrespectful tone; ending with the admonishment that if Sam doesn't agree to the proposal, then he is being "difficult."

After coaching, Kristi was able to send this email with a more respectful manner:

Subject: Request for Schedule Change—Saturday

Hi Sam,

    I know it's really short notice, but I'm requesting a schedule change for next Saturday. I got the dates for my graduation wrong and thought it was for my weekend in two weeks, but instead it is for this next weekend. I was really looking forward to having the boys there. If you don't have special plans with them, I'm wondering if I could pick them up at 12 and have them through an early dinner with Grandma and Grandpa (back 6ish?). Please let me know. If it's not possible, I understand, but if any of the time-frame could work, that would be great.

    Kristi

By practicing constructive email etiquette, Kristi doesn't inadvertently damage the foundations of trust and respect developing in their co-parenting relationship. This email is much more likely to receive a positive response—even if Sam says "no, that doesn't work for me," he's likely to respond more kindly and with consideration.

Time Sensitive/Urgent Requests

Children's needs and schedules occasionally require efficient, expedited responses. We recommend that co-parents work out agreements about how best to handle time-sensitive communications. By email, you might use "Time Sensitive" as the beginning of your subject line. Some parents prefer to reserve texting for time sensitive information; others prefer that their co-parent pick up the phone and call. What's important is that you have agreement about how best to handle these occasional urgent matters, and practice good "business of co-parenting" responsiveness in return.

"Blood and Broken Bones"—Communicating Emergencies

If you're on the way to the emergency room with your child, alerting your co-parent is a priority. In our busy work-day worlds, we often get "voicemail" when we *very much* want to reach a person. There's no time like an emergency with your child when voicemail feels inadequate. But, go ahead and leave a message—calm, factual—provide information on where you're going and why.

You may want to work out with your co-parent that a text message of "911" means "call immediately." He or she can respond to this specific signal for kid emergencies without taking the time to listen to your voicemail.

Requesting Changes in Parenting Practices

What happens if your child is expressing a significant hurt/concern? What if he/she wants to refuse spending time with the other parent? And the concern is repetitive, verified, and you are genuinely concerned? Yet it is not a safety issue, just something you think is unskillful and could/should be handled differently by your co-parent? You definitely feel like you side with your child on this one. How do you listen and help him/her feel heard, and support the need for something different while continuing to encourage his/her relationship with the other parent? Here are some things to consider:

- Do your best to separate your emotions from your child's and listen without judging your co-parent. (This is a vulnerable time for making not-so-loving mistakes if you're not careful, which is to say *your* emotions begin to steer the ship.) Start by letting your child know his/her feelings are important:

* * * * * * * *

"Honey, you're really upset with Dad. What's going on?"

* * * * * * * *

- See if you can get clarity on the problem/issue/concern, and check your assumptions for accuracy:

* * * * * * * *

"So you've told him you're uncomfortable when he comes into the bathroom when you're showering; you've asked him to knock first; and he won't let you lock the door? He just says it's 'no big deal;' he's just grabbing something and going out again? And nothing's changed since the last time you talked about privacy in the bathroom? Is that right?"

* * * * * * * *

- Reinforce that both of you as co-parents care about how he/she feels, and appreciate your child for sharing important concerns/feelings. Instill confidence that problems can be solved one way or another. If the child is old enough to advocate for him/herself, you might start with having the child talk with the other parent. Ultimately, we want kids to know that adults (and kids!) can work things out together without the child feeling helpless, unprotected, or taking a position of refusing residential time.

* * * * * * * *

"I see you are really upset; I'm glad you told me. I think Daddy would want to know HOW much this is bothering you—sounds like he's still not thinking this is as important to you as it is. I'm not sure how Daddy

will want to help solve this—but we'll figure something out. Meanwhile, while we sort this through, I know it's important for you to have time with Dad. I'll talk with him, and you'll still go to Dad's this Thursday. Deal?"

* * * * * * * *

- Communicate with your co-parent without judgement, assumptions, or interpretations—just the facts. Use your child's words. Remember this may be difficult information for your co-parent to hear, especially from you. Be thoughtful about timing and method of communicating. Do you both do better with something like this in email or by picking up the phone? (If the issue has already been a source of deep conflict and remains unresolved, this may be a good time for help from a family or child specialist.)

* * * * * * * *

Mom to Dad: *"Hey Dan, I need to tell you something Jenny told me last night. She was pretty upset and when I asked her what was bothering her, she said .... Does that make sense to you? Do you know what she's talking about? I know we've talked about both girls' need for privacy."*

Dad to Mom: *"I sure do. You know, I've asked her specifically to use the kids' bathroom when she wants to shower, but she insists on using my shower. It's a problem—I can't get into my room or my closet. If she's going to use my shower, she's going to have to live with my coming in if I need something."*

* * * * * * * *

- Offer support; invite problem-solving as a co-parenting team. After sharing the information, give the other parent time to consider before jumping in— trust and allow the other to act thoughtfully. Although you may not get an immediate answer, or the answer you want to hear, in time, your co-parent is likely to make the shifts/adjustments necessary to resolve the tension or issue for your child.

* * * * * * * *

Mom to Dad: *"Got it. Well, sounds like she can't see her way to a solution. I'm not sure why she isn't using the other bathroom. She feels really self-conscious now when you come in while she's showering, and she needs privacy. Would you be willing to sit down with her and work out something different—or can the three of us sit down? I think it's a much bigger deal to her than you might have thought."*

* * * * * * * *

- Sometimes the "something different" that results is a change in how your child copes with an upset/concern/issue with his/her other parent. As a good parent you may have times when you believe advocating—*righting a wrong*—for your child is the single most important step you can take. This is often the case—*except* when you risk your child's relationship with his/her other parent, safety is not at stake, *and* other solutions are available.

• • • • • • • •

Dad to Mom: *"Look, she can have all the privacy she wants in the other bathroom. She shouldn't use my shower. Leave it alone."*

Later, Mom talks to Jenny.

Mom to Jenny: *"Honey, I talked with Dad. He says the problem is you using his shower. So, I'm going to suggest you use the kid-bathroom when you're at Dad's. Is there a problem with that shower? Does your brother stay out when you shower? Does Dad let you lock that door?"*

Jenny to Mom: *"That bathroom's small and there's always towels on the floor—I hate it! Why won't he just STAY OUT and let me use HIS shower?"*

Mom to Jenny: *"Sounds like you're mad about a handful of things— like how sloppy your brother leaves the bathroom. Sweetie, sometimes you simply need to take care of the things that are important to you. Pick up the towels; enjoy your shower with the door locked. Can you follow that plan?"*

• • • • • • • •

Parents aren't and life isn't perfect. As much as we would like to protect our children from difficulties, and want them to have the best, we're left to work with what's good enough in both ourselves and their other parent. There are myriad issues that come up in two-home families. Co-parents have different opinions about religious practice, how money's spent, discipline, on television, and junk food. We have feelings and reactions to new partners entering our children's lives. We have less control than we'd like—and may have more concerns, more guilt, more feelings of protectiveness. We may wish our child's other parent were more empathetic, more considerate, more focused, more aware, more...more...*more than they are.* Carefully choosing battles; respectfully asking for changes in parenting practices when you believe it's absolutely necessary; communicating skillfully informs the course of our co-parenting relationship, and the course of our child's growing-up years.

Modes of Communication

The communication tips covered below are for co-parents. Many may apply to communicating with children also—we'll discuss specifics about being in touch with your children in "What About the Kids and Communication."

Email

Email is an effective tool for communicating information, documenting agreements, and planning schedules. Email is not generally useful for processing emotionally charged issues—the written word can leave a lot of room for emotional misunderstanding. If you and your co-parent process well in email, then that's what's important. If not, *look for an alternative that works more effectively.* Here are some typical communications handled successfully through email:

- Transition updates
- Requests for schedule changes
- Financial information (See Chapter 6: "The Buck Stops Here")
- Co-parenting business meeting notes
- Documenting other agreements

Consider creating an email address specifically for communication with your co-parent. Managing input from your former spouse can be stressful. Having emails cross your desktop at work may be disruptive. Creating a separate email for co-parenting communication allows you to be in the driver's seat on when, how, and where you receive their messages. Plan to check your co-parenting email daily—you pick the time, you prepare and manage your emotions—and do your best to provide cordial and timely responses.

Agreed-upon guidelines for email help co-parents develop well-managed and respectful practices. Co-parents often agree to limit emails to transition days, once a week, or whatever rhythm works best for both. Keep in mind, during the first year or so, hearts are often healing, and less contact is better. The goal is to find the sweet spot between minimizing unnecessary contact for both spouses' recovery, and sufficient contact to co-parent well.

Texts

Text messaging is expedient, immediate, and effective for quick exchange of information. Respect your co-parent's boundaries on texting his/her phone. Without thoughtful consideration, texting can become intrusive and unwelcome. Some co-parents prefer texting over emails and phone calls as a way of managing/limiting direct contact. Co-parents often agree to use texting for the following exchanges:

- Delays of greater than 15 minutes when transitioning children
- Identifying precise location to swap kids at a soccer field, etc.
- Notice of arrival to drop off an expected kid item that was requested
- Courtesy notice that email has been sent that the other parent is awaiting
- "911" emergency notification - *call immediately*

Phone

Phone calls work well for some co-parents—the key is the nature of your co-parenting relationship and shared agreements. Talking on the phone moves a step toward more personal and direct contact with your former spouse. As your relationship becomes more solid and less conflicted, talking on the phone can make problem-solving easier and faster, sharing information about the kids in a way that the written word cannot. Respecting your emotional readiness (and the readiness of your former spouse) helps determine when phone contact becomes a helpful addition to your list of communication modes that work.

In-Person Casual Conversation

When are you and your co-parent ready to sit together and chat at a gymnastics meet? Maybe never. When a marriage has been irretrievably broken, there may be no hope for a casual in-person relationship with your former spouse. And that's OK. When co-parents are able to heal beyond the loss of their partnership and damage often caused during the divorce/separation to the point of casually enjoying and sharing about their children at family or public events, this is very positive for kids.

Many co-parents are surprised by the healing power of time. We often find when co-parents separate and allow ample distance, minimize conflict, and focus on their own lives, being in the company of their co-parent becomes easier—even familiar—over time.

Melissa and Jim divorced when Brandi was 10. It was a difficult, conflict-filled, tumultuous unraveling of family life. Melissa and Jim were unable to move beyond a cursory "hello" at the gymnasium door through Brandi's remaining growing up years. Fourteen years later, at Brandi's college graduation, both parents attended—sitting separately as always. Afterwards, for the first time since the divorce, meeting to congratulate their daughter out on the lawn, the proud parents wanted a family photo with their beautiful new grad. Time had allowed for a bit of healing—and with Brandi's entire adulthood in front of her, it wasn't a moment too late.

Online Family Calendars

Online family calendars help parents share kids' complicated schedules between two homes. Parents' independent access to child-centered information, ease in coordinating schedules and, when age-appropriate, the kids' window into the shared two-home-family schedule, start the list of benefits to having a shared calendar. In the case of families where conflict may be an ongoing issue, calendars reduce contact between parents while communicating in a neutral third party way a shared view of the residential schedule, appointments, and special dates. The shared view helps minimize the misunderstandings that are often generated by each parent keeping a separate calendar. Calendar options range from a simple monthly schedule, others with additional tools like tracking and storing email, bulletin boards, automatic reminders, and filters for content.

We encourage you to match the service that best fits your needs. Examples of calendars created expressly for co-parenting are cozi.com, ourfamilywizard.com, cofamilies.com, coparentcalendar.com, splitschedule.com, sharekids.com, and kidsontime.com.

The key to relationship is knowing yourself—and respecting the other. Forcing yourself to do something you're not ready to do can be emotionally damaging. Forcing your perspective or beliefs on another person can be relationally damaging. Finding your way with your co-parent is the gift you give your children. They don't need you to be best friends, but they clearly benefit from having you both stress-free and wholeheartedly at their concert, even if you're sitting on opposite sides of the auditorium!

> The key is agreement, respectful use, and willingness to modify communications practices as needed by either parent.

Kids and Communication

There is no better time than the present to assist your children with healthy, constructive communication protocols. You and your co-parent model cordial, respectful communication even when *you don't want to!* By teaching your children how to express their feelings respectfully, to problem-solve directly with the person involved (you, your co-parent, sibling, etc.), and to provide adequate and accurate information, you help raise well-adjusted, resilient, and resourceful kids who will be successful, competent communicators.

Kids do best when they know that communicating with their other parent is expected, healthy, and welcome within reasonable limits. Depending on the age of the child, parental involvement is more or less important. For young children, Mom or Dad will have to dial the phone or plan the calls, set up the computer for Facetime or Skype.

Kids and cell phones can create conflict when co-parents aren't in agreement about kids having cell phones. Keep in mind that just because you buy your child the latest iPhone for use on your residential time, it doesn't mean your co-parent agrees with cell phone use on his/her residential time. Phone access to your child does not necessarily mean a cell phone, or a text package, on your co-parents residential time. Unless your co-parent agrees and welcomes the cell phone in his/her home, your child may not be allowed to use it. Please respect the boundaries of your co-parents home and time. If he/she says no to cell phones, then it's no.

As a child gets older and you've agreed that he/she may have a cell phone, establish boundaries on the appropriate amount of texting and Face Time in each household. Be respectful of your co-parents guidelines. As a co-parent, be sensitive to the potentially intrusive nature of texting—not only by distracting your child from whatever he/she is engaged in (or *should be* engaged in), but also for your co-parent. You may have a wonderful relationship with your teen, but texting like a "bestie" on your co-parent's residential time will *not* be constructive or welcomed if you're creating disruption.

A non-residential parent and child can set up routines that make staying in touch easy and predictable—without disadvantaging the residential parent's schedule, homelife, or relationship with the child. This is crucial—and respectful. Establish healthy rules about communicating before a reasonable time at night and after a reasonable time in the morning. Mealtimes should be respected, etc. Ascertain what your child needs based on developmental stage, grieving process/adjustment to separation, and temperament.

Otherwise, once developmentally appropriate, allow older children the freedom to choose how and when they contact their other parent—and allow them the same freedom to contact you. Children rest into their other household, have a rhythm and a sense of safety and security there that doesn't necessarily include you. You're always in their heart, but they may be enjoying what's in front of them without having you on their mind. Obligating children to call or encouraging them to feel guilty through your expression of disappointment or, worse, feelings of *rejection* impair their ability to settle, relax, and *be kids*.

Sometimes parents allow children to have a cell phone or dedicated phone line for talking with their other parent. This can both ease tension about tying up the phone as well as provide the children with privacy to talk freely with their other parent. This set-up doesn't mean there aren't rules for use, but it can facilitate healthy autonomy.

> And lastly, actively support your child to call and share exciting, important information with their other parent—a little prompting, not forcing, is appropriate.

• • • • • • • •

Mason, are you kidding? That's so great!! You got the part you wanted!! I'm really happy for you. You know, Momma would love to hear this, too—want to give her a quick call? I know she'd appreciate hearing this from you.

• • • • • • • •

Highlights in Review

- Healthy family communication supports a strong co-parenting relationship, models crucial skills for the children's own life-skills toolbox.

- Parents and kids often build skills during the post-divorce/separation period out of necessity—settling into a new two-home reality contributes to skill development that likely wasn't needed or hadn't been developed during the marriage.

- By intentionally building effective communication skills, co-parents provide a stronger platform for launching kids.

Chapter 5

"Who's on First?" (Decision-Making)

YOUR PARENTING PLAN may spell out specific aspects of decision-making. Some parents have sole decision-making authority; some have sole responsibility for certain areas and joint in others; a number of co-parents make decisions jointly across many areas, including medical, educational, and significant activity/life-choices for children. Whatever your contractual agreement, meet your obligations with integrity and respect for your co-parent. In this chapter, we'll be talking about the co-parenting executive team as joint decision makers. We'll include day-to-day decisions, responsible informing, emergency decisions, and walk you through important activities/life choices for kids that co-parents face either alone or together.

CEOs—Co-Parent Executive Officers

A two-home family, like a successful company, depends on a functional, productive executive team.

When co-parents struggle, kids *feel it*. Unlike a poorly run company, children can't quit their family and go grow up elsewhere. Learning to co-parent effectively is *for your kids*. The more difficult/conflictual your co-parenting relationship, the more business-like you need to be. By stepping back and

- managing emotions,
- planning effectively,
- focusing on decisions that are essential and necessary,
- employing strategies that maintain decorum,
- keeping children front-and-center,

- responding to their needs in a timely way, co-parents can reduce conflict and build a working co-parent relationship where decisions get made and kids' lives move forward.

As co-parent executive officers making decisions jointly, you share responsibility for implementing decisions and paying the financial proportion agreed upon. There are exceptions, and one parent can agree to pay for something that the other parent supports, but can't or doesn't want to afford, or one parent may agree to ensure trips to baseball practice on the other parent's time (if agreed to). But in general, parents share responsibility for implementing and paying for joint decisions. Respecting the "no, that doesn't work for me" and offering the "yes, of course, I agree" applies to making joint decisions just as it does in all areas of co-parenting. Attempts to push, cajole, manipulate, threaten, act unilaterally or similar power plays in an effort to get your way undermine effective co-parenting.

Without respect between co-parents, joint decision making can break down into judgment, power struggle and impasse. Divorce/separation involves some inevitable tearing from the past. We liken it to cutting a rubber band that was holding two individuals together; both people now cut loose to find their own footing with varying degrees of personal change. Re-establishing common ground over the care of your children, accepting the other's lifestyle changes, and supporting the goal of doing what's good for the kids, helps facilitate a better future. Otherwise, parents continue to struggle with each other post-divorce/separation—holding on to the past, disappointed in the present, and unable to see a future that works.

After the separation, Sylvia bought a long-coveted convertible sports car. Syd couldn't believe it. Every time she set limits on spending for the children's extracurricular activities, Syd accused her of having screwed up priorities. The way he saw it, she chose to buy her expensive car, but didn't want to pay for all the kid activities he proposed. Meanwhile, Sylvia saw Syd trying to buy the kids through promising them anything and everything, with no limits on sports, activities, or entertainment.

Both Syd and Sylvia suffer from difficulty accepting their new circumstances and how each of them has changed. They use criticism and judgment of the other (and "spouse mind") rather than productive problem-solving to reach useful agreements about extracurriculars for their children ("co-parent mind").

A business meeting approach provides structure for joint decision-making. Like any good executive team, you and your co-parent can rely on sound business meeting practices and respectful decision-making skills:

- Set a reasonable amount of time aside for a meeting
- Co-create an agenda and timeline for areas to be discussed and decisions needed
- Keep kids' interests and needs front and center
- Meet in a neutral place
- Come to the meeting rested and fed *(no alcohol, please)*
- Take turns leading discussion points
- Take notes (one person agrees to take notes and distribute afterwards)
- Establish budgets
- Specify how payments will be made
- Resolve logistical concerns
- Determine how the children will be told
- Appreciate each other for the efforts made

These may be new skills; they may seem a bit strange and formal for you and your former spouse; but structure, focus, and a combination of business approach and parent mind reduces conflict and allows co-parents to make effective decisions.

Joint Decisions Made Jointly

Even if you've had an egalitarian, engaged parenting relationship in a one-house family, most parents are unaccustomed to true joint decision making. At the outset of your co-parenting relationship, you're likely to notice all the little and big ways you simply make decisions about the kids without thinking to consult your child's other parent. You've made these sorts of decisions before; what's the big deal? Now that you're in charge of your own home with your children, it feels like none of his/her business. However, the unfortunate outcome of your efficient or automatic response can be to step on your co-parents toes and create animosity and confusion in areas where slowing down and investing in joint consideration and joint decisions would be *best for the kids*.

> Becoming conscious; planning for, working together, and deciding jointly those areas specified/agreed upon for joint decision making, is not only healthy and constructive for your co-parenting relationship and your children, but also may be mandated by law.

Martha and Bill were exchanging information about William's class schedule when Martha mentioned to Bill that she had signed William up for a reading intensive program along with a three-month sensory integration workshop. Bill was taken by surprise "I thought we'd be talking about these things before you just signed him up! Two things: how do you know I can get him to those commitments on my time, and how much do they cost?" Martha was quick to point out, "Bill, this is exactly what he did last year!"

With a deep, calming breath and a bit more discussion, Bill helped Martha see that things were different now. He really wanted to be more involved in William's education and health care decisions; he wanted to be able to meet William's needs when Will's in his care. Equally important, he wanted them to plan together for what each of them can afford now as a two-home family. Martha recognized that Bill was right and apologized—she had jumped ahead in signing William up and forgot to include Bill in the decision.

A Tri-Annual Co-Parenting Business Meeting (introduced in Chapter 4) provides parents a predictable schedule and process for anticipating developmental needs, tracking school events, planning extracurricular activities, problem-solving health/behavioral concerns, and anticipating residential schedule/holiday changes. With practice and planning, co-parents leave their business meeting prepared for the next arc of *life with kids*. And kids experience enormous support as parents provide a coordinated and integrated two-home family life for them! Co-parents may not anticipate every joint decision, so another mechanism, such as an email protocol, will serve to catch those decisions that happen *in between*. An example:

During the January Co-Parenting Business Meeting, Alice agreed to be responsible for getting Shoshana to the pediatrician to follow-up on the teacher's concern about possible attention deficit issues. After the appointment, Alice wrote an email to Ema and let her know that the pediatrician agreed that Shosh would benefit from a trial of medication. Ema wrote back immediately, disagreeing with any medication use before trying other non-medication strategies. Alice was frustrated and felt blocked from doing what the doctor believed was in Shoshana's best interest.

- Alice and Ema are faced with a conflict resolution situation. A discussion ensues. Alice requests that Ema meet with her and the pediatrician. Ema agrees to setting a follow-up appointment.

- Alice requests Ema write out her exact recommendations for how to help Shoshana, and to share them with the pediatrician.

- After further discussion, Alice suggests a two-step approach of trying Ema's preferred strategies for 2 months and get feedback from the teacher, with the agreement that if Shosh's school work doesn't improve, they'll do a trial of the recommended medication.

- Ema agrees; Alice is relieved, and the plan to help Shoshana moves forward.

What happens if Ema won't respond to Alice's email?

- Alice remembers that she and Ema built into their parenting plan that if either parent doesn't respond to an email request within 72 hours (unless they are traveling or out of reach), the requesting parent can go ahead and take action.

- Seventy two hours elapse. Alice gets the prescription filled and Shosh begins taking her medication. Alice notifies Ema in a clear and neutral tone, of the timing and steps she's taken.

What if Alice and Ema can't resolve the conflict?

- The first step is to enter a discussion, if possible, and attempt to problem-solve.

- The next step is to alert your co-parent that you intend to initiate the "conflict resolution process" outlined in your parenting plan. This is often a three-tier process that involves hiring a professional (divorce/co-parent coach or mediator) to assist with resolving the conflict. If that's unsuccessful, the next step might be to engage your collaborative attorneys for counsel and direction. And lastly, perhaps, you can approach the court for help.

"Your Dad and I / Your Mom and I"

In an ideal world, your children will hear you and your co-parent say often, "Your Dad and I/Your Mom and I." As the Co-parent Executive Officers, the more your children sense you and your co-parent communicate about them, are on the same page on important issues involving them and in agreement about their growing-up, the better. The ability to say, "Your Mom and I/Your Dad and I" also helps your children know that there are many areas of their lives that you and your co-parent continue to share concern about and investment in. Kids are reassured when healthy discussions on the "executive level" of the family continue post-divorce /separation about *them* and what's important to them.

• • • • • • • •

Yolanda, age 14: *"Mom, can I go to Homecoming? Not just the game; I mean the dance!"*

Mom: *"That's a good question. Dad and I discussed at our fall planning meeting that this might come up. And we decided that this year you could go with a group—not one-on-one with your date. How do you feel about that?"*

Yolanda: *"That works for me!! Will you pay?"*

Mom: *"As usual, Dad and I believe you should have some 'skin in the game.' We want you to contribute $50 from your babysitting money; we'll cover the rest."*

Yolanda: *"OK...what's my budget?"*

Mom: *"Hmmmm, that we didn't decide—I'll have to get back to you on that."*

• • • • • • • •

Yolanda's parents did a good job of anticipating a normal developmental step. Their planning gave Mom an easy way to field the questions. Yolanda could *feel* the presence of both her parents' involvement in Mom's answer—she knew her Dad was tracking, and sharing in her important events. But what if parents haven't discussed something important yet—and *Jeffrey wants an answer*?

Jeffrey, age 6: *"Daddy, Mrs. Ellen told me I can sleep over at Eli's this weekend, OK??"*

Dad: *"You'd like to spend the night at Eli's house? And, his Mom said it would be OK?"*

Jeffrey: *"Yep—can I go?"*

Dad: *"You know, Buddy, Mom and I haven't talked about you starting "sleepovers" and before we go any further on this, I want to talk with Mom."*

Jeffrey: *"No Daddy! You tell her it's OK! What if Mommy says "no"?"*

Dad: *"Listen, Buddy, I haven't said "yes," and your Mom and I discuss these sorts of things FIRST and together we decide "yes" or "no." So hold your horses, and I'll see if Mommy's available, and I'll let you know as soon as we've had a chance to talk."*

• • • • • • • •

Jeffrey's dad shows respect in co-parenting in the above example.

- Although this is a case-by-case decision on his parenting time, he recognizes that it's also a developmental step—something brand new—and, consequently, wants to include his co-parent in making the decision.

- He reassured Jeffrey that co-parenting decisions like this one will include both parents—he didn't set Mom up to be the "bad guy" by saying, "It's fine with me, but we have to ask Mommy." *No one gets thrown under the bus!*

Holding back permission—or your personal opinion—in lieu of making joint decisions jointly is a learned skill. We ask parents to be careful about aligning with children before knowing if the other parent shares your parenting views regarding areas of joint decision-making. The more comfortable you get with "your Dad and I/your Mom and I" for joint decisions, the better it is for your kids. Will there ever come a time when you'll say to your kiddo, "If it were just up to me, I'd....?" Yes—as long as you're equally comfortable following up with, "...and you know your Mom and I/your Dad and I make these decisions together and that's just how it goes."

Day-to-Day Decision Making

The residential parent maintains autonomy in day-to-day decision making: in managing his/her own household and in caring, feeding, and disciplining kids. This feels like freedom! Especially if you've grown weary of conflicts with your former spouse about child-rearing. Perhaps you came to parenting without realizing how your unique and different family backgrounds and personal styles could create so much tension while raising children. And now, you get to do it *your way*. Here's a classic example:

> Mom believes that children should make their beds, put away their clothes, organize their toys, etc., with increasing responsibilities for their room as they mature.
> Dad believes that children should be allowed keep their rooms however they want—it's their space, and he doesn't care as long as a family of rats doesn't move in.

Both parents could find endless support for their individual perspectives. They could argue about who's right and who's the better parent and who is not. This is unproductive, unresolvable and won't help the children. As it turns out, children growing up in families that require a certain level of household management learn *one* set of skills, and children growing up in families that trust them to find their way to a level of personal space organization learn *another* set of skills. Some children will thrive in one system and struggle in the other.

Matching your daily expectations across households to support what your child needs for successful growth and development is the goal in co-parenting. Stepping away from "my way" and "your way," you examine together the way that helps your child learn what he/she needs to learn, and provides well-rounded, competence-building experiences.

What if you can't agree on what he/she needs or how to get there? Your child sits squarely in the middle between your parenting styles. The ease of transitioning back and forth depends on your child's temperament, age, and on the level of integration and familiarity in his/her two-homes. The older the child, the more capable of negotiating the differences between households—up to a point. Your commitment to following some basic approaches/guidelines/ schedules is not *buckling to the whims* of your former spouse, or *trumping* your co-parent's views to get your way—your commitment is to provide the best possible environments *together* for your children. We want children to use their energy for *being kids* and growing up resilient, secure and happy. Otherwise, they're forced to misspend energy on figuring out how to deal with changes, differences, rules, fighting structure, or floundering in the lack of structure.

Let's look at another example:

Dad lives in a new house and has Lucy's trundle bed all set up with princess sheets, stuffed animals, and night-time monitor on the dresser. He's done a lovely job. Lucy's with him Wednesday through Sunday every other week (along with visits during his 'off week'). She wants to sleep in his "big bed, with YOU, Daddy" and Dad hates to cause her any tears over the short time they have together. It's not that big a deal for him that he loses a couple nights' sleep having her thrash around contentedly through the night; afterall, it's mostly the weekend. Dad knows Lucy's mom wants Lucy sleeping in her own bed, but....but....

Lucy comes back to Mom after "Daddy time" and the battle begins. Like any four-year-old, Lucy has already figured out her argument and comes armed with persistence to sleep with Mommy. But Mom is starting her work week and can't lose sleep and function at her job. Not to mention, a sleep-deprived Mom of a four-year-old is unfortunate for all involved. Something has to be done.

Gabe and Jessie needed help to come up to the 10,000-foot view on Lucy's sleep habits. Even though they were no longer married, Gabe realized that Jessie's well-being as Lucy's mom mattered to him. And once he connected the dot that Lucy's ability to sleep soundly in her own bed actually gave Lucy (as well as Jessie) something important in everyone's two-home adjustment, he could work more diligently with Lucy to sleep in her "big girl" bed. And everyone could thrive.

Allowing what worked in the past to inform the present and provide a foundation for changes in the future supports all members of the family to adjust. How you make day-to-day decisions at your house falls into a broader context of your children's *whole life*, which includes their other household. When co-parents stay cognizant of focusing on daily routines, structures, approaches that can bridge *both* households, kids win.

A solid rule-of-thumb: start with what kids already know. There are a lot of changes in becoming a two-home family, so if we hold a few of the "day-to-day aspects of life" similar to how they were in a one-house family, children can master change in digestible pieces. Think of it from a perspective we're all familiar with: In preschool, snacks happen at 10, quiet time at 10:30, and circle time at 11. Children "rest" into this routine and rhythm, which allows them to use maximum energy for their developmental tasks while acquiring abilities to both tolerate and utilize structure. These skills continue to take on depth and breadth as children progress through elementary school. Around age 12, school structure changes: now children spend their days moving from classroom to classroom for different subjects with different teachers. Kids are now able to master that change. There are many expectations that remain the same whether you're in Mr. Stafford's English class or Ms. Brown's Math class. But there also many things that are different. As students progress, the level of autonomy and self-direction increases and their capacity to thrive with changing expectations unfolds. This same models holds true for children in two-home families.

Holding (within reason) the basic values, structure, and rhythms across two-home families is good for kids. We can't always accomplish exactly what we'd like to see for our children; sometimes we must move toward our co-parent in order to lessen the discrepancy and stress in areas we can give on.

> Louis and Preti use to argue incessantly about how much time the TV was on when they were a one-house family. Louis liked the TV on in the background—listening to sports, news, whatever might be interesting as he moved through chores on a Saturday. This made Preti want to run screaming from the house. She didn't like the noise and resented the kids parking themselves on the sofa rather than getting outside to ride their bikes or pick up a book or help with chores. She felt it was Louis' fault for allowing it.
>
> Now in a two-home family, Preti knew that Louis would have the TV on constantly at his house, as he always had. She began making agreements with the kids about more liberal TV time in her house as long as they agreed to playing outside and reading. She found the diminished conflict and the children's ability to relax with an extra movie here or X-Box game there allowed everyone to settle more easily.

There are very few activities, foods, or ways of being, done in moderation (with the exception of direct health risk), that are more harmful to kids than ongoing strife and conflict.

> We sometimes forget that conflict and high stress is very hard on our bodies, and makes it much more difficult to focus, learn, create, play, rest, love openly—all kinds of things.

Ongoing or protracted strife and upset will inform your child's trust, adult relationship skills, and can, at worst, cause long-term post traumatic stress symptoms. Protect your children from destructive conflict. Feeling safe, secure, loved and contentedly in a relationship with the ones we love is healing for our bodies and healthy for our psyches.

Co-parents' ways-of-being while minimizing unnecessary stress and harmful conflict, is a cornerstone principle. Yes, we may make "loving mistakes;" we work consciously to avoid "not-so-loving mistakes."

Responsible Informing

Responsible informing helps co-parents mitigate the sense that they are being blindsided when the other acts unilaterally on the child's behalf. Communicating *more* rather than *less* about educational, medical, and other important child-related matters with your co-parent is better than under-communicating. Taking significant action without responsible informing may create ill-will, feelings of competition, or a sense of hurtful exclusion.

Jada and Malik were both concerned about their 13-year-old daughter Destiny who was expressing anger over the divorce and threatening to cut herself. Both parents agreed that getting Destiny into counseling was a priority. Malik agreed with Jada to contact his therapist for referrals. A few days later, Jada announced that she had sought referrals from the pediatrician and an appointment at the local teen behavior health clinic.

Malik felt "kicked to the curb." Talking together with their divorce coach, Jada explained that she was doing what "she'd always done" for Destiny. She admitted she neither informed Malik about her thought process and decision to see the pediatrician, nor did she inform or consult with him about the pediatrician's recommendations before moving forward. She realized she had walked right over his efforts, and his desire to help and be part of the process.

Malik had a chance to express his frustration, make clear requests for things to be different next time, and get the information he needed to feel comfortable with the direction for Destiny's care. Now, with more experience and new skills, both parents appreciate the value of keeping each other informed before taking action.

Co-parents who enjoy a positive level of trust may delegate to each other aspects of joint-decision-making for efficiency and division of labor. A good example might be setting dental appointments and following up on routine care. One parent might take the lead on managing and tracking appointments. In all events, co-parents benefit from an established protocol for informing and staying informed when changes occur, new treatment directions are suggested, or follow-up is needed. Example email:

Subject: Brayden's Therapy: Co-Parents' Session Requested

Elisabetta,
Brayden saw Martha today as scheduled. When they were done, Martha suggested that we schedule a co-parenting session before Brayden's next individual appointment in two weeks. I grabbed her Friday at 8 AM opening with the caveat that I confirm it works for you. Please let me know and I'll call her office. If that doesn't work, would you please call her and get a couple of times that do and let me know? Thanks.
Bryan

When allocating decisions to one another, recognize the value of the trust involved—this is an important accomplishment in your co-parenting relationship. Following up with responsible informing reflects this value and reinforces the trust. With information, your co-parent has the opportunity to step in if there's something he/she would like to suggest, or something that needs further clarification or consideration. When your co-parent carries the ball down the field with certain tasks and keeps you informed, appreciate his/her efforts and willingness to loop you in.

Responsible informing may include passing on helpful information with regard to your household, family life, or your children that would prepare your co-parent emotionally to support the kids effectively. Depending on the age of your children, they may do some of this informing on their own, which is perfectly OK for many things: "Dad, we're getting a new puppy at Mom's." But let's consider the decision to introduce the children to the person you've been dating for six months. Would your co-parent like to hear from *you* first or from *your children?* Would it be easier on everyone when the kids come back from their residential time and announce, *"Mom has a new boyfriend"* that Dad can say, *"So I've heard—she and I talked—I understand you are going to meet him this weekend."?* (More on "New Adults in Our Children's Lives" in Chapter 10.)

Sometimes we have extended family information that our former spouse might want to know both as a former in-law and as the children's parent. There will sometimes be difficult health news about a family member or death of a grandparent that has reverberations. Giving your co-parent a heads-up on life changes of this magnitude helps him/her prepare to support your children.

Emergency Decisions

In the case of emergency, dial 9-1-1. Sometimes it's a call from school: your 13-year-old just took a flying dive into the bleachers while playing basketball and momentarily lost consciousness. He's alert now, but the coach is suggesting a trip to the emergency room. Once you're at the emergency room, and you've contacted your co-parent, you'll be asked to give permission for certain medical procedures recommended by the emergency room physicians. You want to be clear what level of decision you can unilaterally make as the parent-on-the-ground, and what level of decision needs to wait for your co-parent. Please consider consulting with your legal team before accidents happen, so that you'll be able to proceed quickly with important decisions.

Kids and Co-Parenting Decisions

Across the arc from childhood to young adulthood, you and your co-parent will confront, work together, and resolve myriad decisions. Many of these don't fit neatly into "education" or "health care" but we find encouraging co-parents to *think ahead* exercises the "joint decision-making" muscle, while preparing co-parents to practice thinking "Your Mom and I/Your Dad and I."

Consider the following list as opportunities to agree on making decisions jointly between you and your co-parent. Anticipating developmental steps and agreeing ahead of time that you'll consult with each other and decide together minimizes future conflict and sets healthy co-parenting expectations. Your children will benefit! Many of the following are not required per se—we offer them for discussion purposes only. Depending on your current relationship with your co-parent, conversation now may or may not be possible, but keep in mind that several of these issues will come up sooner or later. Parents who learn to sit down periodically and make decisions about extracurricular activities together, coordinate schedules and sort out how things will be paid for, assure kids that their lives will go forward even as parents' lives change.

- Swimming lessons/water safety: Would you like to have agreements about ensuring that children learn to swim and have a basic level of water safety?

- Extra-curricular activities involving time, effort, expense: Consider such things as music lessons, dance or gym classes, sports leagues, hobbies, and other child-oriented special interests.

- Dating: As children head into later middle school and high school, you and your co-parent will want to consider how you want to handle dating and ensure your teen's safety.

- Sex education: Do you want to have a conversation about "coming of age" sexuality classes at school, local hospital or faith-based course? Would you both like to participate with your child? Will both of you initiate conversations with your child about sexuality and coming of age?

- Driving lessons: When would you like your son/daughter to take driver's education? Will one of you teach him/her to drive? (The longer a teen can drive with a parent before getting a license, the better.)

- Driver's license: Would you like to establish parameters on earning the privilege to get a driver's license? Grade point average? Ability to pay for gas or contribute to insurance costs? Other ways that your teen shows you he/she's ready/responsible/trustworthy?

- Car: Will your child be allowed to have a car of his/her own? Will the car move back and forth with the child between households? Who will hold title, and who will insure? Who will maintain? What costs will you share in?

- Body piercings, tattoos, or any body alteration or extreme adornment prior to the age of 18: What about pierced ears? Pierced noses or belly-buttons? Will you agree to consult with each other and only sign a waiver if you both agree? How would you like to handle extreme haircuts/color, or trendy dress that might go outside your comfort zone (sagging jeans or mega-goth)?

- Permission to enlist in the military before age 18

- Permission to marry before age 18

- Cell phone possession: Would you like to have an agreement about at what age and under what circumstances your child might have his/her own cell phone? Would you like to agree on some basic "rules" across households— like, it goes on the kitchen counter at 10 PM? Does it make sense to determine if cost will be shared?

- Internet presence: Will you work together on maintaining standards for internet presence, monitoring Facebook pages, Instagram, or whatever is popular with your children? Will you share safety protocols, passwords, etc. for your children's sites with each other?

- Acquiring passports: This usually requires both parents to be present.

- Travel outside of the country with or without a parent: What about that trip during spring break junior year with Madison's best friend's family to Mexico? Would you like to decide those things together? Are you both prepared to give a traveling parent a permission letter to leave the country with your child? Please consult with your legal team if you have concerns about your child leaving the country.

- Gun use: Are you both supportive of your child having access to a gun, learning to shoot, going to a shooting range? Does this include paint guns and B-B guns? Would you like to decide jointly?

- Guns in the home: Would you like to be informed if there's a gun in the home where your child is living? Would you like clear agreements about safety protocols? Would you and your co-parent want to work together to ensure that parents of your children's friends maintain safe gun practices?

- Child-care/babysitters: Will the two of you maintain a list of agreed-upon child-care and babysitters?

- College planning/funding: Will your child go on a college tour? Who will help organize all the paperwork, financial aid forms, edit essays? How will applications and college get paid for? Some children have a college coach— take SAT/ACT prep courses—do you support these services? Will you share in these costs?

- Additional areas: Consider the major decisions you know you and your co-parent will be facing over the next several years. These might include allowing your child to ride on a motorcycle/ATV, on certain types of watercraft, or in a private plane. Bring your list to the next Tri-Annual Business of Co-Parenting meeting. You may agree to delay on some while taking actions on others.

Childcare: Babysitters and Leaving Older Children Home Alone

Childcare can be an opportunity for children to develop positive new relationships, venture into new social situations, and develop new confidence in independent living skills. However, childcare can be a source of anxiety or conflict between co-parents. Following a few guidelines builds protocols for smooth, safe child-care practices in the two-home family.

- Acknowledge and be sensitive to making significant changes in daily routines. If your child has never been in childcare, or has had few babysitters, consider how best to transition him/her into the care of new adults. Parents often find creative solutions to tough childcare considerations when they can work together in the best interest of their child.

> Karen, after being a stay-at-home-mom, felt strongly about keeping two-year-old Nathan out of childcare, but faced having to go back to work. Although Nathan's father did not share the same level of concern, he was willing to be flexible and creative. Together, Karen and Tom enrolled Nathan in three days of pre-school. They each took responsibility for one other day during the week. After several months, they were able to see Nathan adjusting to the new routine and felt confident they could move ahead with adding other days of childcare to his routine.

- Create consistency, if possible, through using family and friends as caregivers. Kids enjoy seeing grandparents, and spending time with family friends and known favorite babysitters. Along with the safety and security, having other adults care for your children strengthens healthy relationships that in turn supports children in their community. If you have the luxury of reducing the number of new caregivers in children's lives during the adjustment post-divorce/separation, that's beneficial for kids.

- Co-parents often share caregivers across homes. When co-parents share a nanny or agreed-upon list of babysitters, they can both feel comfortable with who's caring for the children, and children have familiar and consistent care. Babysitters who know the ropes of caring for your children across both households adds to stability and integration.

- Co-parents can create agreements regarding caregivers. Co-parents often determine qualifications (age, gender, completed babysitting class at local hospital, CPR-certified, good recommendations, etc.?) and personality qualities of those considered for babysitting and childcare. However, without expressed agreement, each parent holds responsibility for childcare during his/her time. If you are in conflict about a shared list or qualifications, please stay focused on ensuring children are safe and adequately monitored. You may have to let the rest go.

- Consider the age and capabilities of each child when leaving children at home alone. There may be legal age restrictions in your area about when a child can be left without adult supervision. We suggest that you contact your local government to ascertain the guidelines in your area. The main concern is *safety*. Parent's need to take time to teach *and practice with* children. Children should know how to handle a full array of risky scenarios, such as being locked out of the house, strangers at the door, injuries and emergencies, such as fire (do they know to immediately leave the house ?). They should be fully competent with all appliances. They should have an emergency adult contact (neighbor or nearby family member) that can respond immediately. And they should always have a means to contact you and their other parent.

- Work closely with older children to ensure that they can manage the independence/freedom and remain trustworthy. In times of big life changes such as divorce/separation, children may be at risk for impulsive/ risky behaviors or open to less-healthy peers/negative peer influences. Set agreements with your older child when left unsupervised regarding how he/ she will structure time, establish rules about activities, freedom to leave the house and how far, and visitors. Parents should find ways to monitor teens to ensure they're handling the independence responsibly.

- Supervising younger siblings adds complexity: exercising care when and assessing if a child has the skill, judgement or attention span to supervise younger siblings. Managing conflict and safely resolving problems requires maturity. Give children age-appropriate responsibility for decisions—don't ask children to be responsible in situations where a mistake/misjudgment would be too costly.

- With age-appropriate independence and responsibility come new life skills and competence. However, when kids are asked to take on too much responsibility, independence becomes a liability. Regardless of age, children need parental attention and guidance on a regular basis. We hope the demands of divorce/separation don't interfere with a child's opportunity to continue in age-appropriate activities. Teens that are suddenly pulled out of their developmental arc to care regularly for younger siblings or take on household responsibilities that trump normal teen life can be difficult. To the extent that we can protect them from being burdened, we'll find that sweet spot between everyone pitching in and each person maintaining his/her own life. When kids cease to be kids, they miss out on the important developmental experiences of their age. Two different examples of children left home alone:

Sarah, 15, has her routine down: she lets herself in the house, makes a snack, then watches some TV. She knows her mom checks her assignments before she gets to use her computer, so she gets on her homework until her mom gets home at 5. Sarah likes having the house to herself—it feels "cool with nobody telling me what to do—I know what I'm supposed to do."

At 2:30, Jared, 16, lets himself in the house; his sisters (7 and 10) follow within the half hour. He makes the little girls snacks and grabs something for himself. Predictably the fighting begins over television and computer. Jared's supposed to help the girls, but he has homework to do and has a hard time getting it done with all the fighting. It's the longest three and half hours before dad gets home at 6:00. Jared really hates trying to keep his sisters in line. He wishes it was like before the divorce when he would stay after school, play sports, or go home with friends. He says he misses having fun.

Keep in mind that older children still need monitoring, even as they argue to the contrary. However mature, teens need to be doing age-appropriate activities, building strong peer relationships, and engaged in school *with adult input*.

> During teen years parents move from "teaching parent" to "trusting parent," allowing healthy teens to test their decision-making ability, their trustworthiness, and moral compass. Our job is to prepare our eaglets to be eagles as they take flight into adulthood.

Children need parents to play a significant role in their lives; divorce/separation often impacts the availability of important parent time. Children in two-home families generally build skills and competencies in self-responsibility, organization, teamwork, etc. out of necessity. This is not a bad thing. As parents, staying aware of the demands placed on kids and how they're coping is essential. If possible, you want kids to stay *in their lives* while you create new ways of running a household as a new team led by one adult instead of two.

Healthy caregivers bring new energy, perspectives, and ways of doing things that enhance/expand your child's world. Keeping changes in primary caregivers to a minimum facilitates the opportunity for the learning that grows out of consistent, positive and enduring relationships.

Highlights in Review

- Healthy uncoupling lays the foundation for an effective Co-Parenting Executive team. Regardless of how spouses feel toward one another, *parents love their kids.* Use that common bond to strengthen constructive, integrated decision-making for your kids.

- Joint decision-making is a skill. Implement "parent mind" plus good business practices to establish practices and protocols that respect both co-parents and works for kids.

- Clarify expectations on which areas of your children's lives you intend to consult, inform, and make decisions together.

- Recognize that your children live between the discrepancies in your parenting styles and home-life structure. To the extent that you both can focus on what works best for your children, and allow the past rhythms to inform their early adjustment to two homes, the better. Over time, kids become more and more capable of transitioning with security and confidence.

- In a two-home family, children often carry additional responsibilities through teamwork with siblings and chores. Self-sufficiency and skill-building are positive outcomes. But *over-reliance* on a child creates stress and disrupts normal developmental progress.

- Children continue to need adult input and supervision even as your time with them may be diminished. It remains an important priority to find ways to stay involved and connected, particularly as your children assert their own independence.

Chapter 6

"The Buck Stops Here" (Managing Finances)

MANAGING PAYMENT FOR decisions made jointly, following the agreements spelled out in your Order of Child Support, means that you're not only co-parent executive officers, but also co-parent financial officers. The back-and-forth conversation about money can be stressful and conflict-filled. Unfortunately, your legal paperwork, which may do a great job of describing what is not always helpful with how.

- How do we know what's owed one another?
- How do we handle both of us wanting to buy clothes for the kids when one of us is receiving child support?
- Who pays for birthday party gifts?
- What about allowance?

> Parents generally have lots and lots of questions even when there's plenty of money. If financial concerns, tight budgets, and unclear definitions are added, it's a recipe for ongoing financial conflict and distress.

CFOs: Co-Parent Financial Officers

Children need protection from adult financial matters until they reach an age when having the right information supports healthy development and skill building. Sharing your financial stress with children, even unintentionally, makes them feel helpless about depending on you and leaves them questioning if they're a burden. The feeling that often emerges when children wish they didn't need something from parents is *shame*. Shame hurts. Shame makes us wish we could go away. Children often feel shame around their parents' financial stress. Protect your children by developing confidence in managing *your* financial stress. A clear message about what you can and can't afford is healthy, followed by increasing confidence that you'll take good care of them. We'll go into more detail about age-appropriate involvement of kids in money matters below.

Parents take good care of kids when they manage the financial matters of raising children successfully and relieve children from anxiety, conflict, and stress about how things will get paid for. Fighting about finances is no different than fighting over your children in any other way. Fighting causes stress. Parents make not-so-loving mistakes when they share with children that their other parent is the one who won't pay for things the kids want, when either use money as a messenger of love or caring, or attempt to lure the children into alliance through money or gifts. Money is a wonderful resource; use it wisely; teach your children well—and implement, "Your Mom and I/your Dad and I" when it comes to financial decisions that are based on joint agreements regardless of who is actually writing the check.

> We-lynh and Chad recognized Kim's love of dance. When they transitioned into a two-home family, We-lynh was uncertain her budget could support the three-times-a-week dance classes that Kim had enjoyed since she was four. Chad offered to cover tuition for the first year, which relieved a huge financial worry for We-lynh. Talking with Kim, Chad was careful to say, "Your Mom and I want you to continue with your dance—so, we have made sure you can re-enroll." There was a small part of him that wanted credit for his generosity—he wanted to tell Kim that HE was the one paying for it—but he knew that making a display of money with Kim would be self-serving, not loving.

Divorce/separation impacts family resources. But other changes do as well: children grow up in one-house families where a parent loses a job, someone gets sick, a parent decides to change careers and goes back to school, etc. All of these life changes impact family resources. Helping children to adjust to budget changes with a positive, constructive, can-do attitudes prepares kids and contributes to their healthy resilience when faced with adversity or change later as adults.

Educate Yourself: Co-Design a Plan and Implement with Integrity

Educate yourself. If you are paying/receiving child support, inform yourself about what aspects of your children's lives/needs/resources are paid for by child support in your state. This may be different from what you think *should be covered*, or different from what your co-parent thinks should be covered, or different from what your sister's child support pays for in California. The first place to minimize conflict is to get a clear understanding of what child support covers and what are shared expenses.

- **Child Support varies from state-to-state.** In general, child support is an exchange of funds that facilitates one parent to meet the basic and necessary needs of the children while in his/her residence while creating a somewhat even playing field based on the financial resources available to each parent. This can include contribution to rent/mortgage, utility bills, and other indirect costs of raising/housing children as well as *direct* costs for food and clothing, etc.

- **Child Support rarely covers everything,** unless clearly specified in your agreements. Typically, child support doesn't cover uninsured medical costs, educational costs, and extra-curricular activities or what might best be described as extraordinary expenses. Again, educate yourself about child support in your state as well as what's reflected in your particular legal agreements.

- **Even when child support transfers from one parent to another, both parents often contribute additional money to support their children.** Understanding that child support is a formula based on incomes, amount of time children spend in each household, and guesstimates of what children need at different ages, recognize that it's a rough model for attempting to fairly distribute resources for the care of children across a two-home family. When we look at child support as allowing children to have the benefit of *both parents ability to support them* while in each household, it's easy to see that each parent also contributes additional financial resources when caring for the children in their own homes.

- **Determining what belongs on the list of shared expenses allows co-parents to set expectations up front and minimize surprises.** Some of these shared expenses may be outlined in your legal documents. Take time together to flesh out what those categories actually mean to each of you. If you agreed that educational expenses are shared, ask yourselves, "does that mean every marker pen for a school project? or are we talking about sharing the costs involved in the School Readiness List handed out at the beginning of the school year? What about field trips? School lunches? What if Elsa loses her TI-84 calculator?"

- **Some parents have agreed to no child support transfer payments—** and have opted for sharing all extraordinary expenses based on a formula (often percentage of income) while fully covering all other basic and necessary expenses in each of their homes separately. For parents who have this arrangement, establishing a comprehensive list of "shared expenses" prepares the co-parent financial officers for the next step: *co-designing a plan.*

CHECK LIST:

☑ I have a clear understanding of what child support is supposed to cover.

☑ I have a list of suggestions of what each parent might cover in his/her own household.

☑ I've started a comprehensive list of shared expenses/extraordinary expenses.

Co-design a plan. You've done your preliminary homework, and you come together in a business meeting to discuss the above checklists. You work together to reach understanding and agreement. You're ready to begin designing a plan for how to handle expenses between the two of you.

- **The expenses we each cover:** Perhaps you agree that each of you will provide all the necessary personal items (identifying what each of you think those are) for your children in your home. (e.g., both parents have Matay's "detangler" in the shower, chewable multivitamins and Children's Tylenol in the kitchen cupboard.)

- **The expenses child support covers:** For parents who have child support transfer payments, this is an important category. You both want to be able to confidently and without stress communicate to the children, "Mom/Dad will take care of that for you." Or, if you've agreed ahead of time, either parent may take care of a particular need and then request reimbursement from the parent who is responsible for the item. One of the particularly tricky areas for many parents is kid clothing purchase. We'll tackle that on p. 116.

- **The expenses we share:** Keep in mind how important it is to ensure agreement about shared expenses. Review your list of what "uninsured medical expenses" means to the two of you. An example:

Blake talked with Daniel about allergy testing for their daughter, Myriah. They both agreed that something needed to be done. Blake told Daniel he didn't think the pediatrician was "any good" with allergies. Daniel shrugged and said, "Fine, take her to an allergist." Blake decided he would take Myriah to a naturopath even though her services were not covered by insurance; he preferred a naturopathic approach over a traditional allergist. When Blake submitted the naturopath's bill to Daniel for his share, Daniel was angry; he had expected to pay only his share of a $15 co-pay at an allergist's.

This could have been avoided if the two dads had conferred with each other about what "sharing uninsured medical expenses" meant, how to come to agreement about uninsured providers, and if Blake had informed Daniel ahead of time about his intention to consult a naturopath.

CHECK LIST:

☑ We've agreed to what each of us will take care of in our own households.

☑ We've agreed to what child support will cover.

☑ We've compiled a comprehensive list of shared expenses looking at what we each think is meant by categories like "uninsured medical," "educational," and "extracurricular activities," anticipating problem-areas before they arise and coming to mutual understanding as best we can.

Develop an expense tracking system. Initially, err on the side of providing too much information and ensuring that your co-parent is confident in your expense-tracking and reconciliation process. We suggest that parents keep receipts and make photocopies to attach to their budget reports for each other. Some co-parents will scoff and say that's unnecessary. If that's true, great. Most parents benefit from building a business protocol with adequate detail, which builds confidence for exchanging funds. There's nothing wrong with handling this aspect of your co-parenting relationship with accurate detail. It may be a hassle to develop, and a new habit to employ, but it's all part of being a reliable co-parent financial officer *for your kids.*

- Consider a separate "kid credit card" for shared kid expense. This helps keep shared kid expenses in one place, and it's easy to categorize and easy to provide to your co-parent. Yes, this means you're doing two transactions at Target from time to time (one for household or personal stuff, one for shared kid expenses), but with a little practice, it's no big deal.

- Keep a folder or envelope in your desk drawer for receipts and other useful expense information. Finding a system that works for you is important. Perhaps a spiral notebook helps you log expenses as they happen; perhaps you're proficient with Excel—both work equally well. Your job is learning to track shared expenses and keep documentation. You'll use this information when reconciling expenses with your co-parent financial officer.

CHECK LIST:

☑ I've figured out whether I want a "shared-kid-expense" credit card and/or will use cash/check to pay for kid expenses.

☑ I have a file/folder/envelope set up to maintain documentation/receipts.

☑ I've determined how I'll log expenses in order to tally total spent for each time period.

Reconcile expenses. Once you have an expense-tracking system, you and your co-parent financial officer will co-create a protocol for when and how to reconcile expenses (unless your legal documents specify this protocol already). You've spent additional money—he/she's spent additional money—and you now have to settle up. How do you respectfully provide information and reconcile expenses?

- Check your documents—is there a protocol already outlined? If so, then you're ready to proceed. If the protocol works well, hooray. Easier than you thought. If the protocol doesn't work well for either of you, you might decide to jointly agree on a protocol that does work. Keep in mind: if anything fails, your documents prevail.

- How often should we reconcile? The answer to this question will be based on a couple of different things:

  ○ How tight your budget is. How long can either of you afford to carry a balance owed between reconciliations? On the short side, parents reconcile each month. On the long side, parents might reconcile annually. At the beginning, monthly helps you get into the swing of how to gather receipts and input into a ledger for reconciling with your co-parent. Once you're confident in the process, you and your co-parent might opt for a slightly longer period between reconciliations; for example, quarterly.

  ○ A typical rhythm might look like this: Each parent prepares a list of expenses and appropriate documentation for the other at the end of each month. You provide the compilation to the other by the 5th of the new month. Review. Ask questions—get answers. Whomever owes the other the balance makes payment by the 20th.

○ Use your "Tri-Annual Co-Parenting" meetings. A natural time to reconcile expenses and plan for who will pay what for the next time block is your Tri-Annual Co-Parenting meetings. Whether you're reconciling monthly or less frequently, you'll do financial planning at these times as well.

CHECK LIST

☑ We've checked our documents and determined if there's a protocol in place.

☑ OR, we've created a protocol we can follow for reconciling finances.

> Co-parents with a high degree of trust and a strong working relationship may have a joint "shared-kid-expense" credit card and/or bank account.

- A joint "shared-kid-expense" credit card: This way, either parent can charge previously agreed upon expenses such as the after-school camp or health care co-pays on the credit card as convenient. At the end of the month, parents pay their portion of the credit card bill and avoid much other reconciling. If you're using an airline mileage card, you both might agree that miles accumulated will be used for the kids' air travel.

- A joint "shared-kid-expense" bank account: Some parents set up a shared bank account for the purpose of paying agreed upon shared kid expenses. Each parent contributes his/her previously established share on a monthly basis and maintains records of how the money is used. If one parent pays all the child care costs, there's no need for reconciling beyond using the shared account to make those payments and providing the other parent with receipts.

Implement with integrity. When either of you assume that you have a right to do something with financial implications for your co-parent without adequate communication and agreement, conflict is likely to ensue. This circles back to "joint decisions made jointly." Remember to map out what educational expenses, uninsured medical, etc. mean in order to avoid unnecessary conflict. When you *avoid* direct communication, *avoid* seeking understanding, *avoid* the other person *in general*, you *invite* conflict, stress, and misunderstanding. Remember: 1) check first, 2) discuss as needed, 3) confirm agreement (in writing if needed), or 4) without agreement, *realize you're on your own if you proceed.*

- If you're including items for reimbursement that you don't have prior agreement for, acknowledge which budget items or receipts they are. This is a business arrangement; be respectful. No mysteries, no surprises. That doesn't mean your co-parent won't agree and happily reimburse you, but he/she has a choice if there wasn't prior agreement *unless specified in your legal documents*.

- Part of integrity is keeping to the timeline you've outlined for your reconciliation process. Keep a strong credit rating with your co-parent financial officer. Don't play games with money or be controlling with money. If for any reason you are unable to fulfill your side of the bargain, be upfront with your co-parent and let him/her know when you'll be able to follow through. Staying current with each other on money owed is very important to the health and well-being of the atmosphere that your children grow up in. Is there stress? Lack of trust? Feelings of deceptiveness? Or, does the business of raising children run smoothly, bills paid on time, activities available, resources procured without anxiety or shame?

- Respecting each parent's right to determine what he/she can and cannot afford is part of healthy co-parenting. If you struggled about money during your marriage, you're likely to continue to have opinions, judgments, and struggles with your co-parent about money once you're divorced/separated. Doing all you can to eliminate money battles in terms of your children's activities, resources, and daily life is part of your uncoupling work and moving forward positively post-divorce/separation. If you are unable to find a rhythm, consider getting assistance through a mediator, co-parent coach or similar to find practices and protocols that work.

Anticipating Expenses

When extracurricular activities are shared expenses, prepare for complexity as children get older and more involved. Parents who discuss how to financially support activities now and in the future help children feel secure as they explore options, develop interests, pursue talents/sports/activities and progress in their capabilities. Ask each other *what do you value* and *what can you afford*? Is there money for music lessons? A dance class? Are horseback riding lessons an option? Do you value children exploring team sports? Will your children learn to swim? (*Swimming is a life-saving skill.*) Will they be allowed to choose one sport or activity each season or multiple sports/activities? Will they be directed to play school sports—or can they tryout for elite teams? How will you pay for transportation, equipment, lessons, and related expenses as they arise? Co-parenting agreement and clarity minimizes children's (and co-parents') frustration and disappointment.

Parents often share the costs of extra-special needs or events in their children's lives. Anticipating how to share costs of everything from braces to B'nai Mitzvah helps co-parents plan and work together effectively as they approach their children's important developmental needs/events. When co-parents are proactive and responsible, children enjoy security that the important things are anticipated, supported, and taken care of by parents. Developing a template today can help guide how you'll work together as special life-cycle events continue even for *adult*-children...like *a wedding*.

> Ezra and Rachel separated before Hannah was 10. Hannah had started Hebrew school in preparation for her Bat Mitzvah, at age 13. Rachel suggested to Ezra that they both agree to a budget now to avoid competing or power-struggling about money later. Ezra agreed that knowing this now would greatly reduce his anxiety about a big expense for something they both will share and want to participate in.

Equally important: when parents are unable to pay for opportunities or events important to kids, *clarity* about what parents can and cannot afford/will or won't "do" financially allows kids to *take responsibility for* areas in their lives that they can affect and manage for their own benefit.

College/post-secondary education funding may be outlined in your Order of Child Support, may be something you'll plan for as the time gets closer, or may be something your child will need guidance to secure for him/herself. Educational research tells us that helping children "see" a future that includes college/post-high-school training as early as elementary school has a dramatic positive effect on student success. Whether as co-parents you'll be able to pay for college in full, or provide some financial support toward your child's post-secondary learning experience, having a plan that sets up your child for success is important. As children enter middle school, you can help kids begin to connect the dots between academic success and options after high school. If you know that our child will need scholarships, financial aid, etc., the sooner you enlist their awareness and understanding, the better. Telling a child in their junior or senior year of high school for the first time that there's no college funding puts your child behind an eight ball of your making. Give your child information and support early enough to make decisions, begin saving, begin working toward better grades and additional achievements, set him/herself up for scholarships, etc. to have access to post-high school education/training. Sometimes strong parenting is setting the stage for your child's success—even when you can't afford something, you might be able to help them find their own way.

Malie and Bud separated when Alea was just two. Bud struggled with addictions, but did his best to stay involved in Alea's life. Neither Malie nor Bud had a college education, so Bud didn't think much about college for Alea—not to mention he believed he'd never have enough money to send her to college. Malie, on the other hand, had wished as a schoolgirl that there would be some way for her to attend college, but there wasn't. She was determined that her daughter would have the opportunity she didn't. Malie bought Alea her first hoodie sweatshirt from their local university when she entered 7th grade. Alea was thrilled. Malie helped Alea dream and imagine going to college; she tied the dream to academic performance, leadership skills, and community service. Although she knew that she would never be able to pay for Alea's college on her own, she was certain she could help Alea in the best ways possible to have options for scholarships and loans to fulfill her college dream.

Co-parents operate on a continuum of cooperation and planning: some parents limit interaction to the bare minimum and others maintain a high degree of coordination. Many factors will inform your particular situation. The practices and protocols we've offered above can be modified and tailored to you and your co-parent. The key factors are:

- Anticipate, plan, and provide for your children as best you can.

- Know what you are financially responsible for based on your legal documents.

- Manage your financial health—know what you can afford in terms of discretionary spending and what you need to say no to.

- Protect your children from unnecessary stress and from adult-level conversations about money.

- Make clear agreements about shared expenses.

- Follow protocols for reconciling finances with integrity.

Jorge invited Brianna to the senior prom. He had been playing sports throughout senior year and applying to colleges, so his personal money situation was tight. He knew his parents rarely discussed things like this together, so he decided to approach each of his parents about "prom funding" separately. Dad knew what he could afford and agreed to give Jorge a flat sum. Mom, on the other hand, told him that she would match whatever he earned. Jorge's parents provided clear, understandable, predictable information about money. Although they were not coordinating as co-parents, they were co-parenting effectively and helping Jorge develop age-appropriate, important life skills.

Kids and Money Matters

Children learn valuable lessons in each household, and that includes learning how money is used, shared, and saved. Each of us comes to parenthood with our own history and experience with money from our growing up years. By the time I was six years old, I knew that my dad did shift work and overtime, what lay-offs were, and what "moonlighting" meant. I watched my parents anticipate work seasons of "feast" and "famine." I knew about clipping grocery coupons, collecting S&H Green Stamps, and counting Raleigh cigarette coupons to redeem prizes. I learned about allowance, chores, paper routes and tithing at church. My mom was the first and only mom to go to work on our street. These were many of the valuable lessons about money and running a household that were part of day-to-day growing up in a small factory town in the Midwest. By the time I was ready to apply to college, my parents had saved what was needed—and by the time my children were ready to go to college, my Mom contributed what they needed. You have a story, too. You have stories about what you learned, whether through adversity or blessing. Now you and your co-parent will pass on lessons to your children. Think about what you want your values and legacy about money to be.

In the first few years post-divorce/separation, each parent is adjusting to a new financial reality. Sifting through myriad feelings and building new skills, parents can be overwhelmed with post-divorce/separation change, adjustment, and the demands of single-parenting. Some things just have to fall through the cracks; some of the things that were important before just don't matter at the moment. As you are able, you will find your way back to an even keel. Surviving turns into thriving. Getting by is replaced with getting on with what's important, what matters, and moving forward. This includes finding your financial balance and helping your children feel secure in their new normal.

Talk frankly with children about what's affordable with confidence, and assist them with resetting expectations as needed. Given the choice between feeling guilty about not being able to afford everything the kids want (or were used to), feeling bitter about your circumstances, or confident in your ability to move forward—choose confidence! Your children don't need you to feel guilty or bitter—they simply need consistent messages and a path forward that makes sense to them. In age-appropriate ways, you can begin to include the children in learning to make wise choices, be smart shoppers, and how to get the most out of money.

Handling Household Allowance and "Chore Money"

Co-parents get to determine if one or both households will be responsible for providing children allowance. We typically think of allowance as a learning tool. This is the money that a parent gives a child for the experience of learning to handle money. Will you save some, spend some, give some to charity? These are all valuable aspects of handling your own allowance. In general, allowance is not tied to any work. Similarly, children don't get paid to do what's expected and responsible for their age around the house. Everyone contributes; everyone pitches in. You don't get paid to be a member of a family and do your part to maintain home.

Each parent may offer extra jobs or chores for children as a way of earning money. Encouraging children's initiative and developing the drive to work and earn their own money provides other kinds of lessons as children mature. Paying children reasonable wages helps kids develop appropriate expectations about work and money. Although school, extracurricular activities, and healthy peer relationships are primary for developing children, finding time for lessons in earning money and money management can be an important day-to-day life lesson as well.

"Skin in the Game": Kids Contributing Their Portion

As children mature, they have the capacity for and opportunity to develop self-empowerment around choices and money management. How many of us grew up hearing, "There's no such thing as a free lunch" or "Money doesn't grow on trees"? Experiencing the connection between *effort* and *reward* is not only taught by achievement in school, but also developed in working toward and securing outcomes such as that special pair of designer jeans, a vacation trip with a friend's family, a particular new video game, a used car at 16—the possibilities are endless. Whether we have plenty of money or not, necessity will always be one of the mothers of invention. Help your children be inventive, empowered, resourceful; provide them opportunities to experience self-sufficiency, to achieve something consequential because they were also personally invested. These are lessons taught through healthy financial participation and money management.

Gracie's passion for dog training had hit a new high. Phil and Susan had supported the dog moving back and forth with the kids since their separation for Gracie's sake. The other kids were simply happy to see the dog, but Gracie was committed to training the six-year-old Australian Shepherd every day, with the goal of taking her to a state-level competition.

Gracie brought a budget to her parents that included the classes she wanted to take, two competitions she would have to participate in before entering at the state-level, with equipment and entrance fees, etc. Phil and Susan discussed Gracie's request at their co-parenting business meeting and agreed that they would each provide Gracie with an opportunity to earn up to $10/week in each household. They would tell her that once she had earned half the amount needed to meet her budget, they would contribute the rest. She had plenty of time to be successful, but she'd have to do some extra work. Phil and Susan were so proud of Gracie's initiative, self-confidence, and grit. With Phil and Susan's forethought and support, Gracie was given the chance to feel amazing accomplishment and self-determination.

Credit Cards and Boundaries

Some parents prefer providing a teen with a credit/debit card over cash for things like snacks, gas, and emergencies. Growing up without basic money management skills continues to plague college students who find themselves in debt with credit cards. If you prefer your teen to use a credit/debit card, consider ensuring they learn to keep a log of what's purchased, or check online regularly to track their balance in order to take responsibility for managing the inflow and outflow of money. If you have clear agreements about what the card can and can't be used for, does your teen live within those boundaries? If not, what are the consequences? Without basic money management skills, credit/debit cards with unlimited balances contribute to a 'magical' attitude toward money: *"It's just always there."* Well, we know that's not true. It's a very hard lesson to learn as an adult.

Teach your children the A, B, C's of money management. How to open, deposit, and manage a checking and savings account. Work with them to develop proficiency at tracking withdrawals (whether by check or debit card) and deposits, and balancing their account on a monthly basis. Budgeting is the next step. Give them opportunities to plan for, budget their own money, and experience the consequences of mistakes. The "C" is for credit. Once teens are skilled with managing cash, a checking/savings account (with debit card), they may be ready to learn about credit and credit/debt management.

Clothing and Budgets

Because clothing is often included in child support, because both parents often enjoy the chance to buy clothes with/for kids, because both parents need clothing basics at each of their homes and because kids often show up for their residential time without jackets and boots just as it starts to pour rain for three days, kid clothing often create struggles in two-home families. Let's break this down into solvable chunks.

- What clothing is covered by child support? Can you and your co-parent agree to what types of clothing will be covered by child support, make those purchases periodically, and distribute basics (underwear, socks, etc.) in both households? When children are young, dividing up the pajamas, play shorts and t-shirts can be fairly straight forward. Every so often, a redistribution may be needed (*how did I end up six pairs of pajamas?*), but in general, parents manage their stock-pile of basics. As children get older, they take over managing clothes for transitions, helping with laundry, and tracking belongings.

- Work with kids to build skills to manage their clothes across two homes. Respect your co-parent by ensuring that seasonal needs like jackets, boots, etc., are available at transitions. It's rarely affordable or practical to double everything kids need. Your efforts for and with each other will make parenting your children much easier. Holding back clothing and putting your child in a situation where the other parent is needing to purchase more clothes on their residential time is game playing, and has no place in healthy co-parenting.

- Co-parents may decide to purchase certain types of clothes separately. This can be particularly helpful when it comes to children having an extra pair of tennis shoes or an extra jacket. Remember that kids' clothes are *the kids'*—and not an opportunity for parents to become territorial. If you've purchased a special outfit that you'd like to stay at your house, that's fine, but make that the *exception,* not the rule.

- Clothes needed for extra-curricular activities and expensive clothing may be shared as well. Co-parents often decide to share the cost of a down jacket, for example. If your daughter is a swimmer, co-parents may agree to share the expense of additional swimsuits.

- Children in two-home families still lose stuff. Kids leave jackets at school, mittens at a friend's, and bathing suits in the locker room whether they are living in a one- or two-home family. Frustrating, yes, but normal. Figuring out how to replace lost or misplaced items amicably is important. Children are works in progress, and we don't want their learning mistakes to become unnecessary sources of tension between co-parents. As children get older, they can assist with a few extra chores to help replace that missing bathing suit. Logical consequences grow strong kids; fighting/blaming between co-parents—not so much.

- Teens oftentimes appreciate a clothing budget and freedom to make their own choices. By their early teens, kids develop fairly clear preferences for types of clothes. They may insist on a particular pair of basketball shorts, or only wear one pair of jeans to school. While providing guidance and setting certain parameters, teens can benefit from a clothing budget. You and your co-parent can discuss the best way to set this up if you think your child is ready for the autonomy and learning available through self-selecting and handling his/her own clothing budget.

Holidays, Birthdays, Gifts

Co-parents decide how much they work together regarding gift-giving on special occasions: do they combine funds, set similar individual budgets, or make completely separate decisions? There are pros and cons to each and every one of these options.

- When Keiran is ready for a new laptop as he heads into junior year of high school, co-parents might agree to pool finances to get him a much nicer laptop for his birthday than either would afford alone. Keiran wins—he has a clear signal that both parents are working together in terms of what's *best for him.*

- When co-parents agree to basic individual budgets for birthdays and holiday gifts, each parent can relax, knowing that neither parent will outspend or compete with money and gift-giving, and kids aren't faced with huge discrepancies between each parent's gifts.

- If parents manage conflict and stress best by maintaining complete autonomy in these areas, kids benefit.

Parents often wonder who's responsible for buying gifts the children are taking to their friend's birthday parties, etc. Like so many of the financial matters we've been discussing, coming to clarity and agreement is key. Parents may determine that these sorts of gifts are covered by child support. Other parents agree that the parent who is taking the child on his/her residential time takes responsibility for the gift. Helping your child have a hassle-free experience around friends' parties is a gift you give him/her.

Highlights in Review

- As co-parent financial officers, you're charged with two primary goals: 1) run the financial aspects of your children's lives smoothly with integrity; and 2) teach them money management, values, and realistic expectations. Work as well together as possible. Prevent kids from feeling shame for needing things.

- Co-parents may approach the above goals separately, but, ideally with clarity and consistency.

- Co-parents benefit from taking the time to ensure shared expectations regarding the purpose of child support, what items they will each take financial responsibility for, and what will be shared expenses.

- Develop a clear protocol for reconciling expenses and follow through with integrity.

- The more business-like and precise the process, the sooner trust will build.

Chapter 7

Co-Parenting at Holidays
and Life-Cycle Events

AS CHALLENGING AS divorce/separation can be, co-parents sometimes find that holidays and special events help them securely lock onto "parent mind" and focus on their children. This can include stepping back and supporting children to enjoy holiday celebrations fully with one parent as much as it can mean stepping in and spending a brief period of time together with your child.

> Co-parents' ability to spend well-defined periods of time together with their children is directly related to the process of "un-coupling," the grieving process for both adults and kids, and the co-parents' ability to trust and respect each other.

New Family Rituals Evolve Over Time

Co-parents find their way into new traditions and kid-centered family events based on family history, state of healing from divorce, and logistics of the two-home relationships. Parents typically consider the children's developmental stage, involvement of extended family, and co-parents' values in planning celebrations. We encourage parents to factor in the children's divorce adjustment when designing holiday celebrations when first separating and the first year or two post-divorce. When parents have the flexibility to accommodate children in this way, kids benefit.

During the Separation/Divorce Process

We ask parents to first reflect on what children are used to, what they've come to expect at the holidays: who's usually there, where do they celebrate, and what's typical? Early in the separation/divorce process, parents often opt for holding established traditions as similar as possible in the first post-separation holiday season.

If one parent lives in the family home, the first holiday celebration post-separation may feel more normal and familiar if the children can be in the family home. Depending on how children are adjusting to their two-home family, co-parents can structure holidays to meet kids' needs as best they can. Notice this is a very different approach—a child-centered approach—than worrying if each parent is getting his/her "fair share" of kid-time.

When inviting the non-residential parent for the kid-centered part of holiday celebrations, maintain healthy boundaries and appropriate roles (host/guest). This facilitates an opportunity for both parents to enjoy the children's special moments. Co-parents may agree that the non-residential parent will come over on Christmas morning at 7 a.m. as the children wake up for Santa gifts, for example. The parent agrees to stay through gift opening and a glass of juice and then excuse him/herself after kisses and cuddles. This book-ended visit supports both co-parents in maintaining "parent mind" for a delineated time period—perhaps 90 minutes to maybe two hours. Parents and kids know how this will work so that expectations are set and everyone can relax as much as possible. Healthy boundaries and follow-through assist children with managing hopes that their parents might get back together, and support the early steps of adjustment to divorce/separation.

> **Special Note:** Be sure that you and your co-parent discuss and agree on being together for a holiday/celebration **before** looping in the children. It's important to respect your co-parent's emotional preparedness and honor the possibility that he/she may want to decline the invitation. Co-parents getting on the same page first protects children from the possible feelings of rejection and disappointment that may follow if a co-parent declines an invitation or proposal. Check and confirm with your co-parent prior to involving kids in the possibility of Mom/Dad coming.

Coaching grandparents, relatives, family friends, and possibly a new romantic partner to support you in celebrating with your co-parent and children helps smooth holiday events. Managing these logistics is a normal part of separation/divorce adjustment. Frustrating, perhaps; stressful, maybe; and typical. Everyone's adjusting. We hope that co-parents don't decide out of hand that there's "no way." There's often a way for both co-parents to support/participate in children's special events to ease everyone's adjustment. Enlist the services of a co-parent coach or mediator if helpful.

- Help grandparents, relatives and family friends understand how setting adult feelings aside for children is healthy, supportive, and allows kids to be free of adult conflict during special moments.

- Help a new romantic partner feel secure that this return to a family event is done strictly as a co-parent and not as an ex-spouse. Reassure that in time, you will ensure he/she's included. Children generally benefit from holiday celebrations with familiar faces in this early phase. There will be plenty of time to include new people once they've adjusted a few steps down the road.

Sometimes divorcing/separating co-parents know that there's no way to share space or have each other in their respective homes. Consequently, they find ways to share kids on holidays in tandem rather than together. To the extent that it's possible, encourage a more relaxed atmosphere about dividing holidays during the separation/divorce process. If you can allow children time with each parent to celebrate their holidays, the loss of family is less abrupt and scary; children are less likely to worry about the other parent, and less likely to feel interfering guilt or concern about a parent's loneliness or OK-ness. Remember, we're making suggestions for this early phase of separation/divorce adjustment.

The First Year or Two Post-Divorce/Separation

Depending on family traditions and the age of children, parents may consider the first couple years post-divorce/separation differently from the longer-term parenting plan/holiday schedule. With younger children, parents often create holiday plans that allow more involvement by both parents at each holiday, whether that's in shared space or in tandem.

Tiffany and Craig agreed that over the next two Christmas seasons, they would maintain the rhythm and activities that they had set in motion as a one-house family. This year, Tiffany would take the kids downtown for a shopping day on December 24th. They would see the Gingerbread House display, get Santa pictures, and walk the corridor of lights as they've done since the children were small. Craig didn't want to spend the entire day together—it was too much for him—but he decided he'd meet them for dinner on Christmas Eve. From there, he would take the children home. Tiffany would come over in the morning at 8 a.m. for Santa gifts. After a few hours she would leave and return to pick up the kids at 3 p.m. for dinner at Grandma's. Both parents felt strongly that holding to these traditions for their 8- and 10-year-old children would support everyone for the first couple of years. They planned that in the second year, they would reverse the pattern, with Craig taking the kids downtown on the 24th, and Tiffany having the children with her for Christmas Eve night and Christmas morning.

Their long-term residential schedule for the holidays looked much different, giving both households more autonomy, separation, and options for new traditions, new senses of family, travel, etc. Their long-term schedule divided the winter break in half and rotated which parent would have children during the first half and which parent would have the children the second half. They both acknowledged that either of them could invite the other parent to participate in holiday celebrations in the long-term if that felt right and worked for everyone involved. Time would tell.

Parents may have a hard time imagining a holiday without their children and have an urge to create holiday residential schedules that insist on regular contact by both parents at every holiday. We ask parents to step back and consider your children's experience of every holiday split—moving, changing, adjusting, doing two of many things: once for Mom, once for Dad. This is *not* adults meeting kids' needs; this is likely kids meeting *adults'* needs. The positive resolution of divorce includes adjusting to changes, loss, and recalibrating your expectations in support of yourselves *and your kids*.

Karen and Frank both cherished their family Thanksgiving tradition: both sides of the family were invited; 14 people sitting around the table, lots of laughter, family antics, and amazing food. Continuing to share the holiday post-separation was not an option given their difficulty managing the current conflict in their adult relationship. Even though it was Frank's Thanksgiving with the girls this year, Karen wanted to talk about dividing the holiday. She wanted to pick up the girls at 5 p.m., which would allow them to attend her delayed Thanksgiving feast. Frank argued that doing so would rush his Thanksgiving plans with his extended family, even though tradition was to have dinner on the table by 2 p.m. He protested that this plan introduced stress rather than enjoyment for the girls. Karen stressed how the girls deserved to celebrate holidays with both parents and both sides of the family.

After much arguing, they looked at the issue from the girls' perspective. Wow, what an eye opener. They could see that enjoying a festive, relaxed Thanksgiving with family was more important for the girls than being shuttled from one household to the other just to celebrate with both parents. They realized they had been arguing for a solution in hopes of avoiding their own hurt and grief over missing their girls, rather than protecting the girls' feelings.

Frank wondered if they should ask the girls which way they preferred the holiday to be celebrated. Karen appreciated his new openness, but she saw how asking the girls put them in a position of either splitting up—one of them wanting to do both and one only wanting to stay in one place—or put them in the position of choosing what they thought Mom and Dad wanted rather than choosing themselves. "No," she said, "this is a decision best made by us, which allows them to relax and be certain they're not responsible for either of our feelings."

Karen and Frank could now strategize how each of them could have a special Thanksgiving break experience with the girls without disrupting or doubling-up the stress. They agreed that whoever had Thanksgiving Day celebrated with family, and the other parent would pick up the children Friday morning and create a tradition of cutting down a Christmas tree. Both co-parents loved the idea that the children would have two different but special traditions during their school break—one with each parent. They would then return to their regular residential schedule for the weekend.

Whether parents create schedules with phases, or move directly to a predictable, well-defined long-term residential pattern for holidays often reflects the flexibility of the divorce/separation process itself. Keep in mind that when you and your co-parent create mutual agreements, when you manage conflict and reduce stress, and you stay kid-centered, the children benefit. It's not an issue of *right* or *wrong*, *better* or *worse*, it's a matter of what works in your family, at this time, and under your unique circumstances.

Sam and Becca had a difficult divorce. They managed to continue to support their son in his activities and move beyond the ugliness of dissolving their marriage. When it came to the holidays, however, they both knew they needed a complete break from one another. They designed parenting plan agreements rotating Rosh Hashanah and Yom Kippur each year—one parent had Rosh Hashanah one year and Yom Kippur the next. Zack was relieved, as both his parents were more relaxed when they weren't forcing themselves to be together. Besides Zack felt that "if we aren't going to BE a family, we're not going to ACT LIKE a family." Zack had both his parents involved in his holidays in a way that, under the circumstances, made sense to him as he adjusted to divorce, and it worked best to manage conflict as well.

The Long-Term

In planning the long term holiday schedule, parents consider how much of their previous, one-home family life to retain for the children (and themselves) while evolving toward separation and autonomy as homelife settles and family life moves forward. Once your two-home family has experience celebrating the holidays and your kiddos have adjusted to the new family structure, vacations and holidays may begin to take on different long-term forms and rhythms. When parents are first in the divorce process, they may not be able to imagine a time that they'd want to travel with their kids to Utah during Christmas. But after someone has recoupled with a partner whose extended family lives in Utah, guess what? So, ideally the parenting plan is structured with this wisdom in mind.

> The intensity and worry that surrounds newly divorcing parents facing so much loss changes enormously once everyone has settled into new rhythms, new-found security, and smoothly running homes.

When co-parents talk openly and honestly about holiday celebrations—what traditions to keep, and which new traditions they want to create—they co-parent based on shared goals for the children and mutual respect for their separate homes. Discussing expectations, helping each other anticipate changes in how your two-home family celebrates holidays, provides both parents opportunity to support children—particularly when introducing a romantic partner into holiday celebrations. If you've been sharing Thanksgiving dinner, is Mom/Dad's new boyfriend/girlfriend welcome? If so, great—set another plate at the table. If not, you may need to move to a new structure for how you celebrate Thanksgiving. When parents talk and figure out how to accommodate or change, children are often spared the abrupt shifts and tension that can arise when one parent makes a unilateral decision without consulting and striving for mutual agreement.

Creating holiday schedules that respect family and existing relationships, while allowing independence for one or both co-parents and/or providing space for new partners, is all part of managing the long-term adjustment for a two-home family. The intersection of all these considerations can be complex. The more capable co-parents are communicating and more accepting of the divorce/separation process, the more positive the negotiations for change will be when adjustments are necessary.

James was relieved that he and Shelly and their three children were doing so well a year and a half after the divorce. He and Shelly were less tense with each other, and contentedly shared most of the first post-divorce year of holidays together for the children. In October, Shelly called to talk about Thanksgiving. She left a voicemail stating it was "her" year, and she would be taking the children away for the holiday. James was stunned and upset. He couldn't understand why she would change something that worked so well last year. He was certain that being together for the holiday was "best for the kids."

After a few days, James called Shelly back. He disclosed his disappointment about her decision and his fear that their hard-earned trust and cooperation would shatter. Shelly took a deep breath and admitted she had been fearful of being upfront about her need for more autonomy — more separation from him. She had been dating Kaiden now for quite a while, and she wanted to include him and help him feel more comfortable. She wasn't sure if it was okay to discuss these issues with James.

Although it was indeed difficult for James to hear, Shelly's openness reassured him that she cared about keeping their relationship friendly and honest. In turn, he felt more comfortable knowing what was driving the plan to change how they'd celebrate holidays this coming season. They checked in with each other about Christmas. They both admitted that they enjoyed Christmas morning celebration with the kids and would continue to invite the other parent for opening presents, but would otherwise celebrate the other festivities separately. Shelly let James know that she might also be including Kaiden, which was something for him to consider.

James recognized the all-too familiar feeling of grief gripping his heart, and wondered if he could face seeing Shelly with Kaiden on Christmas morning with his kids. Time would tell. He didn't have to know or decide right now. Meanwhile he would continue his grief work, and concentrate on un-coupling and moving forward.

In the end, some parents continue many original family traditions throughout their children's growing up years, others completely separate to create new traditions with no overlap between homes, and many two-home families thrive somewhere in the middle. Find what works and what supports adjustment and thriving for adults and kids. Acknowledge your own feelings and deal with them appropriately. Managing your hurt and grief provides freedom to see what's actually best for your kids. Talk directly with your co-parent about what you think might work well. Come up with solutions so that your children can experience tension-free, peaceful holidays shared with the family they're with. Following agreements, maintaining boundaries, and inviting change respectfully with your co-parent helps manage expectations across the arc of post-divorce/separation adjustment.

- Early in the separation/divorce process, co-parents may need complete separation to manage their own feelings, or may choose to provide as typical an experience as possible for their children by coming together for certain aspects of holiday celebrations that are kid-centered.

- In the first year or two post-divorce/separation, co-parents continue to monitor their need for separation while considering which original family traditions they wish to hold in place for their children's sense of integration/comfort/family.

- Longer-term, with co-parents and children adjusting to the two-home family structure, we often see a mix of the old with new traditions. Co-parents often opt for more autonomy, sometimes to include new partners, which influences holiday membership and celebration.

Flexibility and creativity are necessary traits of successful two-home families. Add in good boundaries and clear communication, you have the recipe for successful co-parenting, helping children navigate the ups and downs of two-home family-life over time.

Gwen and Daniel celebrated both the Christian and Jewish holidays with their three children, Max, Leah, and Danielle. As they contemplated their parenting plan and post-divorce life, Gwen admitted that she would prefer to celebrate the Christian holidays and have Daniel take over the Jewish holidays if he chose to celebrate them.

They built a parenting plan that allowed Gwen to have the Christmas half of Winter Break. Daniel simply requested that he be allowed to have the children for every first and eighth night of Hanukkah as long as that didn't interfere with Christmas Eve/Christmas or winter break travel. Gwen was happy with that. As they considered the spring holidays, they realized that in order for Daniel to travel to LA with the kids to see his family for Passover, she may have to miss the occasional Easter, and likewise, if Gwen wanted to travel with the kids over Easter/Spring Break, Daniel might miss having the kids for Passover—but if they were both in town, they would do their best to allow each parent to have the children for their respective holidays.

What About Birthdays?

Children's Birthdays

A child's birthday represents celebrations on two important levels: first is the no-holds-barred celebration of your kiddo as he/she becomes another year older, and second is the annual reflection of your child's birth (that's for you!). There are several ways to honor both of these levels for divorced/separated parents. Recognize that your child's actual birthday may hold particular meaning to one or both of you, and accept that your child's busy, healthy life may preempt exactly how you accomplish honoring and reminiscing. Let's see what can happen with a little creativity and flexibility.

Birthday parties mean different things for kids at different ages:

- For young children, birthdays are often celebrations for the whole family, including extended family and family of friends. For the newly divorced/separated co-parents, gathering grandparents, aunties and uncles and close family friends in one place, like the family home, can be awkward and difficult for the parent who has moved out; simpler, separate gatherings may work better if adjustment has been challenging.

- As children grow older, they become more vocal about how they want to celebrate their special day and tend to focus more on their peers and peer parties on a day convenient for everyone to attend (as opposed their actual birthday). Co-parents may function as hosts for their children's friends, and mutually sort out planning, hosting and paying for the party. They may rotate responsibility each year—one parent hosting and the other as guest—share the responsibility annually, or one parent may be the "birthday planner extraordinaire" to the great relief of his/her co-parent. Ideally, they both attend at least the cake-cutting and gift-opening portion of the party. Co-parents may agree that hosting the party at a neutral location makes attendance more comfortable for both. We do not recommend attempting to throw two peer-oriented birthday parties—one by each parent—as doing so can be stressful and competitive.

- Teens often want even more independence from their parents when celebrating with their peers. Co-parents sort out the where, how and when— co-parents should establish budgets, transportation and supervision as needed. Some teens feel they've outgrown peer birthday parties, which opens the door again for simpler family-based celebrations as the main attraction, whether together with both parents and siblings (perhaps dinner at a restaurant of your teen's choice?), or with each parent's household separately during normal residential time.

Considering children's needs at different ages helps co-parents create celebrations that honor the child while considering each parent's desire to acknowledge the special occasion. Combining those efforts with an honest assessment of the level of tension or comfort in working together, being at the same event, including extended family, etc., can help to guide co-parents' choices.

- Designate which co-parent will be in charge of the peer birthday party. Perhaps you rotate this responsibility in even/odd years. In some families, one parent may have a particular talent for throwing parties, so both co-parents agree that the "party parent" will plan every year.

- When you have multiple children and you both want a chance to take the lead on planning peer birthday parties, we suggest that one parent takes the lead for all the children in one calendar year and then the other in the next. "This is Mom's year to plan your parties; next year will be Dad's."

- During the party, the lead parent is the "duty parent" for the party and the other parent attends as a "helpful guest." Defer, support, be respectful, and your child will have a wonderful party!

The most important goal is to create a birthday party that's fun, enjoyable, and keeps the focus on the birthday boy or girl. If co-parents can participate together for a birthday party and feel glad to be there for their child, that will likely telegraph directly to their kiddo. Conversely, parents who are tense, angry, or sad will likely be sensed by their child. While we applaud both parents' efforts in managing their feelings to share in the day, it is also okay for parents to acknowledge their needs and limitations honestly. Similarly, it helps to acknowledge the needs and limitations of extended family members and friends to participate wholeheartedly in a gathering. Honesty is your best policy, and if you think Aunt Edie won't hold her tongue, perhaps she can celebrate with Junior at another time.

Each parent may still plan a family birthday separate from the annual peer birthday party. Generally these occur during the normal residential schedule and give your child an extra boost of celebrating, gifts, and extended family love. What child argues with two, maybe three, cakes?

What may be trickier is your child's actual birthday. One of you is their "duty parent" and one of you is *not*. Depending on your feelings, you may be content to wait until your residential time to see your kiddo; in the meantime, you'll leave a card, a gift on the porch (if that's acceptable to your co-parent), or text/call a happy birthday wish. Other parents want to know they can cuddle/kiss their baby on his/ her actual birthday even if he/she's turning 15! As school and activities fill schedules, you may need to be creative.

- Perhaps your parenting plan specifies a visit by the non-residential parent on your child's birthday.

- Is it convenient for your co-parent if you pick your son/daughter up in the morning and take him/her out for a hot cocoa on the way to school?

- Is there a window of time after school, before practice, where you can spend an hour together?

- If you wait until after school activities are complete, is there still time to go out and also get homework done? Be thoughtful of your child's stress level.

- Be respectful of the fact that the residential parent may have special dinner plans to celebrate your child's birthday; whatever you do, don't bring Junior back loaded up with a triple hot-fudge sundae.

When birthdays fall on weekends or happen during summer; there are even more potential options.

Anticipating and making room for your child attending another sibling's birthday party on your residential time may become part of family life. Your child may have siblings that don't live with you. Co-parents who can anticipate and plan for children attending sibling's birthday parties is a way you both honor family without splitting children's lives in half. Perhaps this is done through a trade of time, or simply considered a kid activity for your child during your residential time—either works great. The important part is recognizing family through your children's eyes and experience.

Parents' Birthdays

We hate to break this to you, but your birthday may not be as important to your kids as it is to you, or their birthday is to them. Go figure. It's not that kids don't love you, don't get excited to make you a card, give you a present, it's just kids' nature to be more interested when they are the center of attention. Parents do best acknowledging what they want and need around their own birthdays and managing expectations for how children will respond or be involved. Again, your children may or may not be in residence with you on your birthday; you may or may not have a chance to see them on your special day. Take good care of yourself.

- If your children are with you, plan something special—model for them that family, birthdays, and special occasions are celebrated with fun and comfort.

- If your children are with your co-parent, be sure to make plans that feel good to you on your birthday, whether with friends, other family, or by making a special evening for yourself. You may feel your children's absence more acutely on holidays/special occasions; a little planning ahead can help with the missing. Then, when they return, celebrate your birthday together.

- If the children are with you on your co-parent's birthday, help them to fulfill whatever the agreements are for birthdays. At minimum, support them making a birthday call. We encourage you to help the children create a card, make a gift, or take them to the store to purchase a little gift—whatever is in keeping with your family traditions. Remember, they're dependent on you to help them prepare for celebrating their other parent's birthday. If appropriate, consider a generous offer of extra time with the kids for your co-parent on his/her birthday.

More Special Occasions

Mother's Day/Father's Day

Mother's Day and Father's Day mean different things to different parents; most parenting plans designate where children spend time in honor of these two occasions. Take some time to think about how children participated in Mother's/Father's Day in the past.

- Did they make breakfast in bed for you?
- Did they give handmade cards and presents created with the help of the other parent?
- Did the family enjoy an outing together?
- Did Mom/Dad get away for a day to enjoy her/his own kid-free time?

Using the past as a guide helps provide some consistency for children. That said, Mom/Dad may have children with them solo for a special day where new traditions and fun ideas are yet to be discovered.

> When a co-parent assists children in honoring their other parent through planning cards, gifts, activities, children learn valuable relationship lessons and experience a unique kind of support that transcends hurt, upset, and loss.

Your Unique Family Events

Your family most likely has other special occasions and holidays to navigate, separate, integrate, honor, and find new rhythms with. We hope you have found some ideas about how other families come together, separate, honor and celebrate a range of family events. If we can't do it this way, we'll try that way; and with the passage of time, we'll have even more options. Here are just a few of the special family occasions we're aware of that two-home families have found a way to honor and sustain:

- "Gotcha' Day" (adoption "birthday")
- Family Camp (same week every summer)
- Shared vacation home with other families
- Special Fourth of July camping trip

- Honoring Memorial Day

- Dealing with different religious traditions across two homes

Children growing up in two-home families can enjoy all the benefits of ritual, tradition, extended family, and celebration. Co-parents working together to facilitate what's best about family in each home benefits the children.

Highlights in Review

- Post-divorce/separation adjustment evolves over time. How co-parents celebrate holidays and special occasions often reflects this developmental process. What's important in the immediate aftermath of separating gives way to something that may feel appropriate for the next couple of years, which gives way ultimately to a long-term pattern that allows for autonomy, growth and change for adults while maintaining connection and family for kids.

- Keeping holidays and special occasions positive and joyous can be challenging even in a one-home family. That said, doing your best to be honest about your ability to be together to celebrate with your children is important. There's no need to force the river—let time heal, and work with your healing process.

- Flexibility and creativity assist co-parents in finding ways to work together to maximize positive family rituals and traditions for kids.

- A child's peer birthday party is special for the child. When both parents can be present (even if only for a bookended period of time), children feel particularly loved—no one is left out.

- Your children may need to rely on you to help them prepare for their other parent's special occasions; do your best to help kids experience the precious lesson of preparing and surprising the ones they love.

- Co-parents have more control and say about how/when/where they spend time with each other in private spaces and for family events. Done well, children accept and relax into the structure and guidance their parents provide.

Chapter 8

Co-Parenting in Public Spaces

THERE ARE MANY ways children keep co-parents connected—through their school, extracurricular activities, health care needs, life-cycle events—all occurring in public space where they used to be together, and now are not. These common settings may be filled with memories and patterns that may no longer fit. In this chapter we hope to help you find your way through the discomfort and awkwardness to a more satisfying way of sharing public space with respect for each other and the focus on your children.

Emotional Readiness

Taking steps to un-couple, strengthening parent mind, and accepting *what is* will help you manage emotions when participating in public kid events. Some situations more than others may trigger difficult emotions. Developing a calm mindset and logistical coping strategies ahead of time will assist with enjoying your child's public events/activities. As difficult as it may be today to attend events where your co-parent and guests are also present, know that with persistence and experience you'll both find your way to comfortable enjoyment of these events.

Prepare yourself. Start with some helpful mental preparation: 1) Remember that both you and your co-parent belong at your children's public activities and events; 2) be aware that other people may be attending that you would prefer not to interact with or see (he/she/they are also free to attend public events); and 3) know that the only person you can control is yourself. When we want to impose strong expectations regarding what's right or wrong about what others are doing, who should or shouldn't be attending public events, we create our own suffering. Preparing is not a matter of discounting how you feel, it's a matter of building a constructive mindset and healthy coping strategies.

Always 100% parent not always "on duty": a mental switch. Public events can create ambiguity and uncertainty about your parental role and responsibilities. To assist with role clarity, we encourage parents to rely on the "duty parent" model. Ideally, you and your co-parent have discussed respectful boundaries and can maintain civility. The "duty parent" model suggests that the "on-duty" co-parent is in charge of parenting responsibilities while the "off-duty" co-parent maintains a more *guest* role at public events. Even when your children come to you with requests better handled by the duty parent, simply refer the kids back to the parent in charge. They'll learn healthy boundaries, too.

Respecting the post-divorce/separation developmental process. *Healing/recovering from divorce/separation is a process.* Understanding the level of both adult and child adjustment, respecting each other's feelings within reason, and giving stability a chance to take hold helps children relax, focus on their activities, and facilitates parents showing up emotionally available and appropriate for kids.

> Louis and Serena had been dating since he separated from his wife three months ago. Louis's son Brent was playing soccer Saturday morning near Louis's apartment, and Louis was contemplating inviting Serena to the game. He argued with himself: "I really want to invite her—it would be a great chance for her to see Brent without a big introduction or forced meeting." Another part of him said, "Oh, geez, if Phyllis [Brent's Mom] comes to the game, there's going to be holy war." Another voice jumped in: "I'm so tired of her controlling my life;" to which another voice calmly said, "Hey, this isn't about YOU, this is about Brent. How would Brent feel if you bring Serena and it throws his mom into next week?" Louis decided that he'd wait for more time to pass before introducing another person to an already tense and difficult situation. For now, he'll go and support/enjoy Brent playing soccer, and be cordial to Phyllis if she attends.

Adjustment, acceptance, and some measure of comfort will come in time if/when both co-parents are committed to their individual work of moving on respectfully post-divorce/separation. Keeping the focus on your children makes the work of pacing change, respecting each other emotionally, and working through personal grief, worth it.

Sports and Extracurricular Activities

In the catalog of family values, where do we rank an occasion like this?
A curly-haired boy who wanted to run before he walked, age seven now,
a soccer player scoring a winning goal. He turns to the bleachers with his
fists in the air and a smile wide as a gap-toothed galaxy. His own cheering
section of grownups and kids all leap to their feet and hug each other,
delirious with love for this boy. ... The cheering section includes his mother
and her friends, his brother, his father and stepmother, a stepbrother and
stepsister, and a grandparent. Lucky is the child with this many relatives
on hand to hail a proud accomplishment. I'm there too, witnessing a family
fortune. ... I am thinking: I dare anybody to call this a broken home.

—Barbara Kingsolver, American essayist

Enjoy your children when they're participating in school and extracurricular activities. Kid-oriented public events serve as a "bridge" between homes for children. Kiddos often feel uncomfortable or unsure of the new rules of interacting post-divorce/separation. Help your child negotiate that walk with clear permission to enjoy both parents while respecting who's on duty—meanwhile, you keep the spotlight on his/her participation in the activity.

We encourage an attitude that co-parents are welcome to observe, cheer, and touch base with children participating in activities in public space. This also offers an additional touch point for children with the off-duty parent—which is *good for kids.* Please consider the following co-parent protocols that make for positive co parenting during your children's extracurricular activities/special events:

Co-Parent Protocols

- Respect the physical and emotional distance your co-parent wants/needs from you. If your presence creates discomfort, please maintain a healthy and respectful distance from your co-parent at public events like the soccer field. This includes keeping your eyes on your child's activity/event rather than watching/observing your co-parent and his/her guest(s). If the discomfort persists, consider getting some coaching for yourself or better, with your co-parent.

- How you determine who sits with which of the other parents can be done with grace. Your ability to maintain composure can help guide where you sit, stand, or how long you stay at an event. This brings us back to the reminder: the only person you can control is yourself. Your children's activities/events are not a time for a turf war over former relationships with teammates' parents. In time, there will be plenty of space for both of you to relax; in time, you may even find that you can share the same bleacher, cheering section, etc. Make it your goal to find a way to participate that doesn't distract from your child's sense of support by his/her parents both attending.

- When you're the on-duty parent, encourage your children (whether participants or spectators) to greet their other parent. Give them guidance: "There's Dad—go on over and say hi, and I'll see you back here in a few minutes." If you know ahead of time the other parent would welcome the children to hang out with him/her for some portion of an event, practice generosity by allowing/encouraging the children in attendance to move freely between the two of you.

- For the off-duty parent, gracefully accept your secondary role to help reduce tension and ambiguity for your child. Redirect your child back to his/her duty parent for permission to go to the snack shack, or to play over on the swings— consider how you'd respond to another parent's child and you'll be in safe territory, not stepping on your co-parent's duty-parent toes.

- Address your child openly and lovingly with healthy boundaries for the situation. A big hug, congratulations, or whatever is indicated and then help your child move back to the duty parent while assuring him/her that you'll see them again soon (unless you have an agreement that the child can move freely between you).

- At the end of the game, the duty parent can allow 2–5 minutes for the non-duty parent to give a 'high-five' and quick recap of game highlights. However, this is not a time for lengthy discussions, planning for the future, or anything beyond a well-boundaried, respectful few moments, particularly if the duty parent is waiting to load up the car and move on.

School and School Events

Co-parents benefit from strategies for navigating back-to-school nights, science fairs, parent-teacher conferences, end-of-season banquets, and other kid-centered school events. As with extracurricular athletics or recreation sports programs, both co-parents are welcome at school events regardless of residential schedule. Co-parents may decide to split the duty by agreement: "You go this time; I'll go next." But aside from that, both are free to attend.

- Follow the Co-Parent Protocols listed on p. 135 when your children are present. At the science fair, encourage your child to spend some reasonable amount of time hosting his/her other parent. Give helpful directions and allow space for success. Pre-planning with your co-parent can mitigate confusion for your child.

Rick and Mitch both planned to attend Tyson's science fair. Rick was on duty, so he checked in with Mitch about which half-hour he'd like during the evening, offering either 7 - 7:30 or 7:30 – 8. Mitch appreciated both the planning and generosity. He happily accepted the second time slot, which allowed Rick to have the first slot with Tyson. As 7:30 approached, Rick prepared Tyson to meet him in the cafeteria at 8 p.m. when he was done showing Mitch his classrooms and projects. Tyson happily greeted Mitch when he arrived at 7:30 and announced, "OK, now it's YOUR turn, Papa."

- Parent-teacher conferences may or may not be scheduled together. The advantage of meeting together with the teacher is that you both hear the exact same information from the teacher as well as the concerns raised by your co-parent. If you meet separately, you may want to take notes to verify that you understood the teachers feedback, and share them in writing via a transition email with your co-parent.

- At banquets and other more formal events where children are seated with parents, support your child to sit with the duty parent. Leaving these decisions up to the child is rarely a favor, and often a source of guessing and stressing. When co-parents are respectful, give children helpful direction, maintain healthy boundaries, and remain on the same page about supporting kids in public spaces, kids win.

Walt and Barbara carved out very different lives post-divorce. Walt remained "part of the gang" of parents involved in their daughter Erica's activities; Barbara stepped away. When it came to Erica's band banquet at the end of junior year, both parents wanted to attend. Walt arrived first and sat at the table with all his friends. When Barbara arrived, she chose a table where parents of some freshman band members were seated. It was hard on Barbara to feel like an outsider, but she persevered and accepted that she was the one who stepped away from all the parent involvement after the separation. Erica came over to her mom immediately and gave her a big hug and let her know how glad she was that she had come. Erica went back and took a seat next to her dad as the evening presentations began—it was her week at Dad's—and this clarity helped Erica feel confident that she was doing the right thing.

When volunteering in classrooms or for school projects, the co-parent avoids impacting the duty parent's day-to-day relationship with the child. When your support/participation in the classroom enhances your child's school experience and doesn't interfere with co-parent's role in the classroom or impact transitions, then, go for it. Otherwise, be sensitive to any sense of competing or "boxing out" the other parent by signing up first for parent volunteer opportunities. Co-parents may want to discuss rotating volunteer roles at their Tri-Annual Co-Parenting Meeting if issues arise.

High school special events (Homecoming, Prom, Senior Recognition, etc.) bring co-parents together for pictures/gatherings. Teens are particularly sensitive to being singled out or feeling different. As co-parents at a teen-centered event, do your absolute best to be stress-free and easy-going, allowing your teen to move freely with friends, get pictures taken, and share the event without worry for parents' feelings.

Geoffrey's parents had been divorced for eight years by the time he was a senior in high school. They both attended pretty much every athletic event he was in, cheering from opposite sides of the gym. The last game at the end of basketball season involved a special recognition for all the seniors. Each player with a mom in attendance had a rose to present to her; parents walked out to center court with their son where a professional photo was snapped. Lisa and Matt easily wrapped an arm around their son, who stood proudly between them. Parent-mind in action, with Geoffrey as the focus.

Lilah needed two roses for her walk out onto the floor with her parents, because both her mom and her step-mom were there to celebrate her last home game as cheer captain. Her step-mom stood next to her husband while Lilah stood between her mom and dad. "Snap" went the picture of Lilah and her family.

Graduations from kindergarten through college represent milestones for kids and proud moments for co-parents. Our hope for co-parents at these special milestone moments is the ability to come together and celebrate their child. Take pictures for each other; if appropriate, have someone take a picture of you both with your grad for his/her scrapbook or bulletin board. The more parents can relax and focus on their child, the less guilty the child will feel about parents' distress and about parents *"having to come together 'cuz of me."*

Children's life-cycle events, like graduations, are wonderful opportunities for all family members, when everyone can honor and respect each other. However, it's not a time for children to take care of adults' feelings.

> If parents and stepparents/partners are not yet adjusted and accepting of each other, we recommend that primary parents take first position with focusing on the child while stepparents/partners stand back and allow space for the primary parents to support/celebrate their child's accomplishment.

This can be tricky, and it's important to discuss with a loved one ahead of time to assure him/her that the purpose is not to "give in to your ex-partner" but rather to celebrate and care for your child.

Faith Community and Religious Practices

Religion and celebration of faith can be an area of deep divide/conflict if co-parents forget to respect each other's option to determine religious practice. A common concern about a child's religious practice post divorce/separation arises when one co-parent no longer values or shares a willingness to ensure religious education/attendance. As noted, divorce/separation involves "tearing"—and when that tearing crosses religious values and previous agreements/promises about how you'll raise your child together, one co-parent may feel profoundly concerned, anxious and betrayed. Because religious freedom is an important personal choice, there is no recourse but acceptance that your co-parent has a right to his/her own decisions about religious practice and daily activities for your child on his/her residential schedule. That said, co-parents often work out ways that allow a child continuity in religious practice/attendance when valued. For example:

- The practicing parent agrees to take full responsibility for transportation and managing all the logistics of religious attendance—even on the non-practicing parent's residential time, if this works for the co-parent.

- The practicing parent may agree to swap time for the opportunity to have the child/children attend services/activities with him/her if the co-parent agrees.

- The non-practicing parent agrees to religious attendance in much the same way that he/she agrees to any other extra-curricular activity—taking his/her child to the Sunday evening youth group in the same way he/she'd take the child to piano lessons.

- The practicing parent participates with the children during his/her residential time and accepts that the non-practicing or "other practicing" parent will manage the child's activities on his/her residential time.

Certain religious practice milestones for children require education, commitment, practice and ceremony. When co-parents come together and determine that a certain milestone is important for their child regardless of adult religious practice, the commitment is to *the child*. If you've agreed to support your child through the steps of completing a religious milestone, your ongoing attention to your child becomes part-and-parcel with your other foundational parenting practices.

> Your child will depend on both of you to help him/her sustain the commitment and persevere through the practice/challenges that come with obtaining any meaningful accomplishment.

And, of course, attend their special ceremony.

The family-focus of many faith communities can make co-parenting stressful in the early months of post-divorce/separation. With a generally strong value placed on marriage and family, faith communities sometimes struggle with a divorcing/separating couple. The now single-parent/single adult seems out of place. There may be judgments and rumors to dispel. The couple may experience feelings of embarrassment, failure, guilt, unworthiness, and plain old awkwardness or self-consciousness. What was once an easy, welcoming place, may now feel fraught with memories, failure, and uncertainty.

Find strategies for continuing your faith-based life that also supports your child in his/her faith community. When the sanctuary becomes one more place to navigate feelings about how to share space with your ex-partner/spouse, co-parents may find ways to ease the tensions by:

- Having a frank and constructive conversation with the religious leadership about how to separate and respect each other in the intimate space of worship;
- Planning ahead on how to share or divide religious activities/space with your co-parent;
- Attending separate services;
- Attending different communities if that's what makes the most sense.
- As for children, following the co-parenting protocols on p. 135;
- And playing an instrumental role in helping them maintain their *own* community of peers, much like their school friends/relationships, which may go beyond your personal religious practice.

Developmentally, children will come to a point where they express their own thoughts and feelings regarding religious practice. Like every parenting step we take with our children, you will be faced with determining when your children have a say in their religious practice. When co-parents are in alignment on this issue, it's easier to hold boundaries and family tradition. When they are not, the child will use the split to his/her advantage. We encourage parents to recognize that ongoing conflict between co-parents will rarely do good. Trust children to mature into the best people they can and will be, whether they are participating in religious activities when in residence at your home, or their other home, or not at all.

Primary Health Care/Dental Appointments

Talking with professionals about your child's health concerns provides important and necessary information for your child's overall well-being. Reporting updates about your child to the health care provider can be a bit more difficult when children are living in a two-home family. Co-parents who effectively communicate health information through transition emails assist whichever parent is responsible for taking children to see a health-care provider. Most health-care appointments are opportunities to model constructive communication as well as education for your child. When exchanging information about your child, about your child's life with his/her other parent, remember that your child is listening.

- Information shared in front of your child should be child-centered, communicated for the purpose of modeling for your child how to provide that information one day for him/herself. Be accurate and maintain a positive attitude about your child's two-home life (your child builds his/her family life story based on experiences just like this!). Keep developmental appropriateness in mind—as children mature, they are more and more capable of taking responsibility for their health.

- Request adult-level consultation when you need to convey information that may be heard in a negative light by your child about his/her "other parent." Accuracy of information is not an excuse to openly criticize the parenting practices of your co-parent in front of your child—request a moment with the health care provider if there's information of concern that needs to be shared.

Miyako took Cole in for his regular check-up to the pediatric nurse practitioner, Celia. Cole was diagnosed with pediatric hypertension when he was only four years old. Miyako and Rob, Cole's dad, were separated, and Cole was now moving back and forth every other weekend to his dad's. Miyako was explaining the changes and encouraging Cole to contribute his six-year-old version of the two-home family. On examination, Cole's blood pressure was higher than it had been for number of previous visits. As Nurse Celia began assessing what might have contributed to the increase in blood pressure, Miyako realized there was a need for an adult-level conversation. She let Celia know that she needed a few minutes with her alone.

Once Cole was ready, he sat in a chair in the hall. Miyako then shared with Celia that Rob had been taking Cole out to eat much more than they ever did before, due to time constraints and living on his own. Trips for hamburgers and french fries were a form of "male-bonding" and she was feeling like a complete nag—Rob was simply not listening to her concerns. Celia came up with a prescription list of specific low-salt foods. She had Cole come back into the room and went over the list with him of "food choices" when he goes out to eat whether with Mom or Dad. Two copies were made—Miyako would provide one to Rob at the next transition. Maybe this would help—and if not, Miyako would ask Rob to bring Cole to his next appointment.

Benefits: Cole was not exposed to an adult conversation that may have caused discomfort and guilt about the fun he and his dad have, or the tension his mom is feeling about his dad not listening, or her worry about the increased blood pressure. And a plan for both parents to follow was initiated.

Constructive co-parenting at health/dental care appointments and consultations calls out for decorum, trust-building, and agreement that your child is the primary focus. Work out agreements about setting appointments. Rotate appointments to balance the impact on residential time if necessary to spread the responsibility as well an opportunity to participate and be informed. If you find yourselves in regular conflict, consider rotating responsibility on an annual basis, which gets out of keeping score while sharing responsibility and impact. Ensure that paying bills is worked out smoothly.

Peer Birthday Parties

Duty parent responsibilities regarding your children's friend's birthday parties can be delegated, shared, or managed completely on your own. Helping children stay engaged with their friends during each parent's residential time is good for kids.

However disruptive or inconvenient, friend's birthday parties often sprinkle across any number of weekends in the elementary school years. For the co-parent who has limited time with his/her children, this may have a much greater impact than for the parent with more time. When co-parents can coordinate purchasing, wrapping a present, and having the child prepared for the birthday party with directions/invitations, your co-parent is less stressed and your child can enjoy birthday party attendance. This may be another way of practicing generosity if your assistance is welcomed and supportive.

When both co-parents are invited, friend birthday parties are like any other kid-centric event in public. If you both attend, follow your Co-Parenting Protocols. Sometimes parents opt for following the residential schedule when deciding who will attend—in other words, the "duty parent" follows the child to the party. In the event where one parent clearly has a more primary relationship with the family extending the invitation, co-parents may opt to swap time.

> The guiding principle is to practice creativity and child-centered problem-solving when it comes to resolving tension/conflict for kid-centric events.

Kids can't always attend every party—support daily decision-making in each home. As much as we champion kids staying involved with peers as they move from one home to another, there will be situations and times when it's simply not practical or possible. When both co-parents support each other in day-to-day decision-making, children are more capable of settling down and accepting limits and boundaries. "If Dad says, 'not this time,' Mom echoes, 'not this time.'" That way, kids aren't caught in the middle.

Playmates and Their Families

Co-parents generally come to agreements about how to share contact information for each household with children's playmates' families. Make agreements about providing email/contact information to your children's friend's families. Forward pertinent information back and forth; provide hard-copy invitations to each other. Your children depend on each of you to coordinate and assist in making their lives run as smoothly as possible.

Redirecting parents to the co-parent on duty for kid-oriented activities is part of respectful co-parenting. Once you have permission to provide contact information, remember to redirect other parents to the co-parent on duty when invitations are being extended. Playdates/scheduling kid activities needs to be done by the duty-parent. When you involve your child, or ask him or her to relay information, you may create pressure and disappointment. Keep parental information and decisions at the parental level.

> Chris was best friends with his cousin Ben. When his parents separated, things got a little awkward about playing with Ben when Chris was at his mom's. Jim, Chris' dad, talked with his brother and sister-and-law and clarified how important it was to him that Chris and Ben continue their friendship even when Chris was at his mom's. Beth was so relieved that her former in-laws were able to call and invite Chris even on her weekends—and they accepted invitations for Ben to come play with Chris at Beth's as well.

Other Family Events in Public Spaces

Two-home families find creative/supportive ways to deal with important family life-cycle events such as Mom's graduation from college, Dad's community service award, Great-Grandma's 90th birthday, Aunt Delilah's wedding, regardless of residential schedule. When co-parents strategize how kids can attend important life-cycle opportunities on all sides of their family, they can find ways to ensure that children have a rich and integrated sense of family across two homes. This includes important family life events of new partners once those relationships develop to "family level."

> Mom was graduating from university—a special event she hoped her children would attend. Dad agreed to come with the children while Mom participated in the ceremony. Dad understood that although it was "his" time, it was their mother's special moment. Stepping back and allowing the children to put their mom first wasn't easy with his unresolved resentment about the divorce. But to see them enjoying their mom's accomplishments without reservation or worry about his feelings helped reassure him that extending this gesture was the right thing to do.

Highlights in Review

- Attending your children's activities in public space has an emotional dimension that requires preparation and grace.

- Co-parents and guests are free to attend kid-centric activities with respect and healthy boundaries.

- Co-Parenting Protocols provide co-parents and kids with helpful guidelines about who's in charge based on the duty-parent role when both parents are in public spaces.

- School is an important bridge between both homes—parents' ability to navigate shared experiences at school helps children feel safe and secure in their world away from home.

- Faith communities may offer some special challenges due to their family focus. Co-parents may want to look beyond their own religious practice preferences to what supports kids.

- Health-care appointments are a place for constructive information-sharing. Represent your co-parent in a positive light in front of your child.

- Sharing contact information and facilitating peer activities helps co-parents smooth out wrinkles for kids as they transition from one home to another.

- As the family matures, consideration for new family members increases the opportunity for your children to experience the love and celebrations/special events of extended family.

Chapter 9

New Adults in Your Children's Lives

ENDING A RELATIONSHIP, coming to completion with one another, can be a very difficult task all by itself. How deeply we've bonded and attached to one another, the focus and respect we give the process of un-coupling, and the effect the changes have on our children, impact how easily or stressfully we come apart. There are circumstances where the divorce/separation process is further challenged by a new adult in one of the co-parent's lives. The timing for a new romantic interest entering the equation often affects expectations, feelings, and capacity of the other co-parent and children to accept or welcome the new person. Like so many aspects of the divorce/separation process, this, too, can be understood best in the developmental context of divorce/separation adjustment.

Adult Relationships 101

Adult dating relationships have a developmental arc. For some, dating may be a foreign language, a thing of the distant past, and certainly not something you thought you'd be doing at this stage of life. Since you are brand-new at this (again), consider keeping the following in mind:

- **Why should you finish one relationship before beginning another?**
  Notice the word "should," someone "should," but this is not always how life goes. The value of completing one relationship before dating or moving on is in finding your footing first so you don't fall in love too quickly, with unresolved issues, and accidentally hurt yourself and others. Another aspect of completing your relationship prior to including a new person in your life is respect for your current relationship and that person's heart.

- **Premature "we-ness" hampers and restricts the alchemy available in a new relationship.** Coming out of a marriage, you may long to replace the warmth, security, predictability, and comforts of married life.

> When adults rush into the "we-ness" phase of a relationship, they often bring trunk-loads of baggage from their past marriage(s) that later have to be unpacked with their new partner.

We recommend skipping this exercise, and discover the new and fresh ways you get to know someone, date, have fun, and bond—no steps left out. Take plenty of time to evolve into "we-ness" once you've uncovered all the unique aspects of coupling with a new person.

- **Rebound relationships generally don't work out.** When an adult quickly moves from one relationship to the next, he/she may be running from grief, hurt, a fear of being alone, the past—running from him/herself. Running into the arms of someone else is a bit like using that person as a docking station in hopes that any bad feelings will pass while you're "hooked up." At some point, reality sets in and the relationship often falls apart. Then, the person is off and running again—with hurt and confusion left for those in the wake.

- **Falling in love is intoxicating.** There's plenty written on the brain chemistry of lust and falling in love—suffice it to say, our wildly expressed hormones leave us idealizing, daydreaming, making love insatiably; we feel love-struck, closer, more compelled, more special than we ever dreamed we'd feel. (*Thank you brain chemistry and hormones!*) Probably not the best phase for making any important life decisions. How long do we get to wear these rose-colored glasses? About three to four months. If we've made important life decisions during this time, they can be tough to undo.

- **Wherever there's idealization, disappointment follows.** Some people refer to the first phase of falling in love as "dancing in the light"—everything seems perfect and flaws are hidden. During the second stage of relationship development, the *shadows dance,* the disappointments come forward, the flaws are exposed. The real relationship work begins. If all is going well, you'll be having your first real disagreements and learning how to resolve the inevitable conflict of being two separate, empowered human beings. For those who prefer the excitement and intoxication of falling in love, this phase may prove to be too much work and may go looking again for greener pastures. How long does the "reality setting in" stage last? Another three to four months.

- **Emerge with a deepened bond and balanced view of each other— or realize that you're not meant to be.** By about nine months of dating, a couple has a fairly good idea about their relationship. This is often the point that couples determine they want to go forward, or they bring their relationship to an end. It will be in the next year or so together that most couples will determine whether the relationship has a permanent place in their lives.

- **Not every meeting has relationship potential.** Dating is not for the faint of heart. A friend once told me, "It takes 100 at-bats before you meet someone you can go to first base with." If you attach your self-worth and self-esteem to dating, you are likely to need your therapist on speed dial. Be gentle with yourself; wait for the right person, someone safe to explore relationship with, and learn all there is to learn about loving deeply and being loved—and remember to love yourself.

Understanding yourself, respecting your co-parent, and recognizing the stages of relationship development will help guide you when you're ready to blend your love life with your children's lives. Parents are imperfect. Love doesn't happen on a schedule. And guidelines are only helpful when they're applied as guidelines—not as an opportunity for judgment or blame. Our goal is to help you have insight into the typical places where mistakes happen—and help you protect your children from those mistakes you can. Introducing love interests too early or too often is not good for kids. Your job is to vet your relationships before involving children's hopes and hearts.

Introducing New Romantic Partners

The most common question asked by parents about a new romantic interest is: "When's the right time to introduce someone to my kids?" Our general reply: "When you know that this relationship is strong enough and important enough to involve your children." Another important pair of questions: 1) "How will you know if your children are ready to share your attention with another adult, and 2) and ready to accept another adult into their lives?" We wish we had a magic number of weeks, or months, or perfect timing to suggest—but it's complicated. More times than not, the parent asking this question is thinking "I'd like to introduce him/her to the kids *now*." Before you go too far with involving children with a new romantic partner, you might want to consult with your legal team if you have any concerns about how this might impact your separation/divorce process.

First, would your co-parent like to know before you introduce the kids to your romantic interest? Some do, some don't—this is very individual. There's no right or wrong answer to this question—it's a matter of what is more respectful between the two of you: getting an email letting the other know ahead of the introduction, or finding out from the children there was "someone new" at Mom/Dad's home over the weekend. What will allow you to best support your children as they share news that may be exciting for them as well as causing trepidation? Whatever you and your co-parent decide, we encourage that you follow through, stay in integrity with agreements you make, and maintain the trust you're building—even if it's hard, inconvenient, or results in upset.

Introducing can mean anything from "running into a friend of Mom/Dad's at the mall" to "Mommy/Daddy's new boy/girlfriend is coming for dinner" for the first time. We generally distinguish four levels of kid-meeting and involvement in a parent's romantic life.

- "Oh, this is a friend of mine; Ginger and Bradley, I'd like you to meet…" This is something casual, out in public; it may be staged, brief, and generally not repeated. It may occur in the first three months of dating. The parent wants his/her new romantic interest to simply meet his/her children so the new person has a real-life idea of the most important people in the parent's life.

- "Kids, I'd like you to meet someone special I've been seeing…" This is officially letting the children know you have a boy/girlfriend they watch you text or hear you on the phone with. You may do an occasional group activity like all going to a backyard barbeque. But for now, you mostly limit seeing each other to your off-duty time. Likely to occur after 4 - 6 months of dating.

- "Janis is coming over to have dinner and watch a movie with us…" This is beginning to hang-out at home, including him/her in family-level activities, and going out together as a group—no sleep-overs yet. Common by six to eight months of dating.

- "Grant will be here this weekend." This is the point where "sleep-overs" may occur and a more complete integration into home life begins to feel typical or normal. Many parents reserve this level of involvement for after nine to twelve months of dating; some will wait until a formal commitment has been made.

Growth and Development

Like so many things about divorce adjustment, time since separation, age of the children, and the degree to which the children feel stable in their lives has a great deal to do with how they respond and adjust to the idea of one (or both) of their parents becoming involved with another adult. Children have different concerns at different ages. In general, younger children are more accepting of new, kind adults than older children—particularly teens.

- Preschool and early school age children want to know when you "love" someone, if you're going to get married, and if "she/he's going to be my new Mommy/Daddy." Children in this age group "leap to the finish line." They want to know, to label, and to get on with a sense of family they recognize through their friends and limited life-experience. They are concerned about sharing you with someone else (sometimes jealous) and anxious about being treated "special".

- Later school-age children often struggle with wanting to push away and wanting to be accepted/loved/chosen by the new romantic partner of a parent. They may vacillate between wooing behavior and acting up. Underneath, they fear losing you, or becoming less important to you than the new adult.

- Middle schoolers and early teens are typically self-conscious and may withdraw, attempting to keep their lives as normal and under-the-radar as they can. Pre-teens and early teens are working hard at developing their own moral compass, and can be harsh judges of parents' choices. They, too, worry deeply about losing you just as they need to begin separating from you. They may feel protective of their other parent and caught in a dilemma between living their own life and taking care of both of you.

- High schoolers and later teens have already started separating from parents and as a consequence rarely welcome a new partner *(who needs more parents when you're trying to separate from the two who are already raising you?)*. If the new partner is "cool" there could be some general interest, but it's thin and easily lost if he/she should try and set limits on (or display any sort of disapproval of) the middle/older teen. Middle and older teens are often very vocal about having another unrelated adult in their intimate/home space at night or first thing in the morning, "I just feel uncomfortable with him/her here." Sexuality is closer to the surface; confronted by a parent's sex-life can simply feel like "too much information."

- College-age and adult children can vary widely in their acceptance of new partners in their parents' lives. Some are genuinely happy for a parent finding new love. Others carry unresolved grief from losing his/her original family and insist on drawing lines in the sand about who's "real family" and who's not.

Timing, Pacing and Adjustment

When a parent is already involved with a new romantic partner as part of the divorce or early in the separation process, adjustment can be more complicated and stressful for co-parents and kids as everyone attempts to navigate loss, change, loyalties and uncertainty. We're not here to judge—we're here to help with a circumstance that happens and impacts families. We'll talk about it from both sides of the coin: 1) the co-parent involved in a new love relationship; and 2) the co-parent attempting to "hold down the fort" for his/her children while family-as-everyone-knows-it disintegrates.

The co-parent in love with a new partner.

- Each person's situation is unique, but what you may have in common with others who have walked this path, at least in retrospect, is that you were already separating (emotionally) from your committed partner for the last two to five years—even if you didn't know it. This doesn't justify infidelity or betrayal, but it does help explain your imperfection/ humanity. Now, you're in love—or so it feels. You're walking through your divorce/separation process and attempting to assist your children through a major life change with the brain chemistry of someone on drugs—*love drugs,* natural hormones that distort how you think, feel, and see the world. You've never felt life was so *right*—while your family feels like everything is *wrong.* This clash of perceptions can cause enormous pain, misunderstanding, misjudgment, and missteps. Your reaction might be that others are suffering from "sour grapes." Probably not. They're probably devastated.

- Your co-parent is likely to feel shattered and unprepared. This can make co-parenting with you very difficult. He/she may be struggling with each and every transition of the children. He/she is likely questioning your judgment and whether you have any idea of the impact you're having on the kids— maybe even whether you're a fit parent—particularly if you're involving your love interest in the children's lives.

- If you're already living with your new romantic partner, your family may feel "deleted." Your former family members are feeling forced into a situation of your making without choice, preparation, or understanding about what happened. You may feel confused, undermined, and caught between your "old family" and your "new life." You never imagined things could get this complicated and upset, especially when it's born out of *love.*

- Or, perhaps, you've handled your new relationship separate from your divorce/separation process and made stabilizing your children in their two-home family a top priority. We find that parents often just don't know that kids may not simply adapt, fall in line, and accept parental decisions as if everything's going to be OK. A co-parent in love often finds out the hard way that his/her co-parent and children need time, support, and priority to adjust to divorce/separation. And the intoxicating brain chemistry of falling-in-love distorts what you're experiencing and limits responsiveness—actually blinds you—to the very ones you love: your children.

- Create space, time, and energy for your children. They need you; they need to recognize you as their Mom/Dad—not someone else's girlfriend/boyfriend— not someone in love. When everything happens at once, they're left confused and uncertain. "If you can change that quickly about our family, will you do that to me?"

- Do what you can to ensure that you have parent-child time uninterrupted and undistracted by others. Keep in mind that although your own needs are important, your children's needs are more important when they are with you and counting on you as their duty parent.

- Attempt as best you can to hold to routines and rituals that the children are familiar with. Help them cultivate a new sense of security in the face of the family change and the move to a two-home family.

- Help your new romantic interest understand that the time invested in helping your children on the front end of the divorce/separation process will benefit everyone over the long haul.

- Your new romantic partner may be more or less prepared to make space for your former family to adjust, your children to feel secure, and your co-parent to accept the new playing field. Navigating a new relationship through divorce/separation with children requires enormous maturity and trust on the part of the new partner.

The co-parent left to hold things together for the kids.

- You're reeling from a new reality you never imagined. Your former partner is now creating a life with another person that you don't know (or know well)—maybe even "playing house" together with your children. You want to come unglued at the absurdity—and yet, you're called to walk forward, support the children in their relationship with their other parent, and to make sense out of something you hope is just a bad dream you'll wake up from.

- The urge to judge, lash out, insist that you should be the "primary, if not ONLY parent" because your co-parent is behaving/making choices that are bad for kids weighs heavily on your mind. You see yourself as the faithful one, providing stability, predictability; you may be the homework parent, the make-sure-everyone-gets-enough-sleep parent. You have judgements about the morals that your co-parent is modeling for your children. You want to protect your children, limit, and, on some level, *punish* your co-parent for behaving so selfishly. Any of this resonate?? If so, you're completely *normal!* That said, we gently bring you back to some of the important cornerstones of co-parenting post-separation/divorce:

  - Do what you can to take good care of yourself.

  - Actively work on uncoupling and develop your "parent mind" separate from your adult-relationship concerns and emotional hurt.

  - Minimize stress and conflict for your children.

  - Recognize their feelings, while supporting them to see a future when everything will smooth out again.

- Encourage and support your co-parent to focus and prioritize the children. You will have much more influence—your co-parent is more likely to hear you—if you can maintain a constructive, working relationship with regard to the kids.

- For your children, the catastrophe is not that your marriage/partnership is over, but that they could lose a parent. Continuing to support your co-parent's relationship with your children in the face of your hurt and pain may be the single most loving set of actions you'll take during your divorce/separation. Huge. You may not want to. But for kids, however upset, conflicted, and mad they might be, your ability to hold their relationship with BOTH of you as important, worth working through and a *forever* part of the deal, reassures them. They realize you will do everything to protect not only the half of their heart that belongs to *you*, but the half of their heart that belongs to their *other parent*. That's love.

- If your co-parent has "gone off the rails" and appears to be having a crisis—lapsing into adolescence and forgetting responsibilities, you have the opportunity to become the voice of reason for your children until the crisis is over. Trusting the crisis will pass, and your co-parent will re-emerge as the loving parent he/she has been, is another act of love for your children. Consider how you can best "hold down the fort" while your co-parent finds his/her way back into a predictable, contributing co-parent relationship. He/she may need time; your children will need support. If the crisis never passes, you've done what a parent can do to hold the possibility in a constructive, realistic, and supportive way for your children. With maturity, they will put two and two together in a way that makes sense for them.

Amy and Jeff were married for 14 years when they started looking for their dream house. Having just sold the little rambler they moved into years ago in preparation for having children, they rented an apartment while they looked for the "right next-place." Less than a month in the apartment, Jeff confessed to Amy that he thought he might be "in love" with someone else. She stood, deer in the headlights, as he walked out the door. The kids, eight and 10 at the time, had no idea what all this meant. Next thing they knew, Daddy was off vacationing with his new girlfriend, working during his scheduled residential time with them, asking Grandma to take care of them. The kids felt scared, uneasy, and worried about their dad AND mom.

Jeff had no capacity to understand the level of distress he left behind. He grew out his hair, bought a new wardrobe, and started listening to different music. His Facebook page reflected his new status, and pictures were posted from their recent trip to Cabo. Amy was in the makeshift apartment mopping up the mess, working full-time, supporting the children emotionally, and figuring out how to go forward.

Over the next three years, Amy was regularly confronted with how to navigate her own feelings toward Jeff's new "live in" and what she experienced as their approach to "them first" and "she and the kids second." She never gave up, though... "Your Dad loves you bunches; he'll see you on Friday—OH, Daddy had to work today, he'll see you on Saturday."

And eventually, things settled down. Jeff and his new partner married, had a child, and found their way into a new home life. However, Jeff's two older children were still unsettled and confused. That home included blending hers, his, and theirs, and the blending wasn't going so smoothly for them.

With the help of a child specialist, the three adults could hear how much Amy and Jeff's children needed more predictability and direct time with their father. There was no part of this story that was easy for anyone. As it turns out, with a lot of hard work, Jeff and Amy's children are going to be given a chance to have both parents and a stepparent in their lives as they traverse adolescence. Jeff and his wife discovered better ways to address the older two's needs, helping them find their place with their step- and half siblings.

Introducing new partners to children and including them in family life can be a big step forward for kids. Whether early in the divorce/separation process, or later as children adjust, new romantic partners can make divorce/separation real and lasting for children—a kind of finality that parents aren't going to reunite. Along with signaling closure on hopes to be our old family again, a new adult in Mom/Dad's life can bring about new possibilities, vitality, and can expand a child's sense of family. You can see, though, that even a well-timed, thoughtful introduction of a new significant other can mean a whole lot more to your children than you might have anticipated.

> Introducing a "love interest" is not something to take lightly. That said, a healthy, loving person entering your children's lives can be a natural, healthy and potentially positive step toward the future.

Keeping in mind how your children may be experiencing grief—and their comfort with all the changes helps predict their openness to another person. Let's review some critical considerations:

- Children are less likely to feel threatened by a new person when they're comfortable in their relationship with each parent one-to-one.

- Children find it easier to welcome a new person when they feel secure—when structure (schedule) is predictable in each home.

- Children are more able to open up to new experiences and new people when they have passed through the initial stages of grief.

- Children are less likely to react negatively to a new adult once they have digested that their parents will not be reuniting; that they are now a two-home family no matter what or who.

Under the best of circumstances, adding a romantic partner into the equation with your children and co-parent is destabilizing. All growth includes stress and instability for some period of time. There will be reactions, apprehension, anxiety, mixed with curiosity, interest, and hope. We encourage you to remember the dozens of times you've assisted your children through growth challenges. You already have a fair amount of information about how each of them responds to change. Use that information to help them adjust to this change as well.

- Regression, aggression, and rejection are perhaps the most common signs of instability for children. Pacing the introduction and level of inclusion can help children not feel overwhelmed and out of control of what's happening in their lives. At the same time, as the parent, you'll make certain family-life decisions that you believe are in everyone's best interest. Working together to solve problems that arise, listening to concerns and complaints within reason, and giving time for relationships to build between your romantic partner and your children in a step-by-step fashion will help.

- Ready and welcoming for some children, once things have settled down, they want the extra activity and noise associated with more people around their home. Another adult, his/her children, a more family-like atmosphere can help with a kind of post-divorce/separation quietness or even emptiness that some children feel now that "we're not all together anymore."

• • • • • • • •

Jenny, age 12: *"I don't know, it just seems so quiet when it used to be loud. I guess I miss having everyone in the same house getting into*

*each other's space. I used to hate it—now I miss it. When Amanda
and her kids come over, at least there's more stuff to do. It's better."*

· · · · · · · ·

- Your co-parent plays an instrumental role in helping your children adjust to a new partner. When you both normalize that adults re-couple, children get an integrated message that the change is OK. When a co-parent can support kids in developing a relationship with a new partner and openly receive news about special activities, children can let go of fear of causing upset through sharing about their lives. A co-parent can have a negative impact by signaling distress, encouraging reactivity, or worse, catastrophizing the impact of a new romantic partner on the family.

- Respectfully preparing your co-parent can be valuable. Although your adult relationship choice is none of your co-parent's business, you may want to give serious consideration to how to prepare him/her for news of a new love interest. The more he/she feels respected, secure in your co-parenting agreements, and trusts your judgment, the more likely your children will have his/her positive support for the changes in their two-home family.

What about meeting my co-parent's new romantic partner? This can vary from parent to parent. Some of the typical reasons to meet each other include:

- General interest and cordiality—especially if the new romantic partner intends to begin attending kid-centric functions in public.

- When your co-parent would like his/her new partner to provide babysitting/child-care for brief periods of time.

- When the romantic partner is spending the night while the children are in residence.

- Engagement, marriage, or cohabitation.

(For more on integrating a new stepparent for your children, see Appendix p. 224, *How do I Get My Ex to Accept a New Stepparent for Our Kids.*)

Adult Sleepovers

Adult sleepovers may create controversy. Some of the strongest "Mama Bear/Papa Bear" feelings come forward when a co-parent begins talking about having his/her romantic partner spend the night when the children are in residence. More complicating is when a co-parent chooses to cohabitate with a new romantic partner before the separation/divorce is complete—often impacting everyone's adjustment and the residential schedule. In the strictest sense, a co-parent has no control over what occurs at the other co-parent's home unless stipulated in court documents, and/or child endangerment is at issue. To be on the safe side, you may want to consult with your legal team for information on how these decisions might impact your separation/divorce process.

If we step back from any legal considerations and focus on children's needs, we encourage co-parents to take respectful and prudent steps when initiating adult sleepovers. Keep in mind that your children are accustomed to their parents sleeping together, not wired for a new person to be sleeping with their parent. Depending on the age of the child, this can be anything from unnoticed (very young children), disconcerting and uncomfortable (older children) to "too much information" (teens, as we mentioned earlier). Well paced, with relationships built, enough time passed, these normal, healthy steps in adult relationships work better for kids. On an adult level, please consider:

- Moral development, if relevant

- Modeling healthy adult relationship development

- Emotional and sexual safety

Romantic Partner or Stepparent?

Prematurely jumping into a parental role—nurturing, taking care of (bathing, grooming, tucking in at night), teaching life skills—can have a dramatic affect on everyone's adjustment. Please help your romantic partner understand that he/she in not a parent in lieu of your child's other parent when spending time with your children. Inadvertently, this often, for the co-parent, creates feelings of competition, being upstaged, and of wanting to push back and protect children from an untrusted/ unaccepted source of influence. Understandably, the new partner is simply hoping to build relationship, may genuinely enjoy the nurturing/family member role, and may be ensuring you that he/she is serious about your children. His/her enthusiasm, skill and commitment will be welcomed and celebrated in good time, with conscious planning and thorough examination of the pitfalls involved in parenting someone else's children. A smoother transition is more likely to occur when:

- You maintain your role as sole parent with your children until enough time has passed that children are comfortable and your co-parent has had a chance to build familiarity with your situation and how his/her children are cared for with you.

- The romantic partner learns about your children in the initial months of observing you caring for them. He/she learns about your children's rituals, responses, what's familiar to them, how they move through their days—information that can help inform how and when it's time to begin to assist or help and ultimately to fulfill a parenting role.

- You and your romantic partner take steps to learn about step parent/new parent adjustment for and with kids of your (and his/her) children's ages. Learning how to step into a parental role with children who have parents, requires skill, understanding, and a blending of family cultures/values/parenting-style that will not necessarily emerge until you're well into the day-to-day struggles.

Liz felt pulled in so many directions. Her ex-husband Chris and her partner Carla could not have a conversation about six-year-old Maddie without it dissolving into dead-end conflict. It felt like the "battle lines were drawn" with Chris on one side and Liz and Carla on the other—and guess who was in the middle? Chris and Liz realized they had to renew their commitment to protecting their daughter from adult conflict.

With the guidance of a co-parenting coach, Liz and Chris went back to basics and reasserted their responsibility as the principal decision-makers with regard to Maddie. They agreed that once decisions were made by Chris and Liz, the adults in each home would determine how to implement agreements. They also established how either of them could bring a partner's thoughts, feelings, input to the discussions about Maddie without giving that input a vote. Only Liz and Chris were voting members of Maddie's "life-team."

Initially, this was not easy. Carla felt disrespected by being asked to play a secondary role while Chris and Liz partnered over Maddie—even though that partnership was limited to co-parenting. Figuring the new roles/relationship out between Liz and Carla took a lot of reassurance, some practice, and more than a few difficult discussions. Carla was relieved when she was invited into the co-parent coaching to gain insight and understanding into what was happening.

After a few months, Chris began to be less defensive and more open to Carla's ideas, knowing that he and Liz would ultimately make the decisions. Liz felt stronger as a parent and more respected and less stressed about taking care of everyone's feelings. Even Carla had to admit that stepping back and giving Liz room to lead as a parent took much of the stress away from their daily life. She discovered her best role was in trusting Liz's co-parenting relationship, and supporting Liz in her parenting with Maddie in their home—not getting in the middle of Chris and Liz.

Conflict over a new partner can make establishing two-home stability very difficult and tumultuous. Kids end up feeling unsafe and uncertain as they move back and forth between homes where the adults are upset and fighting. Please consult with a co-parent coach, stepparenting counselor, or similar mental health professional to help guide you through this difficult time as quickly as possible, and to diminish the conflict so that your children can have the stability they need.

The combination of decisions made when "falling in love" and the desire to replace the broken family with one that feels better often leads the quick-to-recouple duo into disappointment, struggle, and ultimately the demise of their relationship.

> A difficult statistic that we work with in our business is that 75 per cent of remarriages/recoupling with children do not last—they are often fraught with misunderstandings, broken expectations, and clashes of family hopes and dreams, not to mention conflicts with a co-parent if not handled skillfully.

We bring this to your attention as preventive medicine. Get the help you need to learn about the process of creating a second family. Unpack the baggage from your first relationship first and *then* enjoy all the steps of consciously creating a new relationship, then a new sense of family that includes your children, and hopefully a lasting, loving experience for everyone.

Remarriage/new partnership and skillfully stepping in as a new parent for children in a two-home family can bring joy, additional love, and a valuable expanded sense of family for children. Re-coupling is a natural, normal and healthy step for many adults who have divorced/separated. We encourage co-parents to recognize that the more you resolve your spousal/relationship issues, the more capable you will be at showing your children that your co-parent is taking a step that expands the support and caring in their family for *them*. For the co-parent re-coupling, hold a place of respect for your children's other parent and do what you can to bring ease to the situation.

New Partners in Kid-Centered Public Events

Whenever you attend a child's special event in public, you do so in order to focus on the child/support the child. Sometimes a co-parent and a new partner blur dating with a child's school or athletic event. This doesn't work well generally for either your co-parent or your kiddo. A child-centered event is not the time for displaying public affection, focusing more on each other than the child's activity, or creating any sort of spot-light on your new relationship. Help your new partner appreciate that your child's events are not a proving ground of any sort about your new relationship. Your new partner can help by:

- Keeping a low-profile; confidently attending in support of your parental role.

- Focus on the child and his/her activity.

- Be cordial and respectful to your co-parent if he/she is also attending.

- Be cordial but not overly inviting or overly affectionate/friendly to your other children who may also be in the audience/attending the event with their other parent.

These are guidelines of simple pacing, respect, and relationship-building with the greater family that your new partner is being invited into. In time, the tension and uncertainty will melt away and his/her presence will be accepted, and under the best of circumstances, even welcomed.

Highlights in Review

- Just as the ending of a primary family has stages and phases of adjustment, the initiating of a new romantic relationship has stages and phases.

- Recognizing the brain chemistry changes that accompany falling in love helps parents to practice caution in the early stages of relationship-building in terms of involving their children. Taking the time to adequately vet a relationship before including your children in your love life saves emotional wear and tear on everyone.

- Introducing a new romantic interest or partner into your two-home family system is de-stabilizing. As with any growth spurt, children will need time to adjust.

- Understanding how children might respond to a new adult in your life helps you plan and anticipate how best to help them adjust.

- Your co-parent is a key player in your children's experience of you dating or partnering. The more respected he/she feels, and the better the co-parenting relationship is, the easier it will be for him/her to accept and support (with your children) your changes.

- New partners are not substitute parents. Help new partners understand the value in holding back from nurturing/participating in a parental role, allowing you to parent while the children are in residence.

- During early stages of dating, a new romantic interest keeps a low profile at kid-centered public events. Keep in mind "kids first and for now" when at their events; dating and relationship-building later.

Chapter 10

The Co-Parenting Relationship:
Skill, Acceptance, Maturity

Maturity is the ability to live with unresolved problems.

—Anne Lamott, American novelist

AT THIS POINT, you may be wondering, "how on earth do I get my co-parent to work with me, follow these guidelines, and partner with me—truly partner?" Some of you may feel enormous relief that you have a co-parent who is willing to learn along with you. Co-parenting comes in many different forms, shapes, and degrees of cooperation. Co-parenting often changes over time, responds to changes in circumstances, and generally reflects the level of divorce/separation acceptance. Co-parenting is a unique relationship in that the relationship goes forward as long as children are shared, however thin the thread of connection, and whether we want the relationship or not. And, true of every relationship, the only person we have control over is *ourselves.*

Co-Parenting Relationships Develop Over Time

In the early stages of divorce/separation, parents are adjusting simultaneously to two often conflicting realities: 1) letting go of your partner and all the ways you parented together and agreements you made in one home, while 2) formulating a co-parenting relationship involving what feels like an unnatural separation from your children, new agreements you may have never dreamed of making about your children, and finding skills to integrate children's lives across two homes—all with someone that you may feel very conflicted about. This complexity often results in enormous turmoil and confusion in the early months, setting the new co-parenting relationship into a tailspin. Many co-parents feel "It's just too much."

The strategic use of more separation, not less, in these early months can ease the emotional turmoil and allow budding co-parents a chance to rely on practices, protocols, schedules, and rules to limit conflict, and power struggles. Here in the Seattle area, there is a long beautiful lake that separates Seattle from the closely attached cities of Bellevue, Redmond, and the rest of "Eastside." The I-5 corridor goes up the west side of the lake through the heart of Seattle while the I-405 follows the east side of the lake. I use this metaphor with my newly separating clients struggling with conflict: "I want one of you to proceed as if driving up the I-5, while the other takes the I-405." This metaphor suggests they are beginning to find their individual, uncoupled adult lives with a large lake separating/protecting them as they find their own footing away from their former partner/spouse. "Great—but, what about the kids?" you ask. There are two spans across Lake Washington, the I-90 Bridge and the 520 Bridge. I say that parents will be using the bridges as the place they come together for the first steps in co-parenting: transitioning and caring for their children. Like every alternate route around a city, the 405 eventually reconnects to the I-5 much farther north. Similarly, I suggest that co-parents who allow a period of healthy separation that supports a more complete uncoupling often develop an ease with working together and going in the same direction when raising their children.

There are many factors that shape and form a developing co-parenting relationship. Here are just a few.

- **Divorce/separation adjustment:** how emotionally prepared are you/were you to make these adjustments? Are you an emotionally resilient person by nature or risk-adverse and afraid of change?

- **Level of hurt, anger, betrayal experienced by one or both co-parents:** how difficult is it for you to hear your co-parent's voice and/or see your co-parent? At what level is your trigger-response to your co-parent: mild—you occasionally get triggered; moderate—you often get triggered and work very hard at not getting triggered; or severe—you nearly always end up triggered and overwhelmed emotionally?

- **The divorce/separation process**—how contentious is/was the divorce/separation process? Was a lot of damage created through the legal process? Or, did the two of you mediate/collaborate successfully to a satisfying outcome?

- **Family/friend experience:** if there's been divorce in your family, or among your siblings/close friends, this can shape your expectations and beliefs about what's possible and appropriate in dealing with a co-parent. Are the important people in your life encouraging constructive co-parenting or animosity toward your ex-partner/spouse?

- **Personal feelings and deeply held beliefs:** are you a conflict resolver by nature? Is it easy for you to put your children first? Do you value acceptance? How about forgiveness? Do you tend to hold judgments firmly? Are you plagued by shame, failure, embarrassment?

- **Willingness to get coaching, and use resources:** are you and co-parent open to help, reading, coaching, learning something new when you hit conflict, struggle, or impasse?

These very same factors and how they change over time (or don't change) helps predict the evolving nature of your co-parenting relationship. Although a co-parenting relationship in some form or fashion is non-negotiable as long as both co-parents are involved in a child's life, the degree to which that relationship is engaged and constructive is something that can happen only by mutual agreement. In other words, however much you may value a positive, constructive, engaged co-parenting relationship—you can only invite your co-parent to join you, not force his/her inclination, interest, and/or cooperation.

Accepting that the quality of your co-parenting relationship is limited by what's mutually agreeable to your co-parent can be a frustrating, difficult pill to swallow. What we want to say is, "keep faith." Sometimes, in time, a co-parent softens, changes, accepts, moves on—and then, things can change, shift for the better. Sometimes a co-parent enters a new relationship, gets a promotion, or some other positive change of circumstance, which allows a torn heart/broken confidence/bruised identity to heal and anger to dissipate, and then, things can change and shift for the better. You can only do *your part*; allow time/grieving and adjustment and changes in circumstance to aid your evolving co-parenting relationship.

If all goes well, in time, with acceptance, adjustment, and skill-building, you and your co-parent will spend your efforts and energy coordinating and integrating your children's lives across two homes as seamlessly as possible. Your children may inherit and/or have new siblings across the years, you may develop an appreciation for an expanded extended family and family of friends. You and your co-parent will respectfully coordinate, make decisions, meet financial obligations, and celebrate life-cycle events in an integrated or tandem fashion that support your children. Children can and do thrive in two-home families; they learn a lot about relationships, love, family, and change. They experience responsibility and adaptability in ways they may not have experienced in a one-home family.

The nature of your co-parent relationship is only one part of your child's foundation—an important part, but only one part. You, your co-parent, and the important adults in your child's life each supply a unique and individual opportunity for your child to be nurtured and supported into adulthood. The significance of each individual relationship supporting your kiddo should not be underestimated. Thank goodness for the village.

Marcie's mom and dad decided to divorce as she entered seventh grade. Right from the beginning, things were on tilt. Mom moved out of the family home and lived in a friend's house. She returned home every morning to take Marcie and her sister to school and pick them up after school, but this arrangement quickly fell apart. The conflict between her parents escalated to the point that Marcie was so frightened and hurt that she hated being at home.

Luckily for Marcie, she found her way into a strong, supportive relationship with one of her favorite teachers. Ms. Franklin became a regular anchor during the school day, a mirror to Marcie for the amazing girl that she was—strong, capable, and resourceful. At a time when Marcie's own Mom couldn't be emotionally available to her, another woman stepped in and helped Marcie as she weathered her family's storm.

Impact of Changes in Circumstances

Both positive and challenging changes in either co-parent's life will often create a period of dis-equilibrium for the two-home family. Dis-equilibrium signals an opening for change, a shaking up of a system, sometimes a breaking apart of established patterns. At first, these changes can feel threatening, destabilizing, and like slipping backwards. Keep faith. Changes, shake-ups, and even crisis may signal an opportunity for growth and improved relationship.

When co-parents work together to re-establish a sense of normalcy and equilibrium, the children in two-home families have another positive experience of fielding change, staying flexible, and working together. We have witnessed amazing co-parent responses to everything from losing a job, entering treatment for alcoholism, managing decompensation from mental illness (like bipolar disorder), recovering from trauma from a car accident to responding to an emergency appendectomy. Some of these issues were profound enough to impact residential schedule, decision-making, etc. However, once safety and health issues resolved, the co-parents stepped carefully back into two-home family life with the support, intact relationships with each parent, and rhythm the children were used to. In the face of urgent or emergent needs, family members often put down the hatchet to step up, step in, and allow a healthy, constructive response to family change/crisis.

Lydia discovered a lump in her breast. She told her partner, Mark, but decided not to disclose it to her kids or co-parent at first. As the diagnostics unfolded, Lydia was faced with needing a mastectomy followed by four months of chemotherapy. She knew she had to call Cam, her co-parent, to let him know what was going on.

Lydia and Cam discussed what and how to tell the kids—and decided they would do it together. They wanted the kids to know that Dad was 100 per cent there for them and would be helping as Mom went through treatment. Cam asked Lydia if he could talk with Mark about how best to work together—something that Cam had never been willing to do before. Cam wanted to be able to reassure the kids that the animosity between him and Mark was over and that they would work together during Mom's surgery, treatment, and recovery.

Lydia did as well as could be hoped for through her surgery and chemo. She maintained a positive attitude knowing that Mark and Cam were there for the kids when she couldn't be. And Mark and Cam developed a new respect for each other that would lead them into a very different future.

Positive changes impact co-parenting relationships as well. To witness the value of un-coupling and reestablishing each co-parent's own life, to take responsibility for his/her future and make space for a former partner/spouse to thrive, allows co-parents to face changes with increased resilience and problem-solving. Sometimes, when something positive happens for a co-parent who has been struggling with resentment, grief, unresolved feelings, he/she begins to open up, engage, and move forward in the co-parenting relationship with more ease. Depending on the partner, entering a satisfying, romantic relationship allows the past to take its rightful place in history, opening opportunities for more constructive relationships in the present.

Gwen and Jesse spent the first two years post-mediation in a highly detached, contentious co-parenting relationship over their four-year-old son, Brighton. Gwen had entered a new relationship shortly after she and Jesse separated, and Jesse wanted nothing to do with Gwen, her life, her home, nor did he want to receive communications from her about Brighton except the bare necessities. "Hateful" might best describe their co-parenting relationship—and that went both ways.

Gwen spent those two years getting periodic coaching on how to respond to Jesse's passive-aggressive co-parenting style. She vacillated between wanting to threaten going back into mediation to force him to co-parent effectively and deciding instead to build coping strategies that allowed her to detach, depersonalize, and ensure she was doing what she could to not aggravate the situation.

Then Jesse started dating. He kept it a secret for many months. Gwen found out when Brighton came home from his time with Dad and said, "Daddy has a special friend. Her name is Lisa and we did lots of fun things together!!" As Gwen's divorce coach had predicted, the day would come when Jesse would have something going on in his life that would pull him out of his resentment and anger, when he might want to show what a good dad he was—and put his best foot forward. The time had arrived. Jesse began communicating, he began participating in trading residential time, and wanting to help with health care appointments—and Brighton continued thriving with the addition of Lisa in his dad's life. Gwen was relieved he finally wasn't packing a hatchet of resentment, and they could simply welcome a better co-parenting relationship.

Having faith that a day may come when things smooth out for you and your co-parent means:

- continuing your own growth,

- maintaining healthy boundaries,

- staying respectful/ taking the high road, and

- building skills necessary to move forward and create a positive, optimistic future.

From that position, you'll be ready and able to allow a positive or constructive change on the part of your co-parent to inform your relationship for the benefit of your children. If you're both operating from those general guidelines, your co-parenting relationship is likely to be developing as well as could be hoped for.

Co-Parent Skills

> The business of co-parenting is strengthened when co-parents have a specific skill set for implementing their roles as Co-Parent Executive Officers and Co-Parent Financial Officers.

Throughout the book, we've emphasized these skills in different ways and in a variety of circumstances. We're going to hone in on the entire skill set as a refresher before we describe some of the styles of co-parenting and challenges associated with co-parenting relationships.

Unlike choosing to start a company with a business partner, parents are thrust into the business of co-parenting under some of the most personally painful and stressful circumstances. Whatever skills we might have on a good day may be temporarily lost until stress resolves, hearts heal, and acceptance steps in. Co-parents often find that they build new skills through their transition from partners/spouses to co-parents. This list can help guide you through.

- **Respect:** An attitude of civility should underlie all communication and child-related business. You may not always respect your former spouse/partner, but you can respect the co-parent role and maintain civility toward your co-parent as they execute the business of co-parenting—*even when he/she doesn't.*

- **Tolerance of differences:** The co-parent who can operate from the "80/20 rule" demonstrates a much-needed skill in learning to tolerate the inevitable differences that occur in a two-home family. Have easy conversation about differences if your co-parent is open. If not, let go of 80 per cent of the differences, and only draw attention to the 20 per cent that really have a significant impact on your children's well-being. If none of the differences rise to the level of really having a significant impact, then *let them go.* If you're uncertain which are significant enough to confront your co-parent about, talk with a trusted advisor or your child's healthcare provider to help you discern whether it's worth the potential conflict to bring up the issue.

- **Boundaries/appropriate privacy:** You two adults are separate now. Your lives and homes are separate and deserve all the same healthy boundaries you would give a distant neighbor. Just because your children reside in the house with your co-parent does not afford you special privileges to intrude on, have access to, or secure information about your former spouse/partner or his/her homelife.

- **Integrity/trustworthiness:** As with any constructive relationship, the more you say what you mean and follow through on what you say, the greater the trust you'll earn. Making and following through on agreements, keeping to schedules, handling financial agreements impeccably, all contribute to a positive co-parenting relationship.

- **Child-centered:** Your relationship with your co-parent business partner is focused on your children: their lives, activities, growth and development, and overall well-being. Focusing on your co-parent's parenting style or personal life is not helpful. Feedback is useful only when the other person is open and interested in what you have to say.

- **Skillful communication:** Every relationship benefits from competent listening skills and responsible communication, which means, "I'm responsible for what I say and how I say it." When you take responsibility for how you communicate, you're not blaming or judging or making excuses for whether your communication is skillful or hurtful. Stay on the skillful side of the line both verbally and in writing.

- **Transparency regarding kid-information:** Learning to share a useful amount of information back and forth with your co-parent is a skill and practice. Setting your co-parent up for a successful residential time can be dependent on the quality of your communication about the kids; do the right thing and provide through voice mail or email useful information for your co-parent as he/she takes over for the next shift with the children.

- **Healthy coping:** This refers to being able to manage triggers, step away from invitations to be in conflict or fight, and to stay separate from any drama while responding constructively. When we react to negativity, it's like putting kindling on a fire, which of course only fuels the fire. Learning to hold back, respond skillfully, or ignore negativity are strong skills. Similarly, when we pay attention to positive change, constructive attempts to co-parent in a more productive way, and other signs of acceptance and settling down, we will get more of what we're paying attention to! This is the best part of human nature: given a bit of light, most of us will grow toward it.

- **Optimism about creating a positive future:** Your own conviction about how you'll create the future you want will lay the foundation for that future to arrive—one day at a time. Similar to healthy coping, optimism is a skill of the heart and spirit to trust in a better tomorrow even when today is complicated by challenges. Our sense of personal power to learn what we need to learn, gain the skills, understand the territory, and navigate the trouble spots leads us out of the struggle and into a positive future.

- **Practices and protocols that work:** All the right attitude, communication skills, and strong psychological health doesn't substitute for knowing what to do. When you and your co-parent take the time to use practices and protocols that strengthen your two-home family, kids benefit.

Co-Parent Styles

We've discussed how the passage of time and changes in circumstances can impact co-parents and the nature of co-parenting relationship. As we discuss the spectrum of co-parent styles, we hope to convey that a person and a relationship is a growing, changing entity, however smooth and easy or entrenched and glacial that growth and change may appear.

We emphasize the value of uncoupling in developing individual strength, confidence and skill, which contributes to forming a healthy, working co-parenting relationship. As noted in the list of factors that shape and form a developing co-parenting relationship (pg. 164–165), there are many personal, individual elements that also inform someone's capacity/ability and willingness to engage in a co-parenting relationship. We'll discuss the common styles of co-parents and some of the challenges of dealing with each style, starting with no or low-engagement and progress to styles that involve high co-parenting engagement.

Lone Cowboy/Cowgirl: Giving the benefit of the doubt, this is a co-parent that has never functioned well under rules and places a high value on solitary decision-making and self-determination. There's no intent to be hurtful, or create chaos; the lone cowboy/cowgirl just wants to be the parent he/she wants to be without interference, particularly from you. When you step back, you'll see there's nothing inconsistent with how your co-parent is behaving from the person you coupled/had children with. Challenges include:

- Communication—often a very low communicator—hard to get information shared back and forth, making integration across homes difficult.

- Joint decision-making can be challenging; often delayed due to lack of responsiveness. He/she may make unilateral decisions without thinking much of the impact on you. This can be very frustrating.

- Unreliable for follow-through on requests you might make for how to work with the children on his/her time unless he/she already values the request. When you engage him/her on issues of homework, diet, exercise, TV watching, etc. you are often met with no response.

The Rules—Nothing but the Rules: This co-parent copes best with disengagement and distance. The distance generally doesn't include animosity. You could speculate about what's going on, but it's likely, your co-parent is simply trying to heal, maintain his/her own balance, and prefers interacting with you a little as possible. The rules (your parenting plan and agreements in writing) assist with minimizing contact, negotiating, etc. Challenges include:

- Limited flexibility, which makes the normal ups and downs of raising children and life more difficult to share.

- Integrating your children's two worlds may feel artificial with what feels like a firewall between you and your co-parent.

- Grieving the loss of someone that at one time you may have worked well with.

> The Rules—Nothing but the Rules can also be a useful strategy for a co-parent attempting to deal with a co-parent who is actively hostile, disruptive, manipulative, and/or chaotic. By returning to the rules, relying on the rules, not participating in bending the rules, over time you will render his/her destabilizing efforts less effective.

I'd Rather Fight than Switch: Unlike the co-parent who simply wants distance and disengagement, prefers to follow the rules, and avoids communication, this co-parent is likely to respond to any co-parenting overtures with animosity, disagreement, and frustrating communication intended to create upset, disrupt, and prevent you from having whatever you may be requesting. Think of co-parenting with a puffer fish—he/she is fine until you engage him/her and then all the spines come out. Unfortunately, your child may get caught in this cross-fire—you may suggest you drop by rain boots for the trip to the pumpkin patch and he/she fires back, "You're always trying to control my time—I'll get her ready for her school trips without any input from you." There you are with your seven-year-old's rain boots knowing she'll be heading to a muddy pumpkin patch in her school shoes. Challenges include:

- Giving up—at least, *for the time being*—a treasured value that the two of you would be able to work together in the best interest of your child.

- Not getting hooked by your co-parents animosity, attacks,

misrepresentation of your intentions; actually holding back and *not responding at all* to the negativity.

- Accepting that you can only manage your side of the co-parenting relationship, and giving your co-parent all the space/freedom/autonomy he/she is insisting on this may be as good as it gets.

Generally, the co-parent who's lashing out over attempts to engage him/her as your co-parent is still very hurt, angry, and unable to transition into a business relationship with you. You can wish/want/believe that he/she *should* "be different", but engaging his/her negativity will not contribute to things settling down. Remember: time, changes in circumstances, and eventually acceptance of a new way of life allows co-parenting engagement to smooth out. Your ability to *take care of your side of the street* is your best contribution toward that end.

Good Fences Make Good Neighbors: A healthy co-parenting relationship with strong boundaries and a moderate amount of engagement. Co-parenting from this place allows your children to know that although you need to be separate as spouses, you also know how to come together for the things important to them. If your co-parent wants a strong fence and can be a good neighbor, and you can meet him/her in kind, your two-home family is likely to run smoothly. Challenges include:

- Accepting the fence. Co-parenting is more complex when one parent wants/needs a different level of engagement than the other.
- Adjusting to what may feel like formality between you and your co-parent. When formality or clear boundaries assist with managing conflict and diminishing negotiation, both homes can settle down into their own rhythms without concern for intrusion or disruption. This is good for kids.

Still Crazy After All these Months/Years: We all have friends and some have former spouses/partners who fit this style. This co-parent wants to engage, be involved in decision-making, drop by unannounced and see the kids, spend holidays together without necessarily planning, and he/she tends to be emotional and unpredictable in communication and follow-through. He/she often expresses exasperation about your desire for some predictability, boundaries, respect and wonders: "What's the big deal?!? I just let myself in to your house to make a cup of coffee while I waited for the kids to get home—you act like I went through your drawers." What might have seemed "cute" in a partner, has become enormously irritating in a co-parent with whom you'd like some healthy space and boundaries—and he/she doesn't seem to "get it." Challenges include:

- All the energy that goes into setting healthy boundaries and dealing with the intrusions, whether friendly or hostile.

- Having to explain to your children the differences in your personal styles without throwing your co-parent under the bus (because there are times you'd like to!).

- Re-corralling your kids who have gone from excited to angry when you put your foot down after your co-parent has involved them in some scheme that crosses your boundaries.

A Co-Parent Champion: This is the co-parenting gold-standard—the co-parent who works through emotions and issues with a kind of maturity and capacity that allows children to stay in the center without putting them in the middle. This co-parent focuses on his/her children's healthy development, implements practices and protocols that work, and demonstrates high quality communication. A co-parent champion maintains respectful boundaries, has a moderate to high level of trust with a co-parent who responds in kind, responds with flexibility to difficult situations, and holds an easy nature as he/she moves forward into life with optimism. Challenges? None. This co-parent partner is a *dream come true.*

White Paper Terrorist: We put this category last, as this is by far the most difficult co-parent style, and the one that often requires the most engagement through court involvement. "White paper" refers to all the court documents generated by the negativity. This co-parent is unable to let go and chooses negative, highly involving methods to force relationship. The relentless attempts to harm, interfere, disrupt, threaten and/or deceive you leave little or no room except to respond in order to protect your safety, your relationship with your children, and/or to implement legal agreements.

There's no guarantee for a co-parent who follows The Rules (as described above), that the other co-parent won't take the idea of following the rules and turn it into an opportunity for fighting about the rules. Fighting about the rules blows a hole through the protective aspect of disengagement and boundaries, creating required engagement (often through attorneys and the court system), more conflict-filled communication, and non-productive co-parenting. This co-parent is often suffering from a deeply wounded narcissism/sense of self and is attempting to redeem him/or herself by proving he/she is right. A secondary motivation may be a belief that you deserve to be punished and he/she won't relent until he/she feels justice has been served for the wrongs he/she's suffered by your decisions. If faced with a co-parent who appears determined to insist on negative engagement:

- do your best to follow/respect the rules

- consult with and rely on your trusted advisors

- protect your children as best you can and

- secure emotional support to weather the storm

What if I Worry that My Children are Unsafe?

If you know that your children are in danger, act now. Physical abuse/sexual abuse/battering or neglect should be reported immediately to the police and/or Children's Protective Services. If you have concerns about your co-parent, his/her partner or guests in his/her home, further investigation to ensure safety is important, as difficult as it might be. Still, you don't want to over react and create unnecessary drama or problems that are difficult to unwind. So, what can you do?

> If you are uncertain about whether your children are in danger, consult with a professional as an important, necessary first step.

- Your children's primary health care provider is an excellent source of information, assessment, and recommendations.

- Your legal counsel is another important "go-to" person for whether your concerns warrant further investigation and intervention.

- A trusted mental health provider can assist you in sorting out other steps to consider and whether your concerns rise to the level of more active intervention with your co-parent.

When a Co-Parent's Problem becomes Front and Center

It is beyond the scope of this book to cover all the complex issues that parents and co-parents face. It is important to know that when a parent is struggling with a significant impairment such as a mental health concern, addiction or incarceration, children need age-appropriate explanations from you, their loving guide through life's challenges. You may need guidance to help and to explain things to them.

Child specialists, parenting coaches, counselors, or family therapists are professionals who can help guide you to find ways to offer explanations and clarity for your children. Children feel safer and more secure when they have a child-appropriate way to understand complex adult issues in such a way that maintains respect for and relationship with the parent that is struggling.

The Key to a Difficult Co-Parent: Acceptance

Grant me the **serenity** *to accept the things I cannot change, the courage to change the things I can, and the wisdom to know the difference.*

—Serenity Prayer

Much of what brings a divorced parent into a co-parent coach's office is conflict with a difficult co-parent. There are definitely things that a good co-parent coach can do to assist you and your co-parent *if you're both interested in assistance.* There is an old adage: "You can lead a horse to water, but you can't make him drink." You can bring your co-parent into co-parent coaching or mediation, but you can't *make him/her* change—and neither can the coach/mediator. This can be a sobering reality. Consult with your legal team as needed.

The co-parent coach may be able to explain to a co-parent your requests in such a way that he/she sees the value in making positive changes. The coach may provide workable protocols that neither of you have thought of that reduce conflict, shifting the relationship in a positive direction. Some clients who have been through the litigation process may be required by the court to utilize a co-parent coach in the first year or two post-divorce in an attempt to repair damage from the litigation process and/or ensure a smoother co-parent relationship post-divorce *for the children.* Others may work with a co-parent coach as a first step in conflict resolution as outlined in their parenting plan. Co-parent coaches are there to provide support, guidance, ideas, and skills for you and your co-parent that will help your children thrive in a two-home family.

Along with coaching, we want to offer some other sound support for the day-to-day of adjusting to co-parenting. These are things you can do to make your life with your children as positive and constructive as possible, regardless of what your co-parent may or may not be doing.

Keep a kid focus

When your co-parent is making life difficult, the difficulty can become your focus. The conflict-generating methods of your co-parent begin to fill your foreground and color your residential time with your children. When you are struggling with the commotion and chaos generated by your co-parent, close your eyes, take a deep breath and attempt to see life—*right now*—through your child's eyes.

- What does he/she need, want, or hope for, while he/she's with you?

- What does he/she care about; what does he/she *need* to know?

- How can you help your kiddo *right now,* regardless of the situation with your co-parent?

- How can you set aside the "fair/unfair" framework long enough to simply parent right now the best way you can?

Resist labeling your co-parent's character or behavior

Your co-parent may do many things that frustrate, anger, or sadden you. You may react to his/her behavior from your adult self, who has an opinion about what you consider outrageous behavior, or from your "parent-self," who desires something better for your children. You may have learned words to describe your co-parent: narcissistic, high-conflict personality, manipulative, immature, having a midlife crisis.

Whether true or not, lumping difficult behaviors and traits under a label rarely helps. Labels close us off from focusing on positives while encouraging us to see negatives. When we're invested in a label, we resist seeing anything to the contrary, including healthy adjustment over time. As attorney and family therapist Bill Eddy points out, if you put a normally reasonable person under enough stress, he/she can look like a high-conflict personality. Divorce causes high stress—and as people adjust and accept the changes, they develop many more resources to contribute positively to relationships, including co-parenting.

Consequently, your small overtures of understanding and generosity can lead to real shifts in relationship with your co-parent. When he/she is met with an open door for constructive co-parenting, he/she is more likely to one day walk through.

Keeping an open mind helps you see those important moments of constructive action on the part of your co-parent.

Your children will sense your hope (or lack thereof) in their other parent. Keeping yourself open to possible progress and growth helps your children stay positive and hopeful as well. This is not rose-colored glasses, but a realistic expectation that says, "People can grow and change in time—and we leave room for that to happen—even as we have boundaries and take care of ourselves." This is a valuable lesson for children.

Tammy described her ex-husband Dan in one word: selfish. "He was selfish in leaving the family, and now all he cares about is living life on his terms. My therapist told me he is probably a narcissist."

When Dan would make a request for changes in the childcare schedule for his business trip, all Tammy could see was a re-enactment of their lonely marriage where work came first and she came second. And it went on from there: she saw his requests to have time with the kids when he returned from trips as expecting her to change her and the kids' schedules for his benefit. When he asked to be part of decisions regarding the kids activities, Tammy felt that he was being intrusive and bossy. If you're dealing with a "narcissist," none of Dan's co-parenting behaviors can be seen as healthy, constructive or reasonable.

With some help from a coach, Tammy was better able to separate her experience of their marriage from the present situation. She was able to see his intense focus on work, which had always been a source of hurt for her, as something he needed to do for himself—and not a rejection of her or the kids. Once she could stop taking his dedication to work as a judgment that she wasn't good enough to lure him away from his job, she was able to see his attempts to reach out and become a more active parent to their children. She could see that the kids didn't dwell on his absences; they looked forward to time with their dad and came back happy. Yes, maybe she was the one that would be there to offer the soft, safe, consistent landing after the great, somewhat unpredictable adventures with Dad, but Tammy could begin to see value in both parents' contribution to their children's lives.

Keep an open mind about your co-parent's motives

Your adult relationship with your co-parent has probably led to a long list of beliefs about your ex-spouse/partner as a person and as a parent. However those beliefs may or may not translate into how he/she approaches your children and parenting. It is easy to see a co-parent who is late as one who is disrespectful to both you and the kids. Or a parent who doesn't follow the residential schedule with care as less concerned for the well-being of the kids.

This is not to say your concerns about your co-parents unpredictability or difficulty with follow through aren't valid and important. We want to encourage you to resist *making assumptions* and jumping to conclusions about your co-parent's motivations without more information. There's a clear difference between *intention* and *impact*. You can be certain of the impact of your co-parent's behavior on you, and through listening to your children, on your children. But you will not know the intention without the capacity to listen and understand your co-parent.

> When we separate intention from impact, we're much more capable of working together to find solutions.

Someone who is scattered or on a steep learning curve is often overwhelmed—he/she's not trying to hurt or disrespect…he/she's simply trying to do his/her best with whatever personality, emotional or stress issues he/she's facing! Now, that level of performance may be falling way short. Working together to solve the problem (mitigate the negative impact) is a much different approach than attacking the person.

Jemal was infuriated with Keisha's continued "interference" in her attempts to manage the kids on his time. She volunteered at school on his duty parent days, and she signed the boys up for soccer that went across residential time without asking. She sent long, detailed emails regarding the kids' schedules, their homework and the foods they liked. Jemal insisted that this was Kesha's way of leaving him out as a parent, controlling, and competing for the role of "best parent." He reacted by not reacting: no communication. He ignored her and her emails. He was trying to assert what he insisted was his right to parent without her. In response to Jemal's increasing radio-silence, she actually communicated more—not less, hoping to connect and smooth things out—which drove Jemal even crazier.

Eventually Keisha and Jemal came in for help with their escalating cold war. Jemal learned that Keisha was unable to hear just how much her planning (which was her role in the family before the divorce) was unwelcomed. With the chance to discuss each of their experiences of the communication problems, both Keisha and Jemal could begin a different family life story about the other. Jemal let go of "blaming" Keisha and labeling her as a "control freak" and stepped into problem-solving. Once he was able to acknowledge her contributions to the children's lives, she could relax enough to hear his concerns. He asked for basic agreements regarding joint decision-making and clearer boundaries on his parenting time. Keisha admitted it would be hard for her to step back. With the support of the co-parent coach, she began to understand the importance of treating Jemal as a full-fledged, capable co-parent.

With new agreements in place and better understanding of each other, both parents became more receptive to input. They had agreed to practice saying, "Yes, that works for me" or "No, thank you" to each other's requests/suggestions. Keisha agreed to limiting her communication to transition emails and Jemal agreed to respond in a timely fashion and to provide transition information, too. Most importantly, they agreed to first check out assumptions about the other's intentions when bothered by something, instead of jumping to the most negative conclusions.

Focus on what you can do to help your children

Some of your co-parent's ways of parenting may not change. You will not see eye-to-eye on specific issues that are currently or have always been areas of disagreement. Separation and divorce give both parents freedom to find their own values, practices and approaches to parenting. It can be difficult to shift your focus from changing your co-parent to accepting the limitations or differences between the two of you.

These differences sometimes require explanations to your children: why are things so different here than at Mom/Dad's? The more matter-of-fact about "things in our home" and "things in your Dad/Mom's home," the better. To resist the temptation to tell your children about your disappointment in your co-parent requires *vigilance*. Chalk things up to differences rather than judging those differences as good or bad or better or worse. Children don't need the inside story on your thoughts; they simply need to know how things are going to be—lovingly, firmly and with follow-through.

- Practice what you preach. In other words, continue to parent congruently, in alignment with what you believe is best.

- Meanwhile, treat your co-parent with the respect and civility that you would give to any other person. Model respect through your actions/communications.

Natalie had great difficulty managing her judgements about Rebecca's decision to attend a different church after their separation. Unfortunately Natalie often made disparaging remarks to the children when she found out they attended a new church during Rebecca's residential time. Rebecca's requests of Natalie to stop putting the children in the middle by commenting on her choices had little effect on Natalie's ongoing, negative commentary. Rebecca was concerned about the impact on the children of this persistent tension, and felt undermined as a co-parent.

Rebecca could see two options: to fight back by telling the children her own version of the "truth" about her reasons for leaving the family church—or to stay silent. After cooling off her own anger at Natalie's ongoing negativity, she decided to do her best to remove the kids from the middle. She would remain steadfast in her search for a new church, and normalize Natalie's upset as simply "a difference between me and Mama—neither of us is right and neither of us is wrong."

When the children brought up the issue again by repeating Natalie's accusation that Rebecca was giving up her faith, Rebecca took a deep breath and tapped into her new-found power to normalize the difference. She gently stated, "Yes, you are right. I have changed the way I worship and it is different from Mama's. I know it might be confusing, but I'm glad you two get to go to church with Mama and I'm also glad you get to go to church with me. I don't want you two to feel you need to choose which is "best" or "right"—I just want you to enjoy the time at both. Divorce sometimes means there are differences in both your homes. It might be a little messy sometimes, but its not a bad thing to get to experience new things."

Rebecca could see the girls looked relieved when they said "Okay" and ran off to play. She knew that although they may not get the same message from Natalie, she had released the girls from at least one side of the conflict. She had modeled tolerance and non-judgment, even in a situation where she felt justified to fight and judge back.

Recognize and adjust your **own** attitudes and reactions

Even though your concerns or frustrations with your co-parent may be understandable and valid, you will benefit from examining your own feelings, behaviors and reactions for possible contributions to on-going conflict. Looking to yourself for solutions to a problem does not dismiss or discount the issues with your co-parent. But taking a moment to see if there's something you could do or not do that might shift the relationship in a more constructive direction empowers you. You can still have your frustrations and wish your co-parent would change, but if you can find ways to cope, manage your emotions, respond with civility, and not get hooked by invitations to escalate negativity, you can improve the atmosphere in your home and your time with your children. And when you shift your attitude and responses, your co-parent will (eventually) shift, too.

Every time Terrence heard Jessica bring up money, he felt a surge of anger sweep over him. He went straight back into the emotion surrounding everything he had lost—the house, the significant change in income, the time with their daughter. He had to take a second job to cover the bills. He was furious. He wished that he could stay home and take care of their daughter, not work and worry constantly. It didn't help that Terrence knew Jessica could be irresponsible with money, and she was the one getting a "free pass" on not working—she had another year to stay home with Teresa rather than having to figure out a way to contribute now.

Terrance realized he was having difficulty talking about anything with Jessica: school, activities, doctor appointments, etc., it all brought up his sense of unfairness and frustration. He was tired of feeling this way, tired of being mad, tired of everything feeling bad. Terrance needed help managing his feelings, and knew that grabbing another beer was NOT the help he needed. It wasn't working—if anything, it was making things worse. He called a buddy who saw a counselor to ask him about it.

He made an appointment. With the help of the counselor, Terrance went to work on figuring out how to let go of the past and cope with the present. He learned how to recognize his triggers and to take a deep breath (and lots of other strategies that helped) when he began to feel the familiar rage flash in his chest. He practiced letting Jessica know when he needed a break in their conversations, rather than allowing his emotions to cross the line, which inevitably resulted in him blowing up. Even though he still felt things were unfair, the stress and conflict decreased. He recognized the only way out was to walk forward as best he could.

Jessica seemed to sense his new control and confidence, and became more respectful of his input. Most importantly, Terrance didn't have to experience either himself or Jessica as mad all the time, which helped him to feel that the work of managing his feelings was the right thing to do.

Focus on the positive whenever possible

One of you may be adventurous while the other more of a homebody; or one of you might be rambunctious and loud while the other prefers order and quiet. Parents often differ in their own lifestyles, temperaments, and preferences. Those differences can give rise to conflict over what's best for the children. When we're struggling with unloving feelings or upset, we're more prone to see these differences in our co-parent in a negative light: adventurous becomes *reckless,* careful becomes *overprotective*, structured becomes *controlling*, and involved becomes *intrusive*, etc.

Some differences need to be addressed directly such as those that create undue confusion for your children, disruption in their ability to function through their day-to-day activities, or anything you suspect causes your children harm. That said, whenever possible, see if you can keep perspective on the positive aspects of some of your co-parent's traits that are quite different from yours. Share the positive whenever possible with your children to show support for the gifts of their other parent.

The aspects that drive you crazy, will of course still exist. Sometimes we have to learn how to enjoy (or at least accept, or, learn to ignore) the leopard's spots, rather than taking a paintbrush and ink to them at every opportunity.

> Leopards don't have stripes, will never have stripes, and if you can convince them to **act as if** they have stripes, the changes rarely stick. In general, the conflict involved in continually trying to change someone is more harmful than learning to live with "spots" and developing a civil, accepting relationship.

Co-parents' differences aren't necessarily negative for children. Those differences give children a fuller range of experiences and insights to choose from when deciding for themselves who they wish to become. Both parents become models for and contribute learning lessons to what children use in creating their own unique, individual selves. Eventually as your children become teenagers, they will make fun of you both. Learning to laugh at yourself can be the strongest medicine for learning to accept the differences between you "Yep, I was a monk in a cave in my past life, so I like things *really quiet*. Aren't you lucky Daddy wasn't a monk, too?"

Graciella was utterly frustrated with Raul. All he did on the days he had Alberto was play—no homework, no chores, no structure. Raul would take Alberto to watch his late-night soccer games with no regard for bedtime or the next day's activities. It was exactly reminiscent of their married life, when Graciella was doing all of the household and child-rearing work and Raul was having all the fun with Alberto. She was exasperated that she was no more free from Raul's irresponsibility now than she was during their marriage.

When Alberto came home talking about all the fun he had at Dad's, Graciella couldn't help herself, and would lash out about Raul's lack of "real parenting." She could tell she was hurting and confusing Alberto; Alberto was so happy to be back home with his mom, but she seemed mad at him for having so much fun with his dad. He didn't quite know how to fix the problem; all he knew was that he was upsetting his mom. In time, Alberto became more reserved when he returned from residential time with his dad and more reluctant to share any details of his time there.

Granted, Graciella really wished she had a co-parent to help share the workload of raising Alberto. She wanted more time to be the fun mom, not just the taskmaster she felt she had to be. But as she watched Alberto withdraw from her, she realized that she had dampened his enthusiasm and his safety to share with her whatever filled his heart with fun or concern. She wanted her son to know that his enthusiasm meant the world to her, and got busy reversing her actions.

Graciella started talking with Alberto about the fact that she always knew his dad to be fun and active. She shared with him how proud she felt watching his dad play soccer when they were a young couple. She admitted that she was very happy that Raul included Alberto in his adventures. A wide grin returned to Alberto's face. And she added that it would be very helpfu if they would both do a little homework while Alberto was at his dad's because, after all, one day they both hoped to see him off to college.

Graciella decided to involve Alberto in an age-appropriate way to take responsibility for some of his own work: getting his laundry done, taking his homework to Dad's, making sure he got enough sleep. She reminded him, "Sweetheart, you have to tell your dad if you need more sleep."

She made a concerted effort to drop little compliments such as "Dad's a great soccer player—I bet you're learning a lot from him" and "you have a funny sense of humor like your dad." Alberto really lit up, and began to share more of his life at his dad's with her again—and by Raul's report, visa-versa. The homework issue hasn't resolved yet, but with patience and time, Alberto will develop skills to manage his own work while enjoying time with his dad and thriving in the loving structure provided by his mom.

Highlights in Review

- The co-parenting relationship develops over time. Following the point of separation, with its enormous stress and loss, co-parents often find that their relationship will have many phases as stress diminishes, stability takes hold, and new ways of living begin to unfold.

- Changes in one or the other co-parent's circumstances often have a destabilizing impact on the larger two-home family system. With instability comes an opportunity for a new stability, which can be more positive—or negative. Working through such changes with a co-parent coach can make a huge difference in the outcome.

- Successful co-parenting requires competencies in a specific set of skills. Many of these are strong general relationship skills. Others are specific to co-parents—in particular, having a shared set of practices and protocols that allow for the smooth running of a two-home family.

- Co-parent styles are as unique as each individual. Acceptance of co-parent characteristics that won't change, and finding ways to see positives, will shift the dynamic between you and reduce stress for the kids.

- Do what you can to improve your co-parenting relationship when cooperation from your co-parent isn't forthcoming.

- We can't overemphasize the importance of personal maturity, patience while working through of the loss of the marital relationship, and sticking to co-parenting protocols that work for your children's new two-home family.

- It takes practice to take a breath instead of judge, to use a business-like approach (calm, practical, and results-oriented), and to find new ways of speaking and reacting to your co-parent and children. Keep practicing, and get support when you need it.

Chapter 11

Raising Well-Adjusted, Resilient, and Resourceful Kids in a Two-Home Family

WITH ENDINGS COME beginnings. You have traveled far from the old and found your way into a new sense of family for your children. You've transformed relationships and roles from the past into new ones that fit their needs in two-homes. Your children are making the journey with you and learned a great deal. They, too, have gone through loss, grief and adjustment. How can you help them continue to thrive in their new normal?

Rebuild a Sense of Family Fun

Your kids have gone through a lot of change, most of it not so fun. You may have felt or may still be feeling overwhelmed with just getting family rules followed and schedules kept, meals on the table, and a decent night's sleep. Adjusting to tandem single-parenting and managing a home as a solo adult can take the fun right out of the day-to-day. With enormous respect for what you're doing, know that your children may need a little fun more than they need folded laundry—they may need to help you fold the laundry and have fun at the same time.

> The fun times reinvigorate us and help us remember that despite all the struggle, life with family holds moments of joy and creates sustaining memories.

We find that children often notice the absence of laughter, relaxation, and togetherness in their new two-home families.

. . . .

Natalie, age 12: *"It seems like everyone is so busy and stressed out all the time. I wish we could just laugh like we used to; have fun sometimes. It's sad this way."*

. . . .

Good times don't require a big event, they don't have to cost money, and in fact, it can be small daily silliness or special warm exchanges that lift our hearts and spirits the most. It is said that "Laughter is the shortest distance between two people." Sometimes a newly stabilized two-home family needs to learn to laugh again.

Use existing gathering times, like meals, bedtimes, or car trips to increase the feeling of connection. Times like dinner or the wind-down before bed offer opportunities for togetherness and sharing.

- One family likes to go around the table sharing their best and least favorite part of the day—highlights and lowlights.

- Another family with small children has a "family chant" they created and employ at times of challenge and celebration:

* * * * * * * *

"Who are we? We're the Donovans!
What do we do? We never give up!"

* * * * * * * *

- Build on children's innate curiosity: keep a jar or box of kid-appropriate questions (fun, silly questions, too) and take turn asking family members. It's a simple and fun way to get to know each other more deeply.

- Find 15 minutes and a great children's novel and sit in the hall outside your kids' bedroom(s) and read aloud to them, as they ease their way into bedtime.

- Build pride in the way you and your kids have pulled together: "We're a team of three, making it happen."

Consider creating special events to look forward to year after year that promote sharing and connecting with others. Examples include kids hosting a neighborhood spring egg hunt or "the 42nd Street Summer Olympics," filled with silly games and even sillier prizes. Invite children to come up with ideas, empower them as they build their new sense of home, family, and neighborhood. All that matters is *everyone matters*.

Believe Your Kids will do Great Things

Parents influence how kids see themselves and what kids believe they're capable of. Be an active, intentional contributor to their strong and capable self-image. Obtaining goals takes persistent effort—and also failure.

> Children need parental guidance to build skills to
> deal with failure, wrong turns, and dead ends without
> interference and take-over. Resulting failures should
> be met as opportunities to learn, innovate, practice and
> do better, not give up or give over to someone else.

Allowing your children to struggle with something difficult allows them the chance to have the intrinsic pleasure of hard work well done. Your admiration of their staying power, persistence, creative risks and can-do attitude is much more of a success-builder than focusing on the outcome or goal.

Success can mean many things: academic performance, social confidence, capacity to follow house rules, athletic abilities, learning to manage difficult emotions. To borrow the wisdom of Thomas Jefferson, "There's nothing more unequal than the equal treatment of unequals." Each child is unique. No two children are *equal*. This does not mean that each child needs overly special treatment or shouldn't be held to a set of age-appropriate standards and, at times, expected to *exceed* those standards. This means that helping your child realize his/her potential, work toward goals, achieve, and feel good about progress is what's valuable.

You can help kids reduce anxiety, insecurity, and impatience by focusing on behaviors that underlie success rather than the performance outcome. Find steps toward success, like noticing your child's sustained focus on their homework—for one child that might be 10 minutes on math facts, for another it could be 30 minutes of silent reading. Young athletes need you to be proud of them in uniform, as a good sport, as a kid who sticks with the team and works hard, which is quite different from focusing on minutes played or goals scored. When you focus attention on what you want from your child (no need for 21 gun salutes!), he/she will gradually respond with increasing capacity to grow in the direction of your light. Remember: "you catch more flies with honey than with vinegar." There will be times when you need to set a stern limit but, in general, know that your positive attention is honey to a growing child. Praising for hard work, good attitude, and the courage to try something new helps kids develop necessary skills for self-motivation and self-sufficiency.

Love: The Balance of Nurturing and Discipline

Solo-parenting means you're filling two sets of shoes. You can no longer divide and conquer with one of you playing good cop and the other bad cop. In your own home, *you* have to be *both*. Kids need lots of connection, nurturing, fun, and love, but they also need rules, expectations, structure, and follow-through on consequences. Solo-parenting may mean that you have to grow into a skill set that you might find challenging. Perhaps you need to learn to be more present, warm and affectionate, or be more calm, structured and capable of laying down the law.

Guilt can undermine the balance of nurturing and discipline. Guilt is an insidious emotion that will often take a strong parent off his/her game. Under the influence of guilt, you might allow misbehavior to slip by, or moodiness to rule, or make excuses for poor performance, or indulge regressive behaviors that are counter to healthy adjusting. Kids are kids—not everything they do today is about the divorce/separation. They don't need you to feel sorry for them or blame yourself (or your co-parent); they need you *to parent*.

Stress and exhaustion play a significant role in undermining strong parenting. Remember your own self-care is part of the foundation of healthy parenting, which means putting your own oxygen mask on first. You have to take care of yourself to have the bandwidth and resources to take care of your children. With stress levels high in the adjusting two-home family, a parent may fall apart and yell, react, and default to parenting strategies he/she later regrets. If this happens, go back to your child and apologize; repair the connection, and then return to your original plan: to nurture, teach, and discipline so your child can grow and learn.

When we discipline successfully, we teach and children learn. Parents often equate discipline with punishment. Discipline employs setting age-appropriate expectations and consequences for misbehavior. If in applying consequences or punishments, our children are unable to learn, we're missing the mark. When children are spanked or hit for misbehavior (*even* running into the street), they're so shocked, frightened, or defensive they actually stop thinking, which makes it impossible to learn. Scaring, shaming, demeaning, or harshly excluding children make it very difficult for them to learn. With all the changes, now solo-parenting, and the kids reacting, you may feel at wits' end about what to do. Getting some parent coaching may be a life-saver as you stabilize your home.

Nurturing and discipline represent two key ingredients of strong parenting. Connection and closeness cultivated through fun and nurturing helps motivate kids to follow rules and engenders healthy discomfort when falling short of expectations. Clear boundaries help kids stay safe and feel safe. Our capacity to follow through with predictable consequences for misbehavior reassures them that we care, that we're paying attention, and that we'll take action when needed to protect what we value for them. Children in two-home families need a healthy dose of both ingredients in each home.

Involve Kids while Protecting Childhood

Solo-parenting in a two-home family can be a lot of work. Whether you and your child make a "team of two" or you and your children make a "team of six," teamwork will be the name of the successful two-home game. There's nothing wrong (and a lot right!) about teaching kids the value of pitching in and being a part of the team. It's important, however, to recognize the balance between *involving* and *overwhelming* children. When assigning household chores consider:

- Does my child have the skill to do this chore, or do I need to teach them and provide lots of support at the front end?

- Is the amount of responsibility age-appropriate?

- Am I taking into consideration all the other demands my child is meeting for school and important activities, and developmental needs?

- Do I have the ability to support, reinforce and help ensure a feeling of teamwork?

Tasks such as doing laundry, housekeeping, meal prep and cleanup, and watching younger siblings builds important skills and supports age-appropriate competence. When co-parents work together to build age-appropriate household skills, children in two-home families often outshine their traditional family peers in household competence. Keep in mind that, children also have other tasks to master: maintaining friendships, participating in school, following through on sports activities, having fun and a reasonable amount of down-time. Make sure, if possible, your kids' responsibilities aren't keeping them from participating in these important developmental activities. (For general guidelines for age-appropriate chores, see the Appendix.)

Protect Your Children From Adult Problems

Kids may be smart, emotionally intelligent, almost adult-capable—but deep down they are still growing children. Give kids freedom from taking on adult problems by protecting them from hearing adult issues and emotional concerns. Particularly if your older child asks you to share—or even more seductive, hits the nail on the head about what's going on, be cautious and protect.

Teens, in particular, may make their own loving mistakes and seek to "help" a parent in ways that can actually derail their healthy development and cause them more stress and confusion than anticipated—now or in the future. Because teens can sometimes look and act like small adults, parents can unskillfully invite them into adult business that can compromise their emotional development or psychological safety. This includes:

- Providing emotional support for a parent who is bereft, anxious, or needy as a result of the divorce/separation; stepping in for the absent spouse emotionally;

- Becoming a parent's confidant about adult-related concerns, whether about the other parent, a new romance, finances, or concerns about another child in the family;

- Believing they need to take on adult responsibilities such as raising siblings, handling finances, performing too many or too advanced household chores, often in reaction to a parent who is incapacitated in some way

Kids/teens who absorb adult responsibilities in their struggling family often end up feeling that fulfilling the family's or parent's needs is more important than their own. These kiddos are kicked off the healthy developmental curve in exchange for meeting responsibilities or emotional demands above their developmental preparation. Often in young adulthood, they struggle with insecurity, uncertainty, and confusion in relationships. Rather than dealing with normal peer and age-appropriate issues, this child often feels like she/he holds a "special role" that no one else can understand now—and only later feels *used*.

A child who is torn between fulfilling his/her dreams and taking care of a parent can become fearful, resentful or guilty for what should be a natural, healthy desire for self-interest and independence. Of course the ability to empathize, take responsibility and make independent decisions are wonderful characteristics that we want to nurture and develop in our kids—in *their* lives. As healthy parents, we should usher our kids out of our adult world when they drop by in spite of all their good intentions to help.

The Seven "C's": Helping Kids Build Resilience

(The following boxed material in this chapter is reprinted by permission of the American Academy of Pediatrics. We'll take each of the Seven "C's" and discuss how each applies to the co-parenting experience in a two-home family.)

Kenneth Ginsburg, M.D., MS Ed, FAAP, a pediatrician specializing in adolescent medicine at The Children's Hospital of Philadelphia, joined with the American Academy of Pediatrics (AAP) to author *A Parent's Guide to Building Resilience in Children and Teens: Giving Your Child Roots and Wings* (2010). This award-winning book is an invaluable resource that helps parents and caregivers build resilience in children, teens, and young adults.

Dr. Ginsburg identified seven "C"s of resilience, recognizing that "resilience isn't a simple, one-part entity." Parents can use these guidelines to help their children recognize and use their abilities and inner resources.

▓ COMPETENCE ▓

Competence describes the feeling of knowing that you can handle a situation effectively. We can help the development of competence by:

- Helping children focus on individual strengths

- Focusing any identified mistakes on specific incidents

- Empowering children to make decisions

- Being careful that your desire to protect your child doesn't mistakenly send a message that you don't think he or she is competent to handle things

- Recognizing the competencies of siblings individually and avoiding comparisons

---

As a duty co-parent, your energy and focus is often on efficiently making your household run smoothly, getting meals on the table, and getting kids to activities. A few minutes of focused attention on your child's homework efforts or your guidance as he/she learns a new task or takes on a new chore, is more than simply showering attention or affection—it actually helps your child build competence and a sense of personal responsibility. When you recognize and value your child's initiative, perseverance, or self-management, he/she feels proud of him/herself. When you create opportunities for your child to contribute to the household (learning a new chore, task, etc.) in age-appropriate ways, and *recognize* his/her contribution, you build confidence in your child that he/she is a valued team member.

As children learn to manage their belongings, transition from one home to the other, take responsibility for solving problems with each household (as opposed to complaining to one parent about the other's rules), you set up skill-building opportunities that empower your children to see themselves as capable and responsible. Helping children learn the steps involved in remembering and packing their things, and practicing with them to have difficult conversations, is more time-consuming than taking things in your own hands and just doing it yourself. You'll find that sweet spot between demands for efficiency and continuing the very important job of competence-building by lovingly walking with them through all their mistakes, redos, trials-and-errors, and *one more time*. It's all part of raising resilient and resourceful kids.

▪ CONFIDENCE ▪

A child's belief in his own abilities is derived from competence. Build confidence by:

- Focusing on the best in each child so that he or she can see that, as well

- Clearly expressing the best qualities, such as fairness, integrity, persistence, and kindness

- Recognizing when he or she has done well

- Praising honestly about specific achievements; not diffusing praise that may lack authenticity

- Not pushing the child to take on more than he or she can realistically handle

---

Practice makes better, not perfect. Children are works in progress. The more we help them see their steps toward competence, the more they're able to develop their own confidence. Children are not little adults, regardless of size or age. Their child-like ways, needs and immaturities continue in two homes just as they would in one. Realistic, age-appropriate expectations are essential in building confidence. A reasonable amount of stress strengthens performance and builds skills. Overwhelming stress and/or fear, diminishes growth and blocks thinking and effective problem-solving.

Focus on the best in your child, allow mistakes, prepare him/her to do better with each step of confidence-building. Particularly in the early months of two-home family life, children may need extra support around preparing for transitions. When items are forgotten, approach the mishap with a problem-solving attitude and ideas of how to solve forgetting. Too much pressure too soon will increase a child's sense of failure and exaggerate his/her loss of comfort of living in one home. Remember, this change was something thrust on your children—and they need time to build the skills necessary to confidently navigate a two-home life.

▓ CONNECTION ▓

Developing close ties to family and community creates a solid sense of security that helps lead to strong values and prevents alternative destructive paths to love and attention. You can help your child connect with others by:

- Building a sense of physical safety and emotional security within your home

- Allowing the expression of all emotions, so that kids will feel comfortable reaching out during difficult times

- Addressing conflict openly in the family to resolve problems

- Creating a common area where the family can share time (not necessarily TV time)

- Fostering healthy relationships that will reinforce positive messages

---

Supporting a strong, healthy, integrated relationship with each parent is the foundation of skillful co-parenting. When spouses successfully un-couple and can see the benefit and value of their children having a close and connected relationship with their other parent, the tension, anger, and stress can drain out of family ties for children. As difficult as it may be to imagine, this includes accepting new romantic partners that become a permanent part of your co-parent's life. Finding the spaciousness to accept other loving adults into your children's sense of family creates an atmosphere of safety and emotional security for your children in both homes. This acceptance is not tacit condoning of hurtful behaviour between spouses—this is an act of co-parenting for your children's emotional safety and their healthy sense of connection.

Teaching children that nothing will be made worse by talking about it provides children the safety to come to you with their biggest, scariest problems. When both co-parents agree that there will be no secrets—that a child can safely come to either or both parents with challenges and dilemmas and the co-parents will come together to support and problem-solve with the child—your child will have the same benefit of his/her age-mates in one-home families. Co-parents who continue to see their roles as primary foundations in the face of kid problems, help kids feel supported and held across their two-home family.

Working with your children to understand their feelings, to talk freely with you about their life experiences without harsh or rejecting commentary, supports a flow of communication essential to kids feeling connected. This does not mean that we agree and accept everything that our children dish out, but rather that we listen, guide, direct, and help them clarify their values. We teach appropriate boundaries, communication skills, emotional intelligence, and empathy and respect for others.

▪ CHARACTER ▪

Children need to develop a solid set of morals and values to determine right from wrong and to demonstrate a caring attitude toward others. To strengthen your child's character, start by:

- Demonstrating how behaviors affect others
- Helping your child recognize himself or herself as a caring person
- Demonstrating the importance of community
- Encouraging the development of spirituality
- Avoiding racist or hateful statements or stereotypes

As co-parents, you are two of the most influential forces in your child's developing moral compass. Talk with him/her about values, about what matters in life, how to contribute as a strong community member, about responsibility toward him/herself and others, and about how to care for relationships. You both have something very important to offer. Remember that your child does not need you to make an example of his/her other parent, to blame, criticize, or in any way degrade the other. Children have an innate capacity to ferret out the good and bad characteristics in each of you. What you want to do is help them hold onto what's good in each of you and to do better in the ways that you've failed.

Connection and character make human relationships, democracy, the freedom to be who one is, respect, compassion, honesty, and integrity integral to a full and healthy life. Who better to help your children integrate these concepts than you—and who better to model that learning and self-improvement are lifelong processes?

■ CONTRIBUTION ■

Children need to realize that the world is a better place because they are in it. Understanding the importance of personal contribution can serve as a source of purpose and motivation. Teach your children how to contribute by:

- Communicating to children that many people in the world do not have what they need

- Stressing the importance of serving others by modeling generosity

- Creating opportunities for each child to contribute in some specific way

The change to a two-home family often impacts financial circumstances of the family as a whole. With this change in discretionary spending, children have an opportunity to learn lessons about the value of money, budgeting, and thoughtful use of resources. Children may learn to take better care of their things as they may not be as readily replaced. Siblings share more in terms of toys and clothes than they might have in a one-home family. And children can often learn valuable lessons about how to be generous with others even when they have less.

Kindness doesn't cost anything—and volunteering, lending a hand, and offering to help another in need is the "rent we all pay for living on this earth" as Congresswoman Shirley Chisholm once expressed. Choosing a service activity to do with your children can be as simple as dedicating two hours on a Saturday morning to picking up litter in the neighborhood park and as organized as regular volunteer hours sorting food or serving meals at the food bank. Help your children know that regardless of circumstances, we all contribute to making our families, schools, neighborhoods, and the world a better place. The two "C's" of connection and contribution go hand-in-hand.

■ COPING ■

Learning to cope effectively with stress will help your child be better prepared to overcome life's challenges. Positive coping lessons include:

- Modeling positive coping strategies on a consistent basis

- Guiding your child to develop positive and effective coping strategies

- Realizing that telling him or her to stop the negative behavior will not be effective

- Understanding that many risky behaviors are attempts to alleviate the stress and pain in kids' daily lives

- Not condemning your child for negative behaviors and, potentially, increasing his or her sense of shame

Separation and divorce place all family members under enormous stress, emotional turmoil, uncertainty, and loss. As the adult, you are the guide through the turbulence; you are the one your children will look to for safe mooring when the waves get too high or the storm clouds too threatening. The more you can model healthy coping, constructive stress management, and a basic optimism for a better tomorrow, the more your children can begin to trust that all will turn out OK.

Love, safety, and family connection indemnify children from a world where everything feels too hard. Remind children that tomorrow will be another day—that feelings pass, and new skills will be learned, problems will get solved, and whatever comes to pass, you'll be in it *together*. That's family; that's team; that's what it means to be "the Masons."

If you and your co-parent are worried about your child's risky behaviors, or feeling like you're losing adequate control to keep him/her safe, contact a local family service agency or youth services to find out about counseling for children/teens in your area. This may be one of those times that you and your co-parent do the best you can to come together to support your child very directly. You may need to do some family therapy to help your kiddo address the fears and upset underneath the destructive behavior.

▪ CONTROL ▪

Children who realize that they can control the outcomes of their decisions are more likely to realize that they have the ability to bounce back. Your child's understanding that he or she can make a difference further promotes competence and confidence. You can try to empower your child by:

- Helping your child to understand that life's events are not purely random and that most things that happen are the result of another individual's choices and actions

- Learning that discipline is about teaching, not punishing or controlling; using discipline to help your child to understand that his actions produce certain consequences

When co-parents have:

- a reasonable amount of consistency across homes,
- communication about what's important for the kids,
- cooperation and problem-solving to ensure the children's academics and activities can run smoothly, and
- compromise to keep the focus on the children' needs—not the adults',

they can provide a more integrated and predictable world for their children.

> The four "C's" of co-parenting—consistency, communication, cooperation and compromise— make all the difference in the world for kids.

When co-parents can be predictable, demonstrate self-control with each other, and co-parent effectively, children can settle into their lives and be fully invested in the business of "growing up." Remember: what divorce breaks apart—strong co-parenting rebuilds.

- Children need to know that there is an adult in their life who believes in them and loves them unconditionally.
- Kids will live "up" or "down" to our expectations.

Your love, attention, and approval is powerful medicine for your children. The sooner you can settle down their lives, focus on the present, support loving relationships with each each parent, and help them transition between homes as carefree as possible, the better. Then, with the change of divorce/separation behind them, children can return to building the skills in preparation for a strong adulthood, learning the frustration tolerance that builds tenacity and resourcefulness, and developing the emotional intelligence that strengthens relationships at work and play.

Give Kids the Gift of a Happy Parent

Perfectly happy? No, it just means you give your own needs appropriate importance and take care of yourself. Children, as you know, are keen observers. They will look to you to ensure things are truly okay and, if reassured can once again safely return their focus to their own adventures, interests and dreams. Find time to develop new or nurture old friendships. Have fun, take pleasure in your successes, as well as practicing self-compassion when things don't go so well. Keep patience and faith while you stretch and learn new skills and take on new roles. Finding time for you and restoring joy and confidence in your own life will usher in healing for your children and their two-home family.

Highlights in Review

- Children thrive in a balance of love and discipline, fun and structure, and parents who take the time to find their balance after the transition to a two-home family.

- Laughing, connecting, and creating a sense of community are important for children as they establish their new sense of "normal."

- Stress, exhaustion, guilt, and other difficult emotions impact the quality of your parenting. Self-care is key.

- Teamwork is the name of the game in a two-home family. Teach your children how to contribute to the running of your home, support them in their efforts, and encourage their pride of accomplishment. Simultaneously, protect their normal growth by making time for their kid-oriented activities and appropriate relaxation.

- Protect kids from adult business and issues. Parents take care of kids emotionally, physically, and spiritually—not the other way around. When that balance flips and kids feel pressure or "specialness" in taking on a more adult role with a parent, their healthy development and psychological safety is threatened.

- Consider how you will support the seven "C's" of resilience for your children and the four "C's" of co-parenting with your co-parent.

- "Put your own oxygen mask on first and then assist your children with theirs"—kids are freed from worry when they know their parent is finding his/her way back to being whole and happy.

It is the responsibility of every adult …
to make sure that children hear what we have learned
from the lessons of life and to hear over and over that
we love them and that they are not alone.

— Marian Wright Edelman, American activist for children

Addenda

Additional Resources
for Co-Parents

Books and Internet Resources

BOOKS

For Children

- *Dinosaurs Divorce: A Guide for Changing Families*, Marc Brown and Laurene Krasny Brown (4-8)
- *Boys and Girl's Book About Divorce*, Richard A. Gardner (9+)
- *How It Feels When Parents Divorce*, Jill Krementz (8+)
- *Lets Talk About Divorce*, Fred Rogers (4-8)
- *Two Homes*, Kady MacDonald Denton (3-6)
- *The Family Book,* Todd Parr (4-6)
- *A Smart Girl's Guide to Divorce*, Nancy Holyoke (9-12)

Conflict Resolution

- *Divorce Without Court: A Guide to Mediation and Collaborative Divorce*, Katherine E. Stoner
- *Fighting Fair*, Robert Coulson
- *Getting to Yes: Negotiating Agreement Without Giving In*, Roger Fisher and William Ury
- *A Guide to Divorce Mediation*, Gary Friedman
- *The Good Divorce: Keeping Your Family Together When Your Marriage Comes Apart*, Constance Ahrons, PhD

Parenting in Divorce

- *The Truth About Children and Divorce: Dealing With Emotions so You and Your Children Can Thrive*, Robert E. Emery
- *Divorce and Your Child: Practical Suggestions for Parents*, Sonja Goldstein LL.B and Albert Solnit M.D.
- *When Children Grieve*, John W. James & Russell Friedman

- *Mom's House, Dad's House: Making Two Homes for Your Child*, Isolina Ricci, Ph.D
- *The Co-Parenting Toolbox*, Isolini Ricci, PhD
- *Helping Your Kids Cope With Divorce the Sandcastles Way*, Gart Neuman and Patricia Romanowksi
- *Being a Great Divorced Father: Real-Life Advice from a Dad Who's Been There,* Paul Mandelstein
- *Growing Up Divorced*, Linda Bird Francke

General Parenting Skills

- *123 Magic*, Thomas W. Phelan
- *Parenting With Love and Logic,* Foster Cline and Jim Fay
- *Raising an Emotionally Intelligent Child*, John Gottman, Joan Declaire, and Daniel Goleman
- *Parenting from the Inside Out*, Daniel Siegel and Mary Hartzell

ONLINE RESOURCES

Finding a Divorce Coach/Co-Parent Coach, Child Specialist or Mediator in your Area

- Inernational Academy of Collaborative Professionals: www.collaborativepractice.com
- Academy of Professional Family Mediators: www.professionalfamilymediators.org

General Divorce Resources

- Inernational Academy of Collaborative Professionals: www.collaborativepractice.com
- Divorce Links: www.divorcelinks.com
- Stepfamily Association of America: www.stepfamily.org
- Child Welfare Information Gateway: www.childwelfare.gov
- State-by-State Information and Resources: www.custodysource.com/state/htm

Mental Health Resources

- American Academy of Child and Adolescent Psychiatry: www.aacap.org
- American Association for Marriage and Family Therapy: www.aamft.org

Legal Information

- International Academy of Collaborative Professionals: www.collaborativepractice.com
- American Bar Association: www.abanet.org/legalservices/findlegalhelp/home.html
- The LGBT Bar Association: http://lgbtbar.org/
- Finding a Lawyer: www.findlaw.com
- Reference Desk: www.refdesk.com/factlaw.html
- Law Help: www.lawhelp.org
- National Center for State Courts Pro Se Litigation State Links: www.ncsconline.org

Child Support Resources

- U.S. Office of Child Support Enforcement: www.acf.hhs.gov/programs/cse
- Association for Children for Enforcement of Support: www.childsupport-aces.com

Co-Parent Calendars

- Cofamilies: www.cofamilies.com
- Sharekids: www.sharekids.com
- Our Family Wizard: www.ourfamilywizard.com
- Cozi: www.cozi.com
- 2 Houses: www.2houses.com
- Parenting Bridge: www.parentingbridge.com
- Google Calendar (co-parents successfully share this calendar and it's free)

H-E-A-R-S: Co-Parents' Communication Guidelines

When communicating verbally or in writing:

- Healthy boundaries—respect privacy, be unobtrusive
- Effective—desired outcome: constructive for your kids
- Agreed upon—works for both of you
- Respectful—slow down, consider, manage emotions
- Sustainable—works over time

When communicating by email or text:

- In your kids' best interest—remember, you're writing/speaking to your children's *other parent*, not your ex-spouse.
- Pleasant tone—you'd speak or write with the very same tone to your BOSS.
- Appropriate word choice—this is not the time for four-letter words or other expletives.
- Use bold lettering and ALL CAPS only for highlighting and ease of reading—not for shouting at the reader.
- Be brief, informative, well-organized—do your best to stay within the "200-word rule" for any one subject.
- Use the subject line of an email effectively.
- Be thoughtful about how many communications you send—unless there's something urgent/time-sensitive, your transition email can be sufficient for healthy co-parent communication.
- Repetitive texts or emails are intrusive—please avoid badgering or harassing one another. This is unresolved spousal work.
- Respond in a timely manner to appropriate communications received, even

if all you say is, "Got it. Will get back to you tomorrow" or whenever is appropriate and possible.

- Ignore unproductive emails, texts, or voice messages. Think of any response to negative/unproductive communication as kindling on a fire you're hoping will die-out. *Don't feed the fire.*

Co-Parent Protocols in Public

Boundaries and Respect Allow
Co-Parents to Work Together and Enjoy Kids

- Respect the physical and emotional distance your co-parent wants/needs from you. If your presence creates discomfort, please maintain a healthy and respectful distance from your co-parent at public events like the soccer field. This includes keeping your eyes on your child's activity/event rather than watching/observing your co-parent and his/her guest(s). If the discomfort persists, consider getting some coaching for yourself or better, with your co-parent.

- How you determine who sits with which of the other parents can be done with grace. Your ability to maintain *grace* can help guide where you sit, stand, or how long you stay at an event. This brings us back to the reminder: the only person you can control is *yourself*. Your children's activities/events are not a time for a turf-war over former relationships with team-mates' parents. In time, there will be plenty of space for both of you to relax. You may even find that you can share the same bleacher, cheering section, etc. Make your goal finding a way to participate that doesn't distract from your child's sense of support by his/her parents both attending.

- When you're the duty parent, encourage your children (whether participants or spectators) to greet their other parent. Give them guidance, "There's Dad—head over and say hi—and I'll see you back here in a few minutes." If you know ahead of time the other parent would welcome the children to hang with him/her for some portion of an event, practice generosity by allowing/encouraging the children in attendance to move freely between the two of you.

- For the "off duty" parent, gracefully accept a 'secondary role' to help reduce tension and ambiguity for your child. Redirect your child back to his/her "duty parent" for permission to go to the snack shack, or to play over on the swings. Consider how you'd respond to *my child* and you'll be in safe territory—not stepping on your co-parent's duty-parent toes.

- Address your child openly and lovingly with healthy boundaries for the situation. A big hug, congratulations, or whatever is indicated and then help your child move back to the duty parent while assuring him/her that you'll see them again soon (unless you have an agreement that the child can move freely between you).

- At the end of the game, the duty parent can allow 2—5 minutes for the non-duty parent to give a 'high-five' and quick recap of game highlights. However, this is not a time for lengthy discussions, planning for the future, or anything beyond a well-boundaried, respectful few moments—particularly if the duty parent is waiting to load up the car and move on.

Guiding Principles for Co-Parents: Parenting Plan Options

IN THE WASHINGTON State Parenting Plan, we have a section for "Other" considerations—a place for reminders, guiding principles, guidelines, and what I often refer to as "good co-parenting hygiene." Please find below a list of the typical "Section VI: Other" additions to a Parenting Plan. Perhaps you will want to discuss with your legal team how to include some of these helpful principles and guidelines in your parenting plan. Or, perhaps you and your co-parent will agree to abide by these reminders whether codified in a legal document or not.

Tri-Annual Co-Parenting Planning Meetings: In order to facilitate open communication and planning, the parents may agree to meet face-to-face in a mutually agreeable location (or through other acceptable means) for up to two hours (or extended by mutual agreement) on a tri-annual basis during the months of January, March, and August (additional meetings may be requested and set by mutual agreement). Dad ("odd" years) or Mom ("even" years) will initiate these meetings by e-mail within the first five days of the month. Parents agree to use a divorce coach/family specialist to assist with these meetings if either parent should request it. Parents agree to split the cost of coaching based on percentage of income as recognized in the Parenting Plan Worksheet (Line 6).

- **January meeting:** review the school schedule through end of the school year, special events, developmental needs, health care needs, educational needs, and any other agenda items the parents' desire.

- **March meeting:** prepare for the summer schedule, discuss camps, activities, child-care, vacation-with-parents, address the schedules for Memorial Day/ Labor Day and weekend swapping as needed. Consider plans for Mother's Day and Father's Day. Follow up on any special events, developmental needs, health care needs, educational needs, and any other agenda items the parents desire.

- **August meeting:** review the up-coming school schedule from start of school through end of winter break, special events, developmental needs, health care needs, educational needs, and any other agenda items the parents desire.

These meetings, however, do not supersede each parent's responsibility to keep him/herself individually informed about the children's educational, health care, activity/camp/event schedule.

Residential Arrangements: These agreements are provided for in the best interest of the children. The children's interests are best served by a full and regular pattern of contact with parents, responsiveness and cooperation by both parents, involvement by both parents in all aspects of the children's needs and a reasonably consistent routine of activities, values, and discipline throughout both homes. Absence, inconsistency, and conflict are opposed to the best interests of the child.

Honoring the Residential Schedule: Neither parent will encourage the children to change their primary residence or encourage the children to believe it is their choice to do so. It is a choice that will be made by the parents or, if the parents cannot agree, after consultation with professionals, by the courts.

Flexibility to Meet the Needs of the Children: Each parent acknowledges that as the children grow older, provisions of this plan may need to be changed. When the children reach an age where they are involved with many social, school, and extracurricular activities, their schedule should be taken into consideration. The parents agree to actively listen to the needs of their children and to work together to provide for a schedule and co-parenting arrangement that supports the children's growth and development.

Children Attending Their Activities: Each parent shall have the right and responsibility to ensure that the children attend school and other scheduled activities while in that parent's care. Activities that affect both parents residential schedule are discussed by parents and moved forward by mutual agreement before involving the children. Parents will agree on cost-sharing as outlined in the Order of Child Support for mutually agreed upon activities. Each parent should determine that it is in the child's best interest to miss a scheduled activity for reasons of health and well-being.

Parental Involvement in School and Extracurricular Activities: Both parents may respectfully participate in school and extracurricular activities for the children regardless of the residential schedule.

Parental Responsibility to Stay Informed: Parents shall be responsible for keeping themselves apprised of athletic and social events in which the children participate. The nonresidential parent shall make arrangements with the children's school to obtain duplicate copies of school newsletters, report cards, and any other written materials, which apprise that parent of the children's progress at school. If the information can only be obtained or received by one parent, the parent receiving the information shall provide it to the other parent in a timely manner. All other pertinent information obtained from the school or health care providers will be cc'd to the other parent.

Shared Family E-Calendar: The parents agree to the use of a shared e-calendar to track appointments, activities, schedules, etc. The parents will update the calendar regularly and work together to make this an effective/useful tool for planning the children's lives.

E-mail Communication: The co-parents will rely on e-mail to communicate changes to the residential schedule or other pertinent information as relates to the care of the child. The parents will place a clear message in the subject line, such as: "Request to change residential schedule" or "Dental apt follow-up needed." The parent receiving the e-mail will respond within 72 hours. If longer time is needed to provide adequate feedback, the receiving parent will attempt to indicate when he/she anticipates responding more fully, i.e. "Will confirm whether change in schedule is possible by Friday at 5." Parents will always endeavor to be clear and respectful in their e-mail exchanges. If a parent fails to respond within 72 hours (or however long the co-parents agree on), the sender can move forward without further input.

Text Communication: The parents will consult on the circumstances/appropriate use of text communication. Texts are most useful for alerting to delays in traffic for transitions or for other short informational exchanges.

Telephone Access: When the children are in residence with a parent, the other parent shall be permitted unimpeded and unmonitored telephone access with the children at reasonable times and for a reasonable duration. Parents agree that the residential parent will continue to provide appropriate limit-setting/monitoring of the use of texting/phone in a healthy and respectful/social manner. If either parent should question the limits set by the other, he/she will initiate a conversation from a position of curiosity to understand the boundary-setting of the other parent.

Promoting Contact and Affection toward the Other Parent: Each parent endeavors to promote the emotions of affection, love and respect between the children and the other parent. Each parent agrees to refrain from words or conduct which would have a tendency to estrange the children from the other parent, to damage the opinion of the children as to the other parent, or which would impair the natural development of the children's love and respect for the other parent. Each parent agrees to discourage other persons from uttering such words or engaging in such conduct while in the children's presence. Each parent agrees to be responsible to the impact on the residential parent during transitions at activities—that the contact with the children does not unreasonably interfere with the normal flow of the transition or undermine the residential parent's authority.

Child's Personal Items: The parents agree that the children's personal items are theirs to move from household to household. The parents also agree that there are some items purchased for the children that are part of household furnishings or are for use by the children at their household solely.

Parenting Style, Privacy, and Authority: Each parent agrees to honor the other's parenting style, privacy and authority. Each parent shall encourage the children to discuss their concerns or grievances against a parent directly with the parent in question. It is the intent of both parents to encourage a direct parent-child bond and communication.

Discipline: Both parents agree that the children will be protected from any individual who would use physical/corporal punishment as a means of discipline. Parents will do what they can to prevent any reoccurrence.

Child's Privacy and Maturational Needs: Both parents shall use appropriate and safe parenting judgment during their residential time with the children. As the children reach puberty, both parents will be aware of and guard their unique privacy and maturational needs.

Participation in Religious Activities: Each parent shall be entitled to have the children participate with them in their religious activities. Neither parent shall disparage the other parent's religious activities or attempt to sway the children to their respective religious or philosophical viewpoint.

Gun Possession Disclosure: Each parent will inform the other in the event that he/she maintains a gun in his/her residence. Both parents commit to following the absolute best practices for gun safety in the home in the event of having a gun (locked away with ammunition stored separately). Both parents will maintain responsibility for assessing gun safety with relatives, friends, and parents of the children's peers in the future as the children spend extended time on play-dates, overnights, etc. in others' homes.

Protecting Children from Adult Matters: Neither parent shall advise the children of the status of child support payments, payment for activities, or other legal matters regarding the co-parents' relationship.

Financial Obligation: Neither parent shall financially obligate the other parent regarding the children without the consent of the other parent, unless otherwise provided in the Order of Child support.

Children and Adult Information: Neither parent shall use the children, directly or indirectly, to gather information about the other parent or take verbal messages to the other parent in a non-age-appropriate manner.

Current Residential Information: Each parent shall provide the other with the address and telephone number of their residence and update such information promptly when it changes.

Professional Records: Both parents shall have full access to school, day care, medical and other records of the children.

Authority to Confer with Children's Experts: Both parents shall have equal and independent authority to confer with the children's school, day care and other programs with regard to the children's educational, emotional and social progress.

Child's Passport/Travel: If the co-parents agree to obtain U.S. passports for the children, the co-parents will cooperate in obtaining and renewing the passport(s) when necessary. The parents shall equally share the costs of obtaining the passport(s) and renewing the passport(s). The parent who last travels with the children shall be able to hold the children's passport(s) until the other parent needs the passport(s) to travel with the children, at which point it shall be provided to the other parent, within two weeks of the date of travel, to facilitate travel. If a parent desires to travel internationally with the children, the other parent shall sign those additional forms necessary to do so.

International Travel: A parent shall not travel with the children outside of the United States without the written permission of the other parent, which permission shall not be unreasonably withheld. The non-traveling parent will provide travel authorization within 72 hours of request and make passports available if in his/her possession. Any parent wishing to travel internationally with the children must advise the other parent in writing at least one month in advance, providing a proposed itinerary and contact information for each day out-of-country. (Parents often agree to exceptions for traveling to border countries such as Canada, in which 24 hour notice is sufficient.) Unless the parent receives written authorization, neither parent may travel with the children to a country that is not a signatory to the Hague Convention on the Civil Aspects of International Child Abduction. The U.S. is the habitual residence of the children and a refusal to return the children to the U.S. by either parent shall be conclusively deemed wrongful under the Convention.

Transition Communication Checklist

TRANSITION COMMUNICATION, WHETHER provided by email or voicemail, are intended to help your co-parent be the best parent he/she can be to your child(ren). Consider what information is useful without managing the other household. Be constructive not instructive. If you don't have anything to communicate about many of the areas below, simply say, "School's good; friends are good" as a way of filling in the blanks.

School

- Homework follow-through/special project updates
- School to home communication that your co-parent may need
- Before/after school care updates
- Special events, concerts, awards, to share
- Extracurricular activity updates
- Special needs, tutoring, etc.
- Other

Friendships/Peer Relationships

- Anything to discuss about peer relationships—concerns or things to watch
- Updates on invitations, slumber parties, etc.
- Social networking, phone use/texting, dating
- Other

Physical Health

- Updates on health-care appointments, rescheduled, etc.
- Other health care related issues—exercises, therapies, etc.

- Illness concerns—medications both prescribed or over-the-counter, fevers, rashes
- Physical complaints (tummy aches, headaches, etc.)
- Changes in eating patterns
- Other

Emotional Well-Being

- Any mental health/anxiety-related concerns
- Sleep issues
- Difficulties with behavior
- Other

Discipline

- Self-management and self-organization
- Behavior programs and progress
- Other

Household Changes

- Changes in routines
- Other

Tri-Annual Co-Parent Business Meeting Checklist

Guiding Co-Parents Through the Planning Process

School Schedule/Summer Schedule

- Planning for vacations, non-school days, holidays, camps, etc.
- Parent/teacher conference dates
- Before/after school care
- Extracurricular activities (including sports, arts, groups, etc.)
- Bedtime—ensuring adequate rest
- Other

Academic Concerns

- Tutoring, testing/evaluations, or consults with educational specialists
- Homework issues
- Special projects for this grade level that needs parental management
- Electives: addressing choices and managing equipment like music instruments, etc.
- Other

Social Development

- Discuss peer relationships and exchange contact information as needed
- Anticipate developmental steps like starting to date
- Any behaviors at either home that are of concern
- Celebrate how wonderfully your child is growing
- Other

Physical Development

- Plan for primary care and dental care appointments
- Other health care related issues
- Illness concerns/management
- Self-care progression (diet, exercise, hygiene, etc.)
- Other

Emotional Development

- Self-esteem/self-confidence progression
- Any mental health/anxiety-related concerns
- Behavior management concerns (angry outbursts?)
- Other

Household Changes

- Changes in routines
- Anticipating a move
- Adding new family members (new pet, roommate, partnership)
- Extended family news that impacts children
- Other

Children and Chores

Suggestions for Tasks That Build Children's Skills and Confidence

2-3 years: Simple 1- or 2-step tasks:

- Put toys away in containers
- Put dirty clothes in hamper
- Wipe up spills

4-6 years: Simple tasks with lots of support

- Make bed
- Water plants
- Bring in mail
- Sort silverware from dishwasher basket to drawer
- Empty wastebaskets
- Fix a bowl of cereal

7-8 years: Simpler tasks with little support/More complicated with more support

- Sweep floor
- Dust surface tops
- Clear table
- Sort laundry
- Help prepare lunch for school (putting in snacks, making simple sandwich)

9-10 years: More complicated tasks with support if needed to achieve mastery or for safety

- Load/unload dishwasher
- Vacuum
- Make own simple breakfast from start to finish (toast, cereal)
- Help prepare food (wash, peel vegetables)
- Feed, walk pets

11 years and up: Kid-appropriate, complicated tasks from start to finish without supervision*

- Wash windows
- Clean bathroom
- Do laundry
- Change sheets
- Babysit with adult in home or alone if older (check your states requirements and use good judgment regarding your child's maturity and skill level/training)
- Rake and mow yard

*Keep in mind children's success will grow with age and experience. Be mindful of ensuring that mistakes will not overwhelm or pose a threat to children's emotional or physical safety.

Signs of Kid Distress

SOME CHILDREN MAY need additional support and some children's reactions may need intervention. It takes time for kids to adjust to changes, work through their emotions and upset, and settle down the ways they might act up. However, you should see improvement and increasing stability over time. Our job as parents is to do as much as we can to decrease distracting and unnecessary conflict (particularly with the other parent) and increase day-to-day routine and stability. If things get worse rather than better despite consistency and life settling down, consult your child's healthcare provider. If a child experiences any of the following serious signs of distress, he/she may need additional on-going support/intervention through a qualified therapist or medical professional:

- Significant and persistent sleep problems

- Persistent and frequent body-related complaints (headaches, tummy aches, etc.)

- Difficulties concentrating that significantly impact school or daily life

- Significant behavioral or academic issues at school

- Frequent angry or violent outbursts

- Withdrawal from loved ones and/or peer relationships (for teens, some withdrawal from parental figures is normal, but watch for dual withdrawal from family and peers or a change of long-term friends to new or less socially appropriate friendships)

- Refusal to care for him/herself or lack of self-efficacy (belief in his/her ability to accomplish/succeed) or belief that things no longer matter

- Prolonged loss of enjoyment of previously enjoyed activities

- Drug or alcohol use, reckless behavior, sexual acting out

- Self-injury, such as cutting or eating disorders

- Discussion of suicidal fears, thoughts, or plans

How Do I get my Ex to Accept a New Stepparent for Our Kids?

UNDERSTANDABLY, THE EMOTIONAL terrain of the evolving and changing family can be fraught with fears, concerns, unresolved feelings, and anxiety for all adults. As the co-parent who has moved on, you're often in the position of trying to smooth the waters, to create a path forward for your children—building a relationship with your new partner when your children's other co-parent remains upset, resistant, judgmental, maybe even flat-out angry. Meanwhile, your new partner has his/her own fears about your loyalties, whether your ex will be "in control" or whether the new partner will have a voice on what happens with the children in your shared home; he/she may wonder how much risk is involved in becoming part of your complicated family. You end up straddling two important relationships—your co-parent and your partner—in a seeming "no win" situation. You just want everyone to get along and to get on with your life, parenting your children! Not so fast; not so easy.

Think of this dynamic like a three-legged stool. One leg is your ex's ability to accept your partner. Ideally, you've chosen someone who is capable and loving—and you hope your ex will see that your children are actually lucky to have another invested, caring adult in their lives. You know, and you hope your ex knows, that your partner will never replace him/her as a parent, but rather will augment your children's experience of caring and guidance by a stepparent.

The second leg is your partner's ability to gracefully and respectfully enter an existing system of two primary parents with children. Hopefully he/she has the maturity and confidence to gradually integrate into the children's lives—as opposed to jumping in and establishing dominance, to initially defer to parents for decision-making, to trust and support you as you re-stabilize your co-parent relationship in a way that can include his/her role, and to maintain a cordial/respectful attitude toward your ex.

> Your primary allegiance regarding your children
> is with your co-parent—you two are the
> executive team for your children's lives.

The third leg is you. How you implement decisions and care of the children in your home is between you and your partner. Differentiating between old "spouse roles" and new "co-parent roles" involves learning new boundaries, new protocols and respect for your working relationship for your children. Supporting your partner to know his/her secure place in your life as you work with your "ex" as a co-parent requires leadership, clarity, and reassurance.

Co-parenting and step-parenting are unique and highly skilled roles. Read, learn, get coaching, and beat the odds. Second marriages with children are up against tough statistics: 60 -75% end in divorce. Conflict and unresolved relationship issues can plague the new couple to the point of exhaustion. You, your co-parent, and your partner can do better. *That's what's best for kids.*

Choosing a Family Law Attorney

Hiring a Family-Centered Attorney

By Anne Lucas, MA, LMHC

Most people stepping into a divorce process look for an attorney who is going to successfully represent their needs and interests. They ask friends or co-workers for referrals dependent on their divorce experiences and eventually hire an attorney based on criteria representing "success."

What is success to you? *"That I don't get taken to the cleaners." "That my partner and my kids are able to thrive going forward." "That he/she's lucky if he/she gets every-other-weekend with our kids." "That we get through this divorce as carefully as possible and our children feel secure in their two-home family."*

Parents carefully screen caregivers, school programs and coaches to ensure the adults in their children's lives share their same (or similar) value systems and goals. They want to know that these adults care about the safety, emotional health, and well being of children as much as the parents do. This same vigilance, care, and examination should be used when you interview and hire a separation/divorce attorney. Your divorce is one of the single most important events in your children's lives!

> In a divorce, an attorney is not just representing you. He/she is also representing your children's interests and needs *and* has a major impact on the state of your post-divorce family.

It's crucial that the attorney you select possesses an understanding of what a family-centered divorce means and specifically, what it means for *you* and *your family*. Don't be shy—ask questions. Give directions. Be sure that the person guiding you through your divorce process has your back, has your co-parent's needs in mind, and recognizes that your children's future depends on a safe and sane divorce.

As a psychotherapist and divorce coach, I advise parents to start this process by asking themselves crucial questions. The answers actually set the foundation for your co-parenting. By co-creating a narrative together—your children's "family life story"—you create something to take to your attorneys about how you want the separation/divorce to impact your children and their sense of a post-separation/divorce family. Identify your shared values and goals for your children—make those your "high end goals." List your fears and differences in parenting—you will want the attorneys to help you anticipate and problem-solve these in the future. Be specific about the conflicts you've had in the past and agree you will look for creative solutions to prevent those conflicts in the future.

When you meet with your potential attorney, tell them you want a family-centered divorce and share exactly how that looks to you. Take your high-end goals, your list of challenges and known problem-areas. Explain how you want your children protected from the stress and conflict of divorce—ask how he/she will handle that *specifically*. What will he/she do to support co-parenting, minimize conflict, and prepare for a successful future for your children?

Explore the attorney's belief system about post-divorce families and how they work to set up families for success especially in that first year post-decree. Does the attorney demonstrate an understanding of your challenges as parents—and challenges of parents in general going through divorce? If there is a high level of initial conflict for you and your co-parent, does the attorney talk about firm boundaries, helpful protocols, and clear direction to start with? Does he/she provide a future focus by providing assistance for conflict resolution over time—perhaps recommending a divorce coach? Does he/she have the foresight to build in co-parent coaching or family therapy into your parenting plan as a way of helping everyone adjust to all the change? Is the attorney clear that he/she will encourage a collaborative process in creating a parenting plan that includes *both parents* and attorneys or *parents and a mediator* rather than a plan created solely by one parent?

A parenting plan is a blueprint for the future. It should represent the best of both parents ability to provide for their children's needs. And your attorney should willingly, creatively and legally follow your direction offering guidance and counsel where needed.

Anne R. Lucas, MA, LMHC, is a therapist/mediator/divorce coach who specializes in the life span of couples—premarital, marital, divorce, and remarriage. She is the clinical director and owner of The Evergreen Clinic, a 12 member multidisciplinary behavioral health clinic in Kirkland, WA. Anne is an active member of Collaborative Law, an international dispute resolution process where she practices as a divorce coach and trains attorneys, financial specialists, and mental health practitioners in the US and Canada in the art of Collaborative Law. She is also adjunct faculty at Saybrook University in Kirkland, WA where she teaches and supervises master's level counseling students. Anne currently serves on the board of the Collaborative Professionals of Washington and is a past president of King County Collaborative Law.

Changing Your Parenting Plan

What to Consider When Things Aren't Going Well

By Justin M. Sedell, JD

A PARENTING PLAN (SOMETIMES called a custody decree or residential schedule) is a court order establishing the rules about where your children will primarily live, how much time they will spend residing or visiting with the other parent, and how the parents will divide up important days like holidays, special occasions, and school breaks. In some states it can be very detailed, including rules about how parents are required to make decisions for their children. This is an enormously important legal document. There can be very serious consequences if someone knowingly violates it. In some states penalties for violating the Parenting Plan can include fines payable to the other parent, make-up residential time, or even jail time for the violating parent.

A Parenting Plan is supposed to be a final document. This means that it remains in effect until the children turn 18 years old and under most circumstances it is not supposed to be changed, absent both parents' written agreement. If both parties agree to a change, then they can consult with their attorneys about preparing, signing, and entering with the court a modified Parenting Plan reflecting their agreement.

However, there are certain circumstances where the law allows a parent to ask the court to request changes to a Parenting Plan even when the other parent does not agree. This is called a "petition to modify the Parenting Plan." Because the Parenting Plan is supposed to last until the children were 18, however, the parent asking for the change must prove to the court that there is a legitimate legal reason to modify it. Either parent can file this petition. It can ask the court to change the prior order to increase or reduce a parent's residential time or to change other aspects of the prior Parenting Plan, such as decision-making rights.

Different states have different legal standards and requirements before any contested changes to a Parenting Plan will be approved. For example, some states require the requesting parent to show that there has been a "substantial change of circumstances" from the time that the prior Parenting Plan was entered. Depending on the changes requested, the court might limit the changed circumstances to be those affecting the child and/or the other parent (rather than the requesting parent's own circumstances). It may also limit these to circumstances that were not anticipated at the time that the prior Parenting Plan was filed.

In certain states, a parent can successfully petition to modify the Parenting Plan if he/she is able to prove that the prior order has not been followed for a significant period of time by both parties' agreement and that the children have become so accustomed to the new schedule that returning to the old plan would be detrimental to them. This often arises when one parent has not been exercising some or all of his/her residential time for an extended period of time.

Here are some other reasons that people might consider modifying their Parenting Plan:

- A parent's work schedule has drastically changed, requiring him/her to relocate and/or otherwise making the current residential schedule difficult or even impossible to follow. (You should note that some states have very specific laws about one parent relocating with the children. If you want to move, even if you're only moving a short distance, you should talk to your attorney well in advance to understand the legal process you must follow.)

- One parent has developed a substance abuse problem.

- A parent's mental health is negatively impacting the children in some way.

- The children have been consistently absent and/or tardy to school during one parent's care (while the other parent has always ensured the kids are at school on time every day during his/her residential time) and that this is negatively impacting the children's schoolwork.

- One parent is in a new relationship with someone who poses an actual, credible threat to the children, such as a registered sex offender or someone with a recent violent criminal history, and is exposing the children to that person.

- There has been an enormous level of conflict since the prior Parenting Plan was entered because it requires a level of cooperation and compromise that has proven impossible. For example:

Julia and Doug divorced five years ago. Julia is a police officer with a complicated work schedule that changes all the time. Doug works a regular "9 to 5" office job. Their Parenting Plan says that Julia and Doug must work together to figure out a residential schedule that allows Julia to have the children at least 14 days and nights per month. This has proved to be a recipe for disaster because Julia and Doug can't get along. They fight constantly and they have enormous difficulty reaching agreement about when the kids will stay with Julia. Julia or Doug may petition the court to modify the Parenting Plan to award Julia a set schedule each month so that she and Doug would not have to coordinate and agree anymore.

The list of potential reasons for modification is endless, but the general idea is whether there has been an unanticipated substantial change in circumstances since the time that the prior Parenting Plan was entered. It will be the requesting party's legal burden to prove these changes in circumstances.

You should keep in mind that the court takes all cases affecting children very seriously. Many states do not allow the requesting parent to pursue a request for modification unless he/she can establish at the very beginning of the case that there is a legal basis for it. If he/she is unable to meet that legal standard in the judicial officer's sole discretion then the court may deny the request and dismiss the case. It may even assess a financial penalty against the requesting parent if the judicial officer decides that there was an insufficient legal basis for the case, if he/she believes that the matter was not brought to court in good faith, or for other legal reasons. On the other hand, if the court determines that there is enough information to allow the case to proceed then it may lead to a lengthy legal process that may even require a trial.

If you are interested in pursuing changes to your existing Parenting Plan then you should consult with your attorney to understand your options and chances of success. When meeting with your attorney, make sure to bring a copy of your current Parenting Plan and any other evidence that you have with you. This might include calendars showing the residential schedule your children have been following, emails or text messages between you and the other parent, school records, medical records, or anything else.

Your attorney can help you assess the situation, determine whether modification is a good option for you, evaluate whether there is sufficient evidence to support a petition to modify your Parenting Plan, and assist you to weigh the costs versus benefits of pursuing modification. Your attorney can also help you to better understand how the law of your particular state will apply to your unique circumstances, the chances of success, and whether there might be other options to resolve the concerns outside of the legal system.

For example, many parents are able to successfully resolve any post-Parenting Plan concerns through working with a coach or mediator. Some states even require that you attempt some form of alternative dispute resolution (such as mediation) before you file a case in court. Your attorney will help you understand these requirements and your options.

> Remember that a child's parents are usually the best-suited people to make decisions about his/her future.

The parents' judgment for their own children is usually far preferable to turning over that major authority to a stranger who has never met your children before. That said, there are times when parents cannot agree or when a child or parent's safety is at risk. In those times, the court is there to help make decisions in the best interests of your children.

Although your Parenting Plan is supposed to be a final document, sometimes unexpected things happen that necessitate changes to the Plan even where the other parent does not agree. If you think a change to the Parenting Plan is necessary and that you might meet the above criteria then you should consult with your attorney and better understand your rights, responsibilities, and options moving forward.

Justin M. Sedell is a principal attorney at Lasher Holzapfel Sperry & Ebberson, PLLC in Seattle, Washington. Justin's practice concentrates on the dissolution of marriages involving complex or substantial assets, complex child custody disputes, collaborative law, and high conflict litigation. Justin is an experienced trial attorney who has appeared in complicated family law trials throughout the State of Washington. He is consistently rated by his peers as a "Rising Star" in Washington Law and Politics Magazine, a designation awarded to only the top 2.5% of young lawyers. In addition to his legal practice, Justin is also an adjunct professor at Seattle University School of Law and University of Washington School of Law.

Inadvertently Harming your Child's Relationship With the Other Parent

By Maureen Conroyd, LCSW, BCD

"PARENTAL ALIENATION" IS a term used to describe a pervasive pattern of critical statements, negative attitudes and hostile behaviors of one parent directed toward the other parent in ways that foster in the child feelings of hatred, animosity, fear, and/or unjustified rejection of that parent. Another more subtle, yet alienating process, is when a parent joins with a child in his/her upset with the other parent. Rather than supporting the child to work through an issue with the other parent, the parent steps in supporting and reinforcing the child's attitudes and behaviors of rejection. Even more subtle, yet an extremely confusing form of alienation, is the parent who says with his/her words, "of course I want you to have a good relationship with your mom/dad" while communicating on an emotional level, the pain, loss, obvious anxiety, and/or fear of separation from the child that telegraphs, "He/she left me—don't you leave me, too." A parent runs the risk of getting his/her own emotional needs for revenge, control or emotional neediness met at the cost of damaging the child's other significant parental relationship through:

- Pervasive, ongoing criticism, negative attitudes that include disgust and hatred, and openly hostile/rejecting behavior of the other parent,

- Joining the child in their distress in an inappropriate exaggeration of a developmental upset that's now used to justify and empower the child to act out his/her rejecting feelings, anger, upset, etc.

- Saying the right thing while telegraphing a very different needy, anxious message that the child interprets as, "I need you—don't leave me" or "your mom/dad is not a good person/parent."

The most extreme cases of family dysfunction involving parental alienation are often addressed through legal proceedings in the State Superior Court.

When parents battle for a child's affection and/or attempt to engender loyalties to one parent over the other, they risk wounding the child's love for, attachment to, and identification with that parent. Siblings may get caught in the conflict. If there is more than one child in the family each child may respond differently to the conflict according to their age, temperament, and developmental needs. Some children, especially older children, may act out their grief and confusion and align themselves strongly with one parent expecting siblings to follow. If siblings choose not to follow, conflict and disruption of their day-to-day relationships may ensue. Siblings may attempt to bring balance to the destructive conflict by each aligning with a parent and losing their own siblingship. Kids suffer.

The parent being targeted may respond to this perceived or real threat with a counterattack against the other parent or to defend him/herself. Accusations are made that one parent is being unfair or dishonest while the other parent is blamed for a wide range of poor parenting decisions. Destructive communication patterns or behaviors may surface which contribute to the family's further deterioration.

Sometimes, really good co-parents may inadvertently fall into habits that contribute to the child's thinking that they have to "ally" more strongly with one parent to win their favor, keep their love, take care of Mom/Dad, or keep peace in that home.

> Most parents would be appalled to think that they could engage in any behaviors that might hurt their child.

That is clearly not their intention. Parent's who love their child(ren) want the very best for them and may be unaware of the impact of their behaviors. But. unresolved issues of resentment blame and/or judgment can subtly or not-so-subtly show up in the day-to-day interactions with your child that erodes feelings of trust and closeness with his/her other parent.

Sometimes hostile or manipulative behavior prevents the child from temporarily being with their other parent. This message may convey that the other parent isn't deserving of the same respect or relationship with the child that the other parent enjoys. *"What's the big deal—so we were late getting back! Get over it."* Your child feels the underlying message to the other parent: "You're not worthy of my respect; I'm sick of you; you don't matter."

Sometimes a parent criticizes the other parent within earshot of the child. *"She's such a jerk; he can't be trusted; is crazy; a loser; worthless"*... etc. From a child's point of view, he/she's like each parent in a variety of unique and special ways—maybe in looks, mannerisms, figures of speech, how her brain works, athletic or academic ability. Whatever the identification with each parent, a child is enriched with knowing he/she has two parents who love him/her. To hear his/her parent criticized leaves the child feeling ashamed of him/herself—or worse, like he/she must distance him/herself from that part of him/herself that's *like that parent.*

Sometimes a parent criticizes the child directly for a misbehavior that becomes charged with the parent's anger/blame/resentment toward the former spouse. *"Why do you always have to be late? You're just like your father—he never does anything right, either!"* Or, *"You never finish anything; you're irresponsible, just like your mom."* Here the child is asked to carry the weight of disappointment, betrayal, and loss for a parent over their spousal relationship. The child feels trapped by and a failure because of his/her love and connection to each parent.

Negative statements have a devastating effect on every family member and plant seeds of distrust and discontent. Occasional conflicts and lapses in judgment are understandable. The situation becomes problematic when these actions are repeated over and over and over.

Children don't need to be told or reminded of their parent's faults. Children figure out their parent's strengths and weaknesses on their own. Hearing a parent blamed or put down frequently wounds a child's identity and self-confidence since they share many of each parent's traits. Children often express that *"It hurts my feelings, and it makes me mad."*

Unresolved feelings of hurt, depression, sadness, unmitigated anxiety cause the child feelings of responsibility for the parent's emotional "okay-ness". Sometimes they share their thoughts and feelings—often they do not. Kids suffer on the *inside.*

When a parent leans on a child for emotional support directly or indirectly, the child will often turn away from his/her own developmental process to take care of and support the parent. The child may feel strong feelings about leaving the needy parent; he may become resentful of the other parent; he/she may develop his/her own separation anxiety, making it difficult to leave one parent to enjoy the other. When one parent repeatedly shares his/her sadness and messages how much he/she "misses" the child, the child goes from feeling loved to being burdened by the enormity of the parent's loss, and guilty for enjoying the other parent fully.

When one parent repeatedly blames the other parent for his/her change in circumstance, whether economic, physical, or social status, children feel helpless. Children adjust to each home environment and usually adapt well taking the lead from each parent about the situation. Children feel confusion and perhaps shame over having benefits in one home, however, when they cause distress for their other parent. Rather than supporting and enjoying a child's "good fortune" with their other parent, a parent becomes depressed, negative, accusatory, and resentful. This becomes the emotional atmosphere for the child to navigate, often *alone*.

. . . .

When Sally ran in the house outfitted in Lululemon purchased by her dad, her mom lost her head and yelled, "Your father doesn't know a thing about raising a 16 year old-girl. What was he thinking? I don't even dress like that!" Sally felt embarrassed and ashamed, and, later, angry and confused about what to do with her new clothes.

. . . .

A child's sense of emotional safety may be stunted if he/she hears a constant barrage of complaining and/or blaming. When a parent repeatedly expresses their concerns to the child, the child feels caught in the middle and responsible. *"We wouldn't be in this situation if it weren't that your Mother wanted a divorce—she's the one who makes us live in this rat-hole of an apartment!"* What was once an issue between two adults is now talked about as if the child has some responsibility for a parent's choices: YOUR mother, YOUR father is the problem. In some cases, the child feels persuaded to accept *the parent's view* as his/her own in order to gain relief from the tension or to comfort the distressed parent by joining in the "fight."

A child feels "put in the middle" between his/her parents—and lives in a state of irresolvable split loyalties. When parents blame one another, whether for change of circumstances, for the divorce, for their individual unhappiness, or for "destroying the family," the child is left to figure out how to straddle the gulf created by blame.

> Consider that one side of a child's heart is dedicated to loving one parent and the other side of his/her heart is dedicated to loving the other parent.

When parents insist that the child gets into the blame-game, the child's heart literally hurts as the war goes on inside the two sides of his/her own heart. Split loyalties leave children to navigate between their two parents, two homes, and two sides of their own heart. Children escape into school, activities, peers—some good, some bad.

Sometimes parents unskillfully set children up to make choices that involve rejecting one parent over another, such as setting a family gathering, birthday party, or similar special event that involves the child on the other parent's residential time without pre-planning and agreement. The child is torn—the other parent is set up to be the "bad parent" if he/she says "no." The child may begin to feel used and manipulated as the adults act out their anger with one another through the child.

Children can feel "split loyalties" over enjoying a new step-parent when their other parent regularly expresses hatred, distrust, or negativity toward the other parent's new partner. When a child hears, *"She's just a step-parent—I don't trust her. She had an affair with your dad and ruined our family. You be sure to call me when you're over there—I just need to know that you're all right."* The child becomes anxious and mistrustful; confused and wondering if he should hate his new step-parent. *"What if Mom's right? What if I like my new step-parent? I don't want to hear about affairs! I just want them to leave me alone and stop fighting!"*

Changes in residential schedule are unavoidable. When requesting changes in schedule become a way to instigate conflict, create unnecessary commotion, and/or disrupt either parent's home-life, the child suffers. On-going demands/requests for residential schedule changes, arguing over "right of first refusal" more often reflects manipulative and controlling behavior on the part of one or both parents who are still working out unresolved spousal conflict. Children benefit from a regular, consistent schedule where they adapt to transitions and rest into their two-home family life with each parent. Kids work hard to adapt and manage the challenges that come their way. When parents disregard the children's need to successfully integrate into a rhythm, kids begin to feel unsettled, in the way, a source of the problem, and resentful, *"If I weren't here, they wouldn't have anything to fight about."*

Turmoil and tension often begins during divorce, when parents are feeling threatened by the uncertainty and loss brought on by separation/divorce itself. These are a few of the common ways that a parent harms the relationship with their child's other parent. Unfortunately for children, they need the stability of their relationships with each parent and daily lives more than ever as their parents dismantle the one-home family and try and find new stability in two homes.

In Summary and Recommendations for Next Steps

Intentional or not, these negative parental attitudes and behaviors affect children. Although difficult, the best remedy is for each parent to raise their own awareness of any ineffective habits that have developed out of protracted conflict with an ex-partner. Listen to feedback: from your children, your former partner, or other caring adults. Accept the opportunity to change your perspective, work through unresolved feelings, improve your co-parenting relationship, and ensure a healthy two-home environment for your child(ren). Specifically, we recommend the following steps:

- Recognize that constant negativity is hard on kids and adults alike.

- Blaming and judging your child's parent leaves them helpless—they didn't cause the problem, nor can they solve it. So stop including them in your unresolved past (or present adult issues). Seek appropriate adult support and come to resolution with those areas of your life that aren't working.

- Listen non-defensively to those who care about you that perhaps you're stuck in harmful, negative, and/or controlling patterns with your ex. Blaming your ex without seeing your role in the dance is to miss an important part of the equation for your children's sake.

- Choose a neutral setting to discuss improving your co-parenting relationship with your co-parent for the sake of your children.

- Include a mental health professional (coach, mediator, family therapist) to facilitate a constructive dialogue, change plan, and goal setting.

- Utilize your conflict resolution process in your parenting plan as effectively and constructively as appropriate.

- Involve your children ONLY with the help of a skilled facilitator so that they are not inadvertently harmed by your hoped-for process. Asking children to weigh in on adult issues, residential schedules, living with a stepparent, or to blame one parent in front of the other, or to complain about the behavior of one parent over the other, are all ways of creating split loyalties if not handled very skillfully.

- Act with courage. Learning how to effectively parent and co-parent is a lifelong endeavor.

- Remember, children don't need perfect parents—they need *good enough* parents.

Maureen A. Conroyd has a masters degree in social work and is a licensed clinical social worker. She is a Board-Certified Diplomate in clinical social work. She has completed Mental Health Training for Collaborative Professionals and is a nationally certified mediator. She is an active member of the International Academy of Collaborative Professionals (IACP). She has extensive experience working with adults, children and families in clinical private practice.

ACKNOWLEDGEMENTS

THERE'S NO WAY to fully acknowledge all the important individuals who played a part in bringing this book to fruition. We'd have to start with our original lessons on life and love, learned from our families, parents, and siblings. Each have played essential roles in building our foundation as individuals, appreciation of the complexity of family relationships, and commitment to the importance of family. Along our journey, there have been both north stars and those who gifted us with key challenges. We honor each and every one of you and all we experienced together.

We also wish to thank our amazing Collaborative colleagues for their vision, mentorship, and support, which was invaluable as we hitched our wagon to a movement to put "family" central in family law. At risk of leaving out many valuable and important colleagues who have touched us in ways they may have never known, we'd like to specifically call out a few of our most trusted friends and colleagues:

Felicia Malsby Soleil, whose friendship and professional support have walked in stride with this entire project, as we began to grow Collaborative law in Washington State.

Ann Lucas, for her limitless capacity to support Collaborative Practice and her willingness to reach out to all that seek her advice and mentorship—and for writing an article for this book.

Rachel Felbeck, Don Desonier, and Holly Holbein, Collaborative Practice ground-breakers in the Seattle area, who so generously shared their enthusiasm, lessons, and guidance.

Justin Sedell whose brilliance we were lucky enough to have as a part of this book through his careful review, generous support, and article contribution.

Mark Weiss who sets the standard for thoughtful, wise and compassionate practice and who is continually seeking ways to bring excellence and collaboration to family law.

Mark Greenfield, Nancy Cameron, Diane Diel, Denise Jacob, and Gail Leondar-Wright, who gave precious time and energy to read, comment and improve on, and provide moral support for getting this book across the finish line. You've been an invaluable "brain trust." Thanks also to Maureen Conroyd for her expertise as an experienced and knowledgeable child specialist and co-parenting coach, and her article contribution.

Katherine M. Bell and Alexandra S. Halsey, whose editing skill and commitment to their craft make the reading all that more rich and enjoyable. [Thank you!]

We want to thank Dori Jones Yang for her publishing coaching—like a hand to hold when you're learning to walk.

Thank you to Tillotson "Tilly" Goble for her video production skills—bringing another dimension to the book. And, to Doug Mackey, who's recording expertise and guidance allows this material to be enjoyed by those who prefer to listen.

Kathryn Campbell for her amazing artistic design talent. She is responsible for the beautiful presentation inside and out. [And how perfect, don't you think?]

And, last, but not in any way least, we want to thank all the co-parents and their children who have entrusted us with the honor of coaching, guiding, and assisting them through divorce/separation and beyond.

AUTHOR BIOGRAPHIES

KAREN BONNELL, ARNP, MS is a board-certified clinical nurse specialist with over 30 years of experience working with individuals, couples, and parents. Her private practice is dedicated to working with couples across the spectrum from pre-marital preparation to co-parenting in two-home families to remarriage. As a Divorce and Co-Parent Coach, Karen has dedicated her work to thoughtfully resolving conflicts one person, one couple and one

family at a time. Karen has served on the board of King County Collaborative Law and was a founding member of the Collaborative Professionals of Washington. She is a member of the International Academy of Collaborative Professionals and Academy of Professional Family Mediators. Karen is a regular presenter on topics related to divorce and co-parent coaching, as well as advanced communication skills. Karen lives in the foothills of the Cascade range outside Seattle. She values the lessons learned in the "school of hard knocks" in her experience of creating a two-home family before divorce coaching existed. Her two adult children are her every-day inspiration for the beauty of love, forgiveness, and trust in the capacity of family in all its forms.

KRISTIN LITTLE MA, MS, LMHC is a Licensed Mental Health Counselor in private practice in the Seattle area. She has provided therapy for children at risk and their families within her community for the past 17 years. Currently, Kristin is a board member of Collaborative Professionals of Washington, a growing organization that is dedicated to reducing the harmful conflict of divorce for couples and families. Her private practice as a Collabora-

tive Divorce Child Specialist, as well as her own difficult journey through divorce and single parenting, provides Kristin with unique insights and a compassionate and practical approach for guiding individuals, parents and children through the emotional landscape of divorce. Kristin is a frequent speaker to mental health and legal professional groups on the topic of healthy coping for parents and children in divorce. Kristin lives in the Seattle area with her young son and her loving, large, and complicated two-home family.

Please visit

www.thecoparentshandbook.com

to connect with Karen and/or Kris,
to visit The Co-Parents Handbook Blog,
and learn more about upcoming news and events.

Made in the USA
Middletown, DE
27 December 2016